# Literature and Animal Studies

Why do animals talk in literature? In this provocative book, Mario Ortiz Robles tracks the presence of animals across an expansive literary archive to argue that literature cannot be understood as a human endeavor apart from its capacity to represent animals. Focusing on the literary representation of familiar animals, including horses, dogs, cats, and songbirds, Ortiz Robles examines the various tropes literature has historically employed to give meaning to our fraught relations with other animals. Beyond allowing us to imagine the lives of non-humans, literature can make a lasting contribution to Animal Studies, an emerging discipline within the humanities, by showing us that there is something fictional about our relation to animals.

*Literature and Animal Studies* combines a broad mapping of literary animals with detailed readings of key animal texts to offer a new way of organizing literary history that emphasizes genera over genres and a new way of classifying animals that is premised on tropes rather than taxa. The book makes us see animals and our relation to them with fresh eyes and, in doing so, prompts us to review the role of literature in a culture that considers it an endangered art form.

**Mario Ortiz Robles** is Professor of English at the University of Wisconsin-Madison, USA, and the author of *The Novel as Event* (2010) and co-editor of *Narrative Middles: Navigating the Nineteenth-Century British Novel* (2011).

# Literature and Contemporary Thought

*Literature and Contemporary Thought* is an interdisciplinary series providing new perspectives and cutting edge thought on the study of Literature and topics such as Animal Studies, Disability Studies and Digital Humanities. Each title includes chapters on:

- why the topic is relevant, interesting and important at this moment and how it relates to contemporary debates
- the background of and a brief introduction to the particular area of study the book is intended to cover
- when this area of study became relevant to literature, how the relationship between the two areas was initially perceived and how it evolved

A glossary of key terms and annotated further reading will feature in every title.

Edited by Ursula Heise and Guillermina De Ferrari, this series will be invaluable to students and academics alike as they approach the interdisciplinary study of Literature.

Also available in this series:

**Literature and Animal Studies**
*Mario Ortiz Robles*

**Literature and Disability**
*Alice Hall*

# Literature and Animal Studies

Mario Ortiz Robles

Routledge
Taylor & Francis Group

LONDON AND NEW YORK

First published 2016
by Routledge
2 Park Square, Milton Park, Abingdon, Oxon OX14 4RN

and by Routledge
711 Third Avenue, New York, NY 10017

*Routledge is an imprint of the Taylor & Francis Group, an informa business*

© 2016 Mario Ortiz Robles

The right of Mario Ortiz Robles to be identified as author of this work
has been asserted by him in accordance with sections 77 and 78 of the
Copyright, Designs and Patents Act 1988.

*British Library Cataloguing-in-Publication Data*
A catalogue record for this book is available from the British Library

*Library of Congress Cataloging-in-Publication Data*
Names: Ortiz-Robles, Mario, 1964- author.
Title: Literature and animal studies / Mario Ortiz-Robles.
Description: Abingdon, Oxon ; New York, NY : Routledge, 2016. |
Series: Literature and contemporary thought | Includes bibliographical
references and index.
Identifiers: LCCN 2015046126| ISBN 9780415716000 (hardback
: alk. paper) | ISBN 9780415716017 (pbk. : alk. paper) | ISBN
9781315880389 (ebook)
Subjects: LCSH: Animals in literature. | Human-animal relationships in
literature.
Classification: LCC PN56.A64 O78 2016 | DDC 809/.93362--dc23
LC record available at http://lccn.loc.gov/2015046126

ISBN: 978-0-415-71600-0 (hbk)
ISBN: 978-0-415-71601-7 (pbk)
ISBN: 978-1-315-88038-9 (ebk)

Typeset in Sabon
By HWA Text and Data Management, London
Printed in Great Britain by Ashford Colour Press Ltd.

To G and P, my favorite humanimals

*"The imagination is wild"*

# Contents

# Series editors' preface

Since the turn of the millennium, literary and cultural studies have been transformed less by new overarching theoretical paradigms than by the emergence a multitude of innovative subfields. These emergent research areas explore the relationship between literature and new media technologies, seek to establish innovative bridges to disciplines ranging from medicine, cognitive science, social psychology to biology and ecology, and develop new quantitative or computer-based research methodologies. In the process, they rethink crucial concepts such as affect, indigeneity, gender, and postcolonialism, and propose new perspectives on aesthetics, narrative, poetics, and visuality.

*Literature and Contemporary Thought* seeks to capture such research at the cutting edge of literary and cultural studies. The volumes in this series explore both how new approaches are reshaping literary criticism and theory, and how research in literary and cultural studies opens out to transform other disciplines and research areas. They seek to make new literary research available, intelligible, and usable to scholars and students across academic disciplines and to the broader public, beyond the university, interested in innovative approaches to art and culture across different historical periods and geographical regions.

*Literature and Contemporary Thought* highlights new kinds of scholarship in the literary and cultural humanities that are relevant and important to public debates, and seeks to translate their interdisciplinary analyses and theories into useful tools for such thought and discussion.

Ursula K. Heise and Guillermina De Ferrari

# Preface

Whenever I talk about this project, someone always asks me whether I have considered a particular animal text that, for whatever reason, I have in fact failed to consider. In most cases, the question makes me feel as though I ought to have read this particular animal text; it would have made the book better, more inclusive. This feeling has to do in part with my desire to speak for all animals in speaking of them in this book—a desire that is as illusory as it is symptomatic of our culture's absolute claims on nature—but it also has to do with a certain unease at what the question itself seems to imply about the presence of animals in literature. We all know that there are animals in literature, we even know one or two quite intimately; yet, their presence is hard to quantify and even harder to evaluate critically, such that, in speaking about them, we feel that every animal ought in all rigor to count. Thus, the question, or the fact of its having been asked, implies yet another question: why study animals in literature in the first place?

The relatively recent emergence of the discipline of Animal Studies—a discipline that has emerged from within the humanities and humanistic social sciences—is the most obviously pragmatic answer, especially in the context of the book series to which this volume belongs, *Literature and Contemporary Thought*. But this answer also begs the question of why Animal Studies is itself a relevant or even interesting approach to the study of animals in the context of the highly developed scientific disciplines specifically devoted to the study of animals. The sophisticated descriptive models zoology, and the biological sciences more generally, provide for giving a comprehensive account of animal life are arguably infallible, or at least irrefutable in terms of the methods used to advance its insights. This book takes a rather narrow approach to Animal Studies' burden of proof by arguing that literature, the discipline within the humanities best equipped to account for the figurative character of our engagement with the world, can tell us something valuable about animals that we would otherwise ignore. While literature is neither a natural habitat for animals, nor thereby a repository of reliable knowledge about the anatomy, physiology, and perhaps even ethology of animals, it has nevertheless had more to say about our relation to animals over time than any other discourse. This is so in part because of the rhetorical resources of which literature has availed itself to describe animals in the course of its history, in epics, fables, romances, poems, and stories of all shapes and forms. But literature also has had more to say about our relation to animals because in literature anything can be said, including those aspects of our relation to animals that science, economics, and politics would rather not say.

As you begin to read this book, you too are likely to wonder whether I have included your favorite animal text. We all carry within us a literary animal, a sort of textual daemon or literary familiar, that links us with all the other animals we have encountered in literature and which makes them somehow intelligible to us. For me, it is the axolotl, a translucent newt that lives in the volcanic lakes of Mexico's central plateau and, like this writer was when he first encountered it in a story by Julio Cortázar, exists in a state of adolescence. I am a different person now, but the axolotl's literariness still claims a strong hold on my imagination. During the conquest of the New World, the Spanish chroniclers wrote about the axolotl, describing how the inhabitants of Tenochtitlan considered it a gastronomic delicacy. In the nineteenth century, the French scientists attached to Maximilian's imperial court in Mexico obtained specimens for the Jardin des Plantes in Paris, the very animals whose descendants, in their exile, met Cortázar in his. Now near extinction in its natural habitat, the axolotl only flourishes in the laboratory, where, an object of scientific curiosity, it keeps getting reinvented. The axolotl is in this regard perhaps only the excessive figure for the more general phenomenon I treat in this book: the literary character of our relation to animals.

As you near the end of the book and realize that I have nowhere referred to your favorite animal text, you will probably be as disappointed as I am at having had to exclude the axolotl from its pages. But, if nothing else, such absences tell us something about the paradoxical place animals occupy in our cultural imaginary. Animals are everywhere around us, of course, and yet we would hardly know it if we were to rely on the culture industry alone to provide us with a picture of our relation to animals. This is so in part because cultural representations tend to abstract animals from their natures (Daffy Duck is as reliable a guide to "duckness" as Madonna is to Christendom), but it also has do with the distance, or distances, such representations imply: the historical distance that purportedly separates us from some Rousseauvian "state of nature" to which we can no longer lay claim; the geographical and demographic distance that separates city dwellers from rural inhabitants and all of us from "where the wild things are"; the intangible distance that separates the foods we eat from the animals that lived only to provide it; the awkward distance that separates the drugs we ingest from the animal models that have made them possible; and, what in the end amounts to the same thing, the conceptual distance that categorically separates us from non-human animals. Distance might well be considered a reason for why there is a literary quality to our relation to animals: we are too far removed from the lives of animals to give anything but a fictional account of their lives. Yet, distance is also a formal device that structures our relations to animals, enabling, and at times sanctioning, our often brutal treatment of them. Indeed, in a manner that would be contradictory only if it were not enabling, the stories we tell ourselves about how we relate to animals tend to occlude, or obfuscate, our manipulation of animals *at the same time* that they allow us to imagine what it would be like to be an animal. In Cortázar's "Axolotl," the narrator becomes the axolotl he describes in the very act of making the animal his own by describing it, making of the animal a story and of the story an animal.

In an effort to understand this paradox, this book makes two interrelated arguments: an argument for animals based on literature (on the literarity of animals), and an argument for literature based on animals (on the literal demands animals place on literary representation). In both cases, the views advanced seek a different engagement with difference and a new way of understanding this engagement as a literary phenomenon. Literature helps us imagine alternatives to the way we live with animals, and animals help us imagine a new role for literature in a world where our animal future is uncertain. The arguments in this book thus proceed toward a new version of literary history in which the units of world literature might be construed following the migratory patterns of animals rather than the history of nations; genera rather than genres; biomes rather than languages; taxa rather than texts. Melville's *Moby Dick* (another telling absence in this book) would cease to be read as the symbol of the ever elusive Great American novel and could instead be read as a cetacean epic with truly planetary reach. Or, instead of debating whether Romanticism is one or many, we might instead repair on the breeding habitats of the nightingale to locate the range of the romantic lyric and thereby map its influence. The disappearance of the horse from literature's representational stage might indeed be a better gauge of our modernity than the formal mechanisms that supplanted its role, and thus steam-engine might be a better name for the propulsive style of modern prose than stream-of-consciousness. Dogs' lives might offer a different way of tracking the fate of the individual, as might cats' lives of our vain attempts to cheat death through art. Perhaps the body of vermin literature would give us a better sense of literature's social conscience than the facile pieties we pronounce, so as to settle its scores through criticism. A zoocentric view of world literature might in any case change the terms of the debate and make us more aware of our own animal natures, and thus of literature as an animal invention.

This book does not undertake to be an inclusive survey of animals in literature, nor does it aspire to provide a literary treatment of the animal kingdom as a whole. Yet, it does entertain hopes of being in some measure representative of the manner in which literature has tried to account for animals in its history. The version of literary history you will find here, however, is both partial and idiosyncratic; its principle of selection following the questionable logic imposed by my ignorance, my tastes, and my library. Likewise, the version of the animal world you will find in this book is constrained by its principle of representativeness, which, unlike that of the zoo or the natural history museum, is not premised on postdiluvian taxonomic logics but on the figurative possibilities of the animal, which is to say that the version of the animal world you will find here is also constrained by the limitations—of style, of sympathy, of decorum—that literature has imposed upon itself in its attempts to represent the animal world. It should therefore come as no surprise that literary history and natural history overlap in this book only at the margins. Some animals in this book are merely literary while others are all too real, but, in the manner of a mediaeval bestiary, it does not make a strict distinction between real and imagined animals, not because there is no distinction to be made but because it is hard to locate precisely where it ought to be made. It should therefore be taken as a natural consequence that this book understands animals to be figurative in the most literal manner in which such phrasing can be understood.

\* \* \*

Elephants belong to memories; wolves to packs; giraffes to towers; crows to murders; dolphins to pods. I belong to this enthusiasm: Mercedes Alcalá, Monique Allewaert, Laurie Beth Clarke, Guillermina De Ferrari, Sara Guyer, Ursula Heise, Alex Huneeus, Amaia Huneeus,

Steve Hutchinson, Jacques Lezra, Ion Meyn, Lucas Meyn, D. A. Miller, Frédéric Neyrat, Paloma Ortiz De Ferrari, Michael Peterson, Kellie Robertson, Sadie Straus, Scott Straus, Solomon Straus, Mike Witmore, and Silas Witmore. I am also fortunate to belong to other animal groups: the Mellon Workshop on Animal Studies, which for two years fostered many of the ideas presented in this book, and the Faculty Development Seminar on Animal Studies, which challenged and expanded the reach of these ideas in a climate of warm collegiality. I had the great fortune of counting with the support of Sara Guyer at the Center for the Humanities and Susan Freedman at the Institute for the Humanities, both at the University of Wisconsin-Madison, in the creation of these animal groups. I am also grateful to the Graduate School at the University of Wisconsin-Madison for providing summer support, and to the English Department, whose chairs during the book's period of gestation, Terry Kelley and Caroline Levine, were instrumental in making animals count in literature. I also want to thank Ruth Hilsdon and Elizabeth Levine at Routledge for their patient efforts in bringing this volume to term. Special thanks go to Guillermina and Paloma, who have been indulgent without measure with the author, and his animal antics, during the writing of this book.

# 1   What is it like to be a trope?

This book is about the relation between literature, one of the oldest of human endeavors, and animal studies, one of the newest disciplines within the humanities. It seeks to find common ground between two very different approaches to the same question, or sets of questions pertaining to how humanity defines itself, and to whether or not this definition has something to do with the animal world. In mapping out this common ground, the present book will endeavor to address these questions by describing the new discipline called animal studies in terms that will be familiar to students of literature: What kind of characters do animals play in literature? What sorts of narratives do they inhabit? What is their figurative status? Why, how, to whom, and for whom do animals speak?

Animals have always been part of literature, but their presence, perhaps like that of dogs in some human cultures, has been as marginal as it has been constant. In the great epics of antiquity, Gilgamesh, the Hebrew Bible, and Homer, animals play significant, even necessary, roles, but no one would claim that these, the earliest of literary works, are essentially about animals. They are, if anything, about how humans became human. Indeed, from this perspective, literature can be said to be about how humans describe themselves as *not* animals. Yet, as the example of Ovid so vividly illustrates, this act of self-definition often entails using the figural resources of literature to imagine what it would be like for a human to be an animal, or for an animal to be human. In imagining such metamorphoses, the categorical distinction between humans and animals that literature would otherwise seem to be making becomes suspended in the metaphorical nature of language. Literature serves to separate humans from animals, but also to confuse and conflate them. In Franz Kafka's *The Metamorphosis* (1915), Gregor Samsa is a human who, in becoming an animal, also becomes the living metaphor of his life as a human, which has resembled up to the point of his transformation that of the vermin he inevitably becomes. The presence of animals in literature, marginal yet constant, suggests that literature is that discourse whereby humans simultaneously declare their difference from animals, and take the measure of their suggestive similarities.

This might lead us to conclude that we are literary animals in the sense in which Aristotle speaks of humans as political animals. We certainly imagine ourselves as uniquely equipped to produce works of astounding verbal beauty and, at times, of plodding verbosity in which we render the world we inhabit as a world we share with animals. But, in the more than three millennia of literary history, literature has always represented animals without for all that speaking *for* them. Literature can be said to be literary to the precise degree that animals are made to speak *in* literature and, therefore, it might be more accurate to say that animals are the ones that really speak *for* literature. Modern science poses the question of whether animals have use of language; no one ever asks if animals use language poetically. This book will try to imagine what it is like to listen to animals as they speak in literature through the verbal inventions of humans. It will thus seek to defend a somewhat paradoxical thesis: *animals as we know them are a literary invention.*

## Animals are as old as literature

Animals are as old as literature. This is to say that animals have been represented in literature since its beginnings. From the earliest epics, fables, parables, and plays, animals have donned a great variety of guises to become the privileged presences that show us how to be human. But it is also to say that animals are there at the very origins of literature. In most cultures, origin myths involve the separation of humans from a natural state in which the distinction between humans and non-humans has not yet been determined. In the story of Genesis in the Hebrew Bible, for instance, Adam is given the task of naming the animals and, in carrying it out, becomes their overseer. In Eden, animals are not only named, however; they are also made to speak, as the example of one particular serpent best illustrates. The flood that seeks to make up for Eve's heeding of the serpent's call also becomes an opportunity for animals to be renamed, or at the very least reorganized, by the human who saves them under divine dispensation. Genesis, then, can be said to stage the origin of human culture as an event in which the act of naming separates humans from animals. At its own origins, literature tells us of humans' invention of animals *as* animals. To say that animals are as old as literature, then, is also to say that they are not any older than literature.

But it is not only on the fictional plane of myth that humans can be said to have invented animals. As Jacques Derrida's use of the awkward neologism "animot" (a combination of "animaux," the plural of "animal" in French, and "mot," the word for "word") suggests, the single term "animals" is something of a fiction since it is used to group together a vast multiplicity of living beings. The strict division Western culture establishes between humans and animals may itself be the product of a certain form of us-and-them literality whose origins are in fact literary in nature. This division can be traced back through the history of Western thought in the different iterations of the definition of the human as a privileged species of animal that has or has had something extra or supplementary appended to its animal nature: the human is a political animal (Aristotle); a promising animal (Nietzsche); an animal with soul (Descartes); a time-keeping animal (Heidegger); etc. In all of these cases, humans are distinguished from their non-human cousins on the basis of cognitive, spiritual, intellectual, and linguistic considerations. Most of us would likely agree that humans, endowed with big brains, are capable of doing things that other animals cannot accomplish, but it is also true that other animals are capable of doing things that humans can only dream of doing without the aid of technology, or at any rate of doing them better: flying, swimming, running, smelling, hearing, etc. It might indeed be worth considering in this context to what extent technology is guided by humans' desire to become more like animals, or at the very least to make use of animal attributes that they don't otherwise possess. Moreover, the ability of certain animals to do certain things very well would distinguish them from other animals that are not capable of doing them as well as they can, or of doing them at all. We might imagine a category in which bats, for instance, are defined as echo-locating mice, flying mice, or cave-dwelling mice, but we would not thereby be usefully distinguishing bats from, say, centipedes. The problem, in other words, is not that the categorical distinction established between humans and animals is not based on factual difference; it is that the difference thus defined would seem to make us categorically distinct from all other members of the animal kingdom. The difference between humans and mollusks is just as marked as is the difference between camels and sparrows. We all share a common origin, as Darwin postulated, but in nature difference is all there is. What's more: difference is the very principle of evolution.

To suggest that the category "animals" is a human invention is thus not to deny the variety and diversity of life. On the contrary: it is to remark that the categorical distinction made between humans, on one side, and non-humans, on the other, is a figment of our imagination, a conceit that, by creating a rigid binary, in fact denies difference on a larger scale. There are of course many mechanisms, some discursive, some logical, some habitual, and others technological, that humans have devised to make this distinction hold and which have determined the way we have related to animals throughout history. The use of animals for food, clothes, tools, transport, war, labor, sport, devotion, and, of course, art has been made possible by the right we arrogate to ourselves to lord over the non-human world. Whether we imagine ourselves as the benign stewards of the planet, as the fearless captains of industrial progress, as disinterested pioneers in the search for knowledge, or as the selfless leaders of human emancipation from need, the fact remains that our relation to non-humans has most often been premised on our willingness to assert our domination over nature. The invention of the animal has thus been instrumental in the development of human culture by creating the conditions of possibility of our own invention as civilized beings. William Cronon's contention that "wilderness" is a human invention is to the point here, for, even though many animals exist within the domains of human civilization, these domesticated beings serve as a reminder of our unnatural regard toward the non-human world, which only exists "out there" in the "wild" nature of our imaginations.

But Cronon is also right to insist that the human invention of wilderness is a historical phenomenon, pertaining to specific human cultures and to specific moments in human history. If I maintain that animals are a human invention in a general sense, it is not because this particular invention has no history of its own; it is because I take the strict separation between human and non-human worlds to be a structural necessity for first positing, and then advancing, the idea of civilization. Daniel Defoe's *Robinson Crusoe* (1719) is instructive in this regard for it tells the story of a shipwreck who must reinvent his life by wresting from nature the means to satisfy his basic needs and, in doing so, to reestablish his difference from nature, thereby claiming the authority granted by civilized life to control it. Critics have read Defoe's novel as an allegory of the foundation of political sovereignty based on the concept of colonial protestant individualism, but little attention has been paid to the fact that Crusoe's process of reinvention is entirely premised on the domestication of animals—goats, cats, a parrot—and the use he makes of them for food, clothes, shelter, and companionship. (He makes his famous umbrella, the most over-determined symbol of his civilized individuality, out of animal skins.) Crusoe's story of human refashioning is all about the individual distinguishing himself from the other—non-humans, savages, cannibals, Friday, Spaniards—through a series of separations, the aim of which is a life of independent sovereignty in a state of nature.

To be sure, our conception of animals has changed drastically over time and continues to vary significantly from one culture to the next. Yet, most historians who study the history of human–animal relations agree that, at least in the West, the advent of industrialized modernity was decisive for the history of animals. Human–animal relations, as Harriet Ritvo has shown, underwent a radical transformation at the end of the eighteenth century when animals became "objects of human manipulation" as new economic realities, new technologies, growing global commerce, and abrupt demographic shifts increased the demand for animal labor and animal products. At the same time, the disappearance of animals from everyday life for the vast majority of urban dwellers made the presence of animals in cities as pets, zoo specimens, museum displays, and circus performers ever more imperative. These new roles for animals, categories that were largely created by a political logic that was for the first time based on biological quantification, changed the nature of the relation that had been established over thousands of years between humans and animals, giving rise to a new entity: the modern animal. Indeed, we can adapt Michel Foucault's famous claim (1970) that "man" was invented at the turn of the nineteenth century to assert that the modern animal was invented at the same time; the two inventions are in fact part of the same process.

This historical "mutation," as Foucault terms it, reconfigured our relation to animals in the form of an apparent paradox: on the one hand, a generalized cultural disavowal of the scale at which animals are killed in industry, science, and sport; on the other, the proliferation without precedent of discourses about animals through the development, institutionalization, and dissemination of knowledge about the natural world. Under different rubrics—natural history, comparative anatomy, phylogeny, embryology, genetics, ecology, etc.—the emergence of the biological sciences in the nineteenth century marks a decisive turn in the development of our knowledge of living beings and of the discourses that describe, catalog, and rationalize our complicated relation to animals. The institutional origins of literature as we know it today can also be traced back to this same period as a new referential relation to the world is inaugurated with the development of the two forms of literary empiricism that, *mutatis mutandis*, constitute for us the field of literature to this day: Romanticism and Realism.

Nature was of course a constant referent for the Romantics, but, despite the conspicuous presence of songbirds in its poetry, it is a nature that is oddly devoid of animal life. Romantic poetry occupies a landscape of the mind, which, excited by what it perceives in nature, emits through recollection a song that, though figured as the voice of a nightingale, is all poetic invention. The imagination is more subdued in Realism since, less spectacularly endowed with the power of composition, it is directed at the representation of social life. It arguably shares with the experimental sciences that are coming into being at the turn of the nineteenth century a binding empirical disposition toward reality, but Realism trains its considerable powers of description on human nature rather than on its relation to the non-human world. Modernism can be said to entangle these two modes of empiricism, inventing new representational forms to express, in a mode that may be described as a realism of interiority, the meanderings of consciousness as it records the social world it inhabits. As it enters the second half of the twentieth century, the mind can now only reliably reflect itself as it sings of a longing for songs of nature. To be sure, there are animals in this literary tradition, some even as famous as Moby Dick, but when we refer to modern literature we are not in general thinking of animals. It is mostly at the margins of this central canon—in children's literature, in genre fiction, in memoirs—that we find traces of the literary animal. Like droppings on the forest floor, these traces of the animal in literature suggest a number of possible tracks, histories, plots, and scenarios that both blur and reaffirm the double structure that at once binds human to non-human, and keeps them categorically separate from each other.

The history of modern literature is thus the history of an absence; an absence made all the more poignant by the cultural embeddedness of animals during the same period. But this paradox is not limited to the history of literature. To assert that it is would be to consign animals to the domain of representations and to forget that there are "real" animals out "there." Indeed, the human invention of the animal as a form of figuration informs other domains of knowledge, not the least of which is science. The most recent example of this form of figuration is the Anthropocene, the new epochal concept postulated by atmospheric chemist Paul Crutzen to account for the transformative influence of human action on the life of the planet. The dating of the Anthropocene is a matter of some dispute among geologists and environmental scientists, but, to the degree that the expansive scope and accelerated rate of humans' environmental impact can be traced back to the use of fossil fuels, it can be argued that it began with the Industrial Revolution. Our collective actions have altered the atmosphere, acidified the oceans, transformed the earth's biomes, and caused the extinction of plant and animal species on a scale that has reshaped the very fabric of life on Earth. We may no longer believe in the existence of unicorns, but, thanks to human action, the passenger pigeon, the Tasmanian tiger, and the dodo exists today only as museum relics. With our discovery of microorganisms, the myth of miasma was summarily debunked, but species new to humans are being located every day on a scale that suggests our current knowledge of the animal world, not to mention the very concept of species, could well be up for grabs. Scientists have catalogued approximately 1.8 million species, but estimates as to the total number of species in the world vary so widely as to make the prospect of settling on a figure an exercise in wishful thinking (Giller 2014). Of course, the enormous diversity of life on earth has a history of its own, most of which predates us and much of which still escapes us.

Darwin's theory of evolution offers a powerful model for giving an account of the history of animals, but the narrative he started is constantly being amended, revised, complicated, and expanded with the aid of new models, new technologies, new discoveries, and new scales of engagement with the natural world. Darwin himself, in a famous passage that appears at the end of *On the Origin of Species* (1859 [1964]), relies on analogy to posit a single origin of species: "Analogy would lead me one step further, namely, to the belief that all animals and plants have descended from some one prototype" (484). Indeed, we seem to have only an inkling of the magnitude of the task ahead of us if we are determined, as a species, to give a full account of the complexity of life on earth, a quantity that baffles the imagination. In a manner that may be more acute for science than for literature, but not for all that less figurative, we have to invent the animal in order to understand it.

It will have by now become clear to the reader that when I say that animals are a human invention I am not suggesting that koalas and seahorses, fantastic as they seem, do not exist at all, nor that, in describing them, we abstract them out of existence. The argument I am proposing is not, therefore, culturalist in the narrow sense of the term; rather, it seeks to account for the discourses that have made possible a view of nature—usefully defined by Kate Soper as "everything which is not human and distinguished from the work of humanity" (1995, 15)—that is, if not entirely accessible, certainly open to human manipulation. Animals exist in nature, to be sure, independently of human agency, but human agency deigns itself capable of apprehending all of nature. When we consider that human manipulation of animals has created, literally invented, many different forms of animals through domestication, husbandry, cloning, genetic engineering, and habitat destruction, however, the notion of human agency takes on a disturbingly literal character. Some animals have been invented specifically for use in scientific research. The JAX® mouse, for instance, is a commercially successful line of inbred mice used in genetics, cancer, and pharmaceutical research, and the OncoMouse™, a "transgenetic" mouse that contains a piece of human DNA, is used in breast cancer research (Rader 2004). Other inventions, such as the cloned sheep "Dolly," are scientific curiosities that, like Frankenstein's monster, seem to exist for the sake of showing that they can be invented rather than with human wellbeing in mind, since cloning large mammals seems to have little practical applicability at the present time.

But the human manipulation of animals is not limited to the laboratory. The vast majority of animals killed for food (more than 8 billion chickens are killed in the United States every year), have been modified chemically, physically, and genetically to such an extent that it is not an exaggeration to say that they have been invented in their present form. Similarly, domestic pets have been selectively bred so excessively that some breeds have developed traits that, as James Serpell notes, may well appeal to our "anthropomorphic perceptions" about companion species but that, on occasion, also endow them with severe health problems (2005, 129). The English bulldog, for instance, once a symbol of poise and athleticism is now so physically malformed that it has difficulty breathing and, on account of multiple deformities, most bulldogs must now be born by cesarean section (129). The destruction of habitats through agricultural and urban development, moreover, creates conditions that lead to the creation of new species when they do not cause outright extinction. Wolves and coyotes, whose habitats have been drastically altered by human encroachments, are interbreeding to produce hybrid offspring—the so-called coywolf—that are better adapted than their parent species to survive in an ecological niche created by humans (Velasquez-Manoff). Similarly, invasive species typically become invasive through human agency, irreversibly altering the ecosystems into which they enter and often causing the displacement or extinction of native species. The case of New Zealand is instructive in this regard. In the eighteenth century, British colonists began to introduce mammals in large numbers into New Zealand with devastating consequences for the distinctive fauna and flora of what had until then been an isolated environment that, in the absence of pressure from predators, had favored bird species (Kolbert 2014). As these examples show, humans have intervened decisively, if perhaps unwittingly in some cases, to create new animal species. To suggest that these inventions are in some way literary may of course obscure the extent to which the consequences of our actions on the natural world are all too real, but it is also important to recognize that the human imagination is nevertheless at work behind the invention of animals.

The point of enumerating different instances of animal manipulation by humans is not to establish a causal link between literature and what I have been describing as the human invention of the animal. Rather, it is to make the more general, and more generally applicable, claim that there is something literary about our relation to animals. When we are guided by empirical methods to describe animals, we must often fall back on figurative speculation (an apt way of describing literature) to begin to fathom the complexity of the natural world and of our roles within it. When we subsume this unfathomable animal kingdom under one single rubric, we also make visible our propensity to want to make it our own as well as our desire to use our enormous powers of invention to shape it for the benefit of that other abstraction we call "mankind." When we take all this into account and consider our relation with the so-called animals, we finally understand the immense need we have for literature to make us see with clear eyes how animals have always been part of our imagination, inventing us as much as we have invented "them."

## History for animals

The selective visibility of the animal—everywhere visible in culture and the popular imagination, yet hidden from view in factory farms, laboratories, and high art—suggests something else about our complicated relation to animals: that it is also socially determined. The hunter and the circus goer, the professor and the pet owner, the child and the worshiper, the fishmonger and the silk weaver, the sheep herder and the cartoonist, the ecologist and the shoemaker will each have a different view of what animals are and of how we ought to treat them. To the extent that literature directs its energies toward a description of the social, there is probably no better way of understanding the selective visibility of animals than by submitting our ideas about the treatment of animals to the literary pressure of tropes, plots, and personifications. But before suggesting how literary history provides the grounds for making this argument, it is worth examining the political history of human–animal relations as they have developed over the last two hundred years, beginning with what is their most visible formalization in the context of what we today generally refer to as animal rights.

The history of humans' concern for animal welfare dates at least as far back as Thomas Aquinas, but like those of John Locke and

Immanuel Kant several centuries later, his argument for the benign treatment of animals had more to do with the effect this form of behavior has on humans than for the sake of the animals themselves. "He who is cruel to animals," Kant wrote, "becomes hard also in his dealing with men" (1980, 212). These arguments seem to recognize humans' uneasy conscience regarding our treatment of animals, but this recognition does not yet amount to entertaining the possibility that animals be understood as rights-bearing beings. It is to Jeremy Bentham, the founder of utilitarianism, that we must refer when we talk about the origins of animal rights in the West. In a famous passage written in 1781, Bentham rhetorically associates animal rights with the abolition of slavery:

> The French have already discovered that the blackness of skin is no reason why a human being should be abandoned without redress to the caprice of a tormentor. It may come one day to be recognized, that the number of legs or the villosity of the skin, or the termination of the *os sacrum*, are reasons equally insufficient for abandoning a sensitive being to the same fate. What else is it that should trace the insuperable line? Is it the faculty of reason, or perhaps, the faculty for discourse?...the question is not, Can they *reason?* nor, Can they *talk?* but, Can they *suffer?*
>
> (Bentham 1781, 283)

Bentham's argument was highly influential at a time when animal welfare was beginning to be seriously debated and remains, to this day, a lodestone of the modern animal rights movement. Contemporary philosopher Peter Singer, whose *Animal Liberation* (1975) is one of the founding texts of the discipline of animal studies, updates and considerably expands Bentham's insight to argue against what he calls "speciesism," the discrimination of non-humans based on species difference. Bentham's utilitarian argument envisioned a less encompassing form of moral considerability for animals than does Singer's; Bentham, for instance, found suffering acceptable in animals used for scientific experiments if these could be shown to be beneficial to humans. But this difference perhaps reflects the debates into which Bentham intervened rather than the premises upon which they base their respective arguments, since Singer also subscribes to utilitarian principles in calling for the liberation of animals.

Bentham's argument paved the way for the gradual adoption of laws aimed at regulating the human treatment of animals in Britain. This incremental logic can be observed in the sequence of Parliamentary Acts that gave legal form to the growing political demand among Britons to face humans' ethical responsibility towards animals: the Act to Prevent the Cruel and Improper Treatment of Cattle of 1822 (also known as Martin's Act); the Cruelty to Animals Act of 1835, which was repealed and replaced in 1849, 1850, 1854, and 1876; the Wild Animals in Captivity Act of 1900; the Protection of Animals Act of 1911, which was amended in 1921, 1934, and 1954; the Abandonment of Animals Act of 1960; and the Animal Welfare Act of 2006, which consolidated the different types of animal rights legislation. The passage of these acts over the past two hundred years, together with the vigilant efforts and vigorous lobbying of organizations such as the Royal Society for the Prevention of Cruelty to Animals (founded in 1824) and the Victoria Street Society (founded in 1875), ensured that animal baiting, staged animal fights, unregulated animal vivisection, and other practices common to the eighteenth century in Britain were gradually outlawed or at least restricted.

Today, many countries have adopted some form of animal welfare legislation, and several drafts of a Universal Declaration on Animal Welfare (UDAW) have made their way through various levels of United Nations committees. The history of animal rights legislation in Britain is thus not unique, but it is exemplary in two respects. In the first place, it parallels the development and consolidation of industrial capitalism at the site of its greatest expansion in the nineteenth century, and therefore offers a historical index of the exploitation of animals in the modern world system. It also provides a time-line for visualizing the ways in which animals have come to occupy a significant, if not yet central, place in our political culture. It is tempting to write the story of legislative accomplishment as a narrative of redemption in which the cruelty we associate with traditional practices such as bear baiting, cock fighting, and horse flogging has gradually given way to a more enlightened attitude toward animals that makes us recoil before the abandonment of domestic pets, the abuse of cattle, and the neglect of circus animals. Yet, despite real advances in the amelioration of suffering for animals—the introduction of anesthetics in experimental situations, the development of more humane methods for killing livestock, the enforcement of laws regulating the use of animals in sports, the limits placed on hunting and fishing, etc.—the rate and pace of animal use has dramatically increased over the last two centuries. Indeed, the parallels between economic development and animal rights suggest themselves less as a narrative of mutual accommodation than as one of instrumentality, such that it is worth wondering if the history of animal protections is also the history of the protection of vested interests. Indeed, cultural historians such as Kathleen Kete suggest that animal rights legislation in the nineteenth century reflected class bias, restricting animal abuse among working class communities that depend on animals for their own survival while turning a blind eye to upper-class traditions such as horse racing and fox hunting that involve the cruel treatment and exploitation of animals.

Second, the incremental nature of animal rights legislation in Britain serves as a reminder of how the line that separates human from non-human animals is constructed. If the history of animal rights traces our engagement with the ethics of animal manipulation, it also demonstrates that logical and discursive barriers exist that may prevent us from engaging with animals ethically. Ludwig Wittgenstein goes so far as to argue that even if a lion could speak, we would not understand what it said, so different are human and animal as to make the bridging of the ontological chasm that separates us an impossible as well as a pointless task. Contemporary philosophers have not always found the task as daunting as all that, however, and a considerable body of work already exists that attempts to give account of humans' troubled relations to animals. I have already mentioned Peter Singer's utilitarian arguments against speciesism, but other philosophers have vigorously argued in favor of moral considerability for animals using other approaches. Tom Regan, for instance, argues for animal rights on the grounds of similarity: animals (at least those with certain cognitive abilities) are subjects of a life with inherent value and thus bear the same rights as humans. Mary Midgley argues that our consideration for animals ought to be measured using a reasonable scale (she uses the figure of concentric circles) according to which animal suffering is always weighed against whatever real advantages we might derive from it. Moving away from the Aristotelian view of biological exceptionalism for humans, Alasdair MacIntyre argues that some animals (dolphins, higher apes) are "dependent rational animals," and should thus be counted along with humans in our conceptualizations of community. Martha Nussbaum offers another sort of Aristotelian argument for moral considerability on a sliding scale, but on the basis of whether an animal can be said to be autonomously flourishing.

I will refer to some of these claims in more detail in subsequent chapters, but it is perhaps worth offering general remarks at this stage about philosophy's logical investments in the question of the animal. The manner in which the distinction between human and non-human animals is drawn has always been a condition of possibility for formulating a stance toward things from the point of view of humanity, a stance I take to be a defining characteristic of philosophy.

The historical time-line of philosophy's negative regard for animals, of course, stretches back far into the past for much longer than the time-line that reflects our efforts to counter such negative views by taking account of animal suffering. As I mentioned in the first part of this introductory chapter, the form of this negative regard is in one respect common to the Western philosophical tradition as a whole in that humans have been defined as animals endowed with certain characteristics that distinguish us from the rest of the animal kingdom (logos, soul, *techne*, time, deceitfulness, etc.), and which ostensibly render us superior to other animals.

Continental philosophy has had a longer engagement with the question of the animal, negative though this engagement has been in comparison with that of modern Anglo-American philosophers. Indeed, when one refers to the human–animal divide as a discursive construction in Western thought, one customarily refers to a tradition that stretches from Aristotle to Heidegger. This is not to say, of course, that contemporary Continental philosophers have not had something to say about the problem of the animal, but it is fair to say I think that their engagement has not been in any significant manner invested in animal rights discourse. In the work of Gilles Deleuze and Félix Guattari, for instance, the aim has been to conceptualize a new mode of considering the human subject as a process of becoming in which the distinction between human and animal, individual and group, community and pack, is fluid. What they call a "becoming" is a state of filiation in which what counts is not the category of species as a pure concept but the notion of a multiplicity as it bleeds into another multiplicity. Similarly, Derrida argues for a reappraisal of the animal from the perspective of the limitrophe region, marking the distinction between human and non-human as a region of limitless difference. The political implications of these formulations are, if evidently less pragmatic, no less rigorous and rather more radical than those we find in the Anglo-American tradition since they call for a wholesale reconsideration of what it means to be human, and, in particular, of what it means to be human with respect to non-humans. Animal rights discourse, from this perspective, is not as effective a strategy for undoing the human–animal divide as is its radical deconstruction: to demand rights for animals is to posit a degree of continuity or similarity between humans and animals so as to be able to make moral arguments about inclusiveness. Moreover, to the degree that animal rights discourse operates within a reparative logic whereby humans bestow (human) rights on those that never possessed them, it also tends to reaffirm the very distinction it seeks to overturn, since animals are at least implicitly defined as lacking reason,—as lacking, that is, the right to demand rights—when their fate is decided on the basis of a gradualist program of legal and political reforms that can well ameliorate animal suffering, but does not thereby change the nature of the relation.

But the discursive construction of the human–animal divide, however porous and unstable it has been shown to be by contemporary philosophers, is not of philosophical interest alone, if by "philosophical interest" we understand a rarified, constrained set of logical conventions that pertain exclusively to humans. It represents a stance toward animals that makes visible our commonplace assumptions about what our relations to animals ought to be like and, in doing so, helps to give shape to our conceptual authority over them. Quite apart from the question of whether certain philosophers would have understood their discourse as making possible the physical manipulation of animals, it is possible to argue that, historically speaking, the construction of a strict division between humans and animals enabled the manipulation of animals by making them not only inferior to humans but, to the precise degree that they do not possess the attributes that make humans distinctive, also incapable of objecting to how they are treated.

Italian philosopher Giorgio Agamben has coined the term "anthropological machine" to describe the discursive apparatus that both installs and polices the ontological difference Western thought posits between human and non-human. For Agamben, the distinction between human and animal is first established within the human. Citing the eighteenth-century French physiologist Xavier Bichat, Agamben argues that there are two "animals" within the human: an "internal" animal that is construed in biological terms alone, and an "external" animal that is distinctively human. The difference between the external and internal animals is not rigid; indeed, it passes within the human as a mobile border that creates a "zone of indifference" in which the distinction between human and animal is suspended. This exclusionary zone makes possible, by means of reversal, two symmetrical figures, each of which is inscribed as "bare life": the humanization of the animal in pre-modern times (the slave, the savage, the wild man), and the animalization of the human in modern times (the human in a vegetative state, the racial other, the Jew). The anthropological machine does not invent animals, or "animots," quite in the manner I described above; rather, it produces a form of animality that is thoroughly human. For Agamben, it conditions the very possibility of politics: the conflict between human and animal is the "decisive political conflict, which governs every other conflict" (2004, 80).

Indeed, beginning at the end of the eighteenth century, a whole new political order comes into being that is premised on the animalization of the human. "Biopower," Michel Foucault's (1978) name for this new political dispensation, operates by putting into motion a form of political rationalization that is based on the statistical capture of biological variables within a given population (birth rates, life expectancy, infant mortality, health risks, etc.). This "avalanche of numbers," to use Ian Hacking's suggestive phrase, creates the necessity for categories under which to tabulate different members of society (by age, sex, occupation, and so on), inventing, in the process, categories that now become the markers of difference within a population. Through a process Hacking calls "dynamic nominalism," these markers in turn invent the members of the category, who are now objectified according to specific traits that are deemed to be biological and thus "natural." Among these, there is perhaps none more slippery and insidious than the category of race, which, under biopower, becomes an overdetermined biological category that pertains to the "internal" rather than to the "external" human animal, even though the dividing practices to which it gives rise are carried out on the basis of "external" factors alone.

In his description of the anthropological machine, Agamben suggests that the totalitarian experiments of the twentieth century constitute the complete animalization of the human, and that modern human societies take on biological life as their sole political task. Agamben is not the only thinker to imbricate the history of animal manipulation with the political history of human societies. In one of the notes appended to their book *Dialectic of Enlightenment*, Max Horkheimer and T. W. Adorno make a suggestive argument about animals and power: "The Fascist's passionate interest in animals, nature, and children is rooted in the lust to persecute. The significance of the hand negligently stroking a child's head, or an animal's back, is that it could just as easily destroy them" (2002, 253). Political power, in this telling, is exercised through the threat of violence, but is premised on humans' drive to dominate nature, which here appears as the vulnerable figures of child and animal. Peter Singer, Jacques Derrida, and J. M. Coetzee make another suggestive connection between political power and animal subjection by drawing parallels between modern factory farms and Nazi concentration camps, which, according to some historians, operated using technologies of mechanization that can be traced back to the Chicago stockyards. But the historical conjunction of animal manipulation by humans and Nazi ideology runs deeper since the implementation of a eugenics program to select for so-called Aryan features was of a piece with programs to develop, through selective breeding, animal breeds that would manifest the mythic values by National Socialism. The so-called Heck cow, for instance, was developed under the auspices of Hermann Göring in an effort to restore the biological unity of the aurochs, now lost to time, and to place it at the same time in its original habitat, which was identified in the form of an old-growth forest in Poland that had been recently annexed by the Germans during WWII (Wang 2012).

It is worth reflecting in this context on whether selective breeding in domestic animals, practiced though it might be for sound agricultural reasons or for rather more questionable anthropomorphic ones, operates as the horizon of possibility for the division of human populations into racial categories, as though these were in fact biological distinctions on the order of species. Selective breeding in domestic animals is, of course, as old as domestication itself, with most modern breeds of cows, dogs, cats, pigs, and so on, having long lost their own ancestral "aurochs." Darwin himself of course made use of the detailed knowledge garnered from his breeding experiments with pigeons to confirm his theory of evolution. But the ability to create new breeds and select for specific traits among domestic animals does not mean that the distinctions among breeds are other than morphological, nor does it imply that "pure" animal breeds, like noble lineages among humans, should constitute an ontological difference from the mongrelized masses, even as both practices, animal husbandry and racist ideology, seem in this context to each provide grounds for the other. Eugenics, which had broad appeal in the United States before the Nazis made it their own, had its roots in the work of Francis Galton, who sought to apply the findings of his cousin Charles (Darwin) on human heredity, and counted C. C. Little, the inventor of the JAX® mouse, among its most fervent practitioners. The practice of eugenics is a justifiably condemned practice among humans, not because it is not possible to favor specific traits through sexual selection—this is in fact one of the pillars upon which Darwin's theory of evolution rests, even if, unlike human societies, nature does not operate according to design, intelligent or not—but because it is unethical.

Animals are certainly not accountable for the atrocities humans visit upon other humans, but the customary use of animal tropes in political rhetoric—perpetrators and victims are often qualified as "beasts" or "animals"—suggests that animals play an important symbolic role in politics; a role that, as the history of human–animal relations that I have hastily sketched so far indicates, is not solely symbolic. The threat of violence that underwrites the sovereign's discourse of power is premised on the quotidian power we exercise over nature, as though "negligently stroking" an animal's back. For Cary Wolfe, as long as it is institutionally taken for granted that it is all right to systematically exploit and kill nonhuman animals simply because of their species, then the humanist discourse of species will always be available for use by some humans against other humans as well, to countenance violence against the social Other of whatever species – of gender, or race, or class, or sexual difference.

(2003, 8)

But the discourse of power is also premised on the threat embodied by the sovereign, who presents himself as a beast whose unpredictable, irrational, ferocious, and even monstrous power is premised on an exalted form of animality. In the series of lectures collected under the title *The Beast and the Sovereign*, Jacques Derrida notes that the animality of the sovereign is an artificial form of animality, for the sovereign, exercising power through fear, must appear to be both beastly and invented by humans. Citing Hobbes's *Leviathan*, Derrida suggests that the state, personified in the figure of Leviathan, is created by "art" as an "Artificiall Man" that has to be understood as an animal-like monster (2009, 27). Derrida does not put it in these terms, but if we try to describe the figure of Leviathan as a trope, the trope of "anthropomorphism" falls short of describing Hobbes's figure since the state is not figured as a person, exactly, but rather as an artificially created animal that is meant to stand in for an ("Artificiall") person. It is, in short, a species of catachresis in that the state is posited as an unnatural beast that nevertheless rules over nature. But, for Derrida, this is not the only figural dimension of political rhetoric since politics itself is staged as a moral tale whose model is the animal fable. He uses the example of La Fontaine's fable *The Wolf and the Lamb* to show that political logic functions as a form of storytelling which entails not only the discursive elaborations of power but justifies and explains its actions as well. To be sure, the moral of La Fontaine's fable—"The reason of the strongest is always the best"—is apposite in the context of sovereignty, but animal fables, as a genre, have a more general political function since they constitute a fictional modality whereby the state makes known its power and its authority. Sovereignty relies on this fictive modality, or, better, "affabulation," to offer a narrative of its power, but also to conduct its policies since political action, including repression and war, are transacted within the moral universe of the fable.

Anthropomorphism and "affabulation" are two of the ways in which animals are figured in political discourse. Far from entailing a merely "symbolic" use of animals, however, political discourse is premised on humans' mastery over nature, with "real" animals always occupying the referential endpoint of this discourse, supporting in their vulnerability the rhetorical erasure to which they are submitted. This is also applies to the animalization of the human under biopower since to govern (oneself as well as others) on the basis of biology is already to consider oneself to possess mastery over biological processes, a mastery only arrived at through massive manipulation of animals. Animal rights discourse, in contrast, assumes that the politics of inclusivity that characterizes modern liberal societies can be extended to include animals, as though animals had always been excluded from the purview of human law and justice. The political history of human–animal relations, as the examples above suggest, is intricately tied to the figurative and literary dimensions in which they are represented. Animals, to paraphrase Marx, "cannot represent themselves, they must be represented" (1996, 117). The slippage between representation as a "speaking for" those that cannot speak for themselves (Marx uses the verb *vertreten* in German) and representation as a depiction, portrayal, or presentation (*darstellen* in German) is at work in the anthropological machine, which tends to reabsorb political action (as performative speech) into description (as constative speech). The challenge for animal studies is to disentangle the descriptive—empirical, philosophical, scientific, social, etc.—from the properly political. It is unlikely that animals will speak for themselves, and if they ever do, as Wittgenstein's example of the lion suggests, we may never be able to talk with them, but we must nevertheless attempt to create conditions that could make it possible. We can do this not only by conducting experiments designed to find ways of communicating with primates or dolphins—this form of research has certainly deepened our knowledge of how certain animals use symbolic systems—but also by carefully analyzing the ways in which animals have been described, portrayed, personified; in short, invented. It is through literary reading that this is best accomplished, not because there are no animals "out there," but because we have only had access to them through a screen of tropes.

## Tropes and taxa

Tropes—figures of speech such as metaphor, metonymy, irony, and so on——speak to us in myriad ways. Thomas Nagel is probably right in saying that it is impossible for us to know what it is like to be a bat *for* the bat, but we can readily imagine what it is like to be a bat for *us* as we do routinely with things we don't know. Tropes help us make informed approximations; "our conceptual system," as George Lakoff and Mark Johnson argue, "is largely metaphorical" (2003, 8). So, when we try to understand animals perhaps the more pertinent question to ask is:

what is it like to be a trope? In an often quoted essay, "Why Look at Animals?" John Berger suggests that the first metaphor was animal and that the relation between humans and animals was from the outset conceived of as a metaphoric relation. To say that the relation between humans and animals was always metaphoric, however, is not to suggest that it is abstract or non-existent; rather, it is to remark that tropes mediate our understanding of what we have in common with animals, and what we do not have in common with them. That is, tropes allow us to mark differences as well as to make associations with animals.

It may seem foolhardy to suggest that we should consider animals as tropes, given the precarious lives many animals lead in the Anthropocene. To think of animals as mere tropes rather than real, living entities has no doubt contributed to the ease with which we have killed, and continue to kill, wittingly and unwittingly, unconscionable numbers of animals. Indeed, as the argument I have thus far been making about the human invention of animals suggests, the trivialization of the animal through figure comes at a steep price for humans as well since it facilitates, licenses, and indeed sanctions certain types of atrocities perpetrated on humans by other humans. But to think of animals as mere tropes is not only a means to denigrate animals and humans alike; it is also to understate the power of tropes themselves. Tropes are the cognitive referents on the basis of which we make sense of the world, and which, in doing so, help us shape it. Here animal studies can provide a valuable lesson for literary scholars: the constant, if marginal, presence of animals in literature not only impels us to reconsider the significance of animal tropes, or, rather, of the animal-as-trope; it also pushes us to reassess the character, morphology, physiology, and force of tropes themselves, of the trope-as-animal.

What would it be like to imagine literary history as the history of the trope-as-animal? What if the history of metaphor—one way of thinking about the history of literature as a whole—were conceptualized as the history of the species of trope that refers to animals? The first thing to note about this imaginary genealogy is that the animal kingdom as it is described by the natural sciences is not proportionately represented in literary history. It is by no means surprising, of course, to discover that the animals represented in literature are those that exist in closest proximity to humans. This includes domesticated animals, to be sure, but also those with which we have historically had the most frequent contact: animals we hunt, animals we collect, animals we eat, animals we pet, etc. That horses, dogs, cats, parrots, pigs, and other domesticated or socialized animals are the most frequently represented is thus hardly surprising. Similarly, animals of the sort environmentalists have dubbed "charismatic megafauna" (apes, lions, tigers, eagles, elephants, wolves, bears, owls, etc.) inhabit a relatively ample literary terrain. Proportionally speaking, very few sea creatures make it into the literary canon, Moby Dick acting here as the large exception that proves the rule. Few insects, and no worms, grubs, mollusks, or microbes that I can think of can claim the status of literary "character." Scale, proximity, and familiarity indeed seem to determine the literary selection of animals, but even within the broad categories that are represented in literature, there is no self-evident reason for why certain animals attain the status of character while others languish in literary obscurity. Is there something like a coefficient of representability that might help us account for the fact that some animals are literary while others are not? Is there a measure we can use to understand the distribution of animals across the literary landscape?

Let's consider genre, the category most frequently used in literary history to classify the great variety of textual species. We find animals in every genre, of course, but if we were to construct a scale of genres arranged according to the presence of animals, we would have to settle on two or three genres that seem to aggregate animals in larger proportion than other genres: animal fables, the pastoral, and children's literature. Next to these, we would have to include genres in which animals are in some way important, but do not determine the basic characteristics of the genre: epics, chivalric romances, nature poetry, "it" narratives. Then we would need to include all the popular sub-genres of the realist mode that often include animals, but that are not centrally concerned with animals: naturalism, colonial romances, science fiction, frontier tales, adventure stories. Kafka lends his name (which means "crow" in Czech) to a unique generic moniker, the Kafkaesque, that comes to subsume all animal genres with dark bureaucratic efficiency. This partial classification is useful in that it allows us to visualize the distribution of animals in literature: lots of animals in minor genres (children's literature, so-called genre fiction, "it" narratives, etc.), but not so many in the dominant genres. Inasmuch as this pattern mirrors the status of animals in culture at large—marginal but constant—this form of classifying literary animals is not terribly productive since it shows us what we already know.

Or else consider one of the most traditional formal categories of which we avail ourselves when we read literature: plot. Can we talk of animal plots the way we talk about the marriage plot, the inheritance plot, or the revenge plot? To be sure, many animal plots are anthropomorphic in nature: the lion and the mouse, the crow and the fox, the hare and the tortoise represent human stances and moral positions for which animals serve as mere generic proxies. Fables focus on forms of behavior we can observe in nature—foxes *are* cunning; hares *are* quick; lions *are* fierce—but these forms of behavior are presented as an array of abstract and essentialized attributes that offer humans moral options, implying all the while that humans are capable of adopting the whole range of positions, while animals can represent only one. Other anthropomorphic animal plots endow animals with more complex characters, but they are driven by human action rather than animal behavior. The hunting plot—one of the oldest, if not the oldest, plot of all—traces the relation between hunters and hunted as a special relation that sometimes blurs the distinction between humans and animals. Melville's Captain Ahab, Hemingway's Francis Macomber, and Faulkner's Isaac McCaslin, to mention only one important strand of American literature, view their prey (whale, lion, bear) as though it were human, turning the hunt into a formidable contest in which the predominance of the human is understood to be at stake. The call-of-the-wild plot offers another perspective on the human–animal relation, though it functions on the basis of a distinction that structures human rather than animal societies. Jack London's misleadingly chiasmic tales of dog-wolves and wolf-dogs are premised on the notion that, as Buck and White Fang cross the boundaries between nature and civilization, what seems to be in play is the very limit of human's invention of nature, since for the animals the difference between being wild and being domestic is transacted through instinct rather than fancy. Many texts, of course, stage the crossing of the nature–culture boundary in the opposite direction, and it is the pull of civilization that seems to be instinctual. The myth of the wild child or *enfant sauvage*— domesticated in the story of Mowgli or Tarzan—traces the progress of the animal–human as it sheds its animality to become a member of the human community to which he always belonged, if not, as in Romulus and Remus, to become the founder of civilization itself.

Another way of understanding the animal plot is to think of plot itself as an animal. In the *Poetics*, Aristotle famously compares a well-constructed plot to a beautiful living creature:

> A well-constructed plot ... cannot either begin or end at any point one likes.... [T]o be beautiful, a living creature, and every whole made up of parts, must not only present a certain order in its arrangement of parts, but also be of a certain definite magnitude. Beauty is a matter of size and order, and therefore impossible either in a very minute creature, since our perception becomes indistinct as it approaches instantaneity; or in a creature of vast size - one, say, 1,000 miles long - as in that case, instead of the

object being seen all at once, the unity and wholeness of it is lost to the beholder. Just in the same way, then, as a beautiful whole made up of parts, or a beautiful living creature, must be of some size, but a size to be taken in by the eye, so a story or plot must be of some length, but of a length to be taken in by the memory.

(Aristotle 1984, 6)

Aristotle's analogy offers a possible category for analyzing plot. If scale and form are the elements we need to look for in narrative construction, could we imagine different types of plots in which the shape of narrative could be described using animal tropes? There could be a linear though winding serpent plot, a circular though prickly hedgehog plot, a plot as angular as the legs of a praying mantis, a Bildungsroman plotted from caterpillar to chrysalis to disillusioned butterfly, an elephantine structure so large as to rival the cetacean plot, which, perhaps swifter and more buoyant, would also be less memorable.

If we read Aristotle's analogy literally, the notion of an animal plot also puts us in mind of another facet of literary history that is routinely neglected in accounts of the rise of literary cultures. The history of literature cannot be considered apart from the animal products that have made possible the production, dissemination, and preservation of literary objects. It is not an exaggeration to say that quills, parchment, velum, glue, ink, pigments, hair, leather, and many other animal products are integral to the material history of literature; the animal "parts" of the "beautiful whole" of living literature. To classify the history of literature according to the animal materials that have been used in the creation of texts would give us a very different account of the uneven development of literature, and of its unequal planetary dissemination than the one we now have by allowing us to measure the relative permanence and portability of writing against the migration patterns and species distribution of specific animals.

What if we were to classify literary animals according to mode of representation? The categories could include: Animals that are represented as though they were human (talking animals); animals that are not real (fantastic animals); animals that appear as symbols (symbolic animals); animals that are real (real animals); etc. In this taxonomy, the category of talking animals would include all those animals that are anthropomorphically represented to stand in for human attributes or abstract ideas. Fantastic animals would include well-worn mythic animals like unicorns, dragons, and phoenixes, as well as human–animal hybrids such as mermaids, centaurs, and werewolves. Symbolic animals would be those that do not appear in literature in any concrete way but rather operate as symbolic repositories for human actions, human figures, and human anxieties: warriors, evildoers, monsters, racial others, and women are often referred to as animals. Then there are animals qua animals: the horses, dogs, cats, apes, and birds that routinely if uneventfully make their way through literature. These different forms of representation entail distinct figurative functions, each of which bears a specific relation to its referent (the animal as such), but they tell us little about how we are to read them.

Quoting "a certain Chinese Encyclopedia" called "The Celestial Emporium of Benevolent Knowledge," Jorge Luis Borges offers the following animal taxonomy:

> (a) those that belong to the emperor; (b) embalmed ones; (c) those that are trained; (d) suckling pigs; (e) mermaids; (f) fabulous ones; (g) stray dogs; (h) those included in this classification; (i) those that tremble as if they were mad; (j) innumerable ones; (k) those drawn with a very fine camel's-hair brush; (l) *et cetera*; (m) those that have just broken a flower vase; (n) those that at a distance resemble flies.
>
> (1999, 231)

This taxonomy suggests itself not only as an affront to the very question of order (this is how Michel Foucault reads it), but also as a challenge to reading since this taxonomy is as much a literary taxonomy as it is an animal taxonomy in which the animal referent seems to recede into the distance.

What then if we classified literary animals according to the readers who read animals? For some readers, nature poetry without nightingales, robins, and blackbirds is inconceivable; pastoral poetry without sheep unimaginable; chivalric romances without *chevaux* (horses) unseemly. For some readers, of course, literature is *only* about animals. Children typically learn about literature and animals simultaneously, finding in the symbolic universe of words and pictures (I paraphrase from memory here) a veritable treasure trove of familiar tropes, shapes, and colors that make the distinction between human and animal hard to discern. The question of whether the anthropomorphic representation of animals refers us back to a prelapsarian Eden in which child and beast coexist in harmony, or instead, accounts, from an early age, for our subsequent propensity to keep us categorically apart is less important, I think, than the fact that the animals so represented are not animal-like at all. The best example of this are Lewis Carroll's *Alice* books in which the improbable Mock Turtle and the March Hare stand in for cultural constructs that would deny their animality. That they are also the material expression of sophisticated puns (the Mock Turtle has the body of a sea turtle and the head, hoofs, and tail of a calf—turtle soup made from beef broth; the March Hare is as mad as the saying that would vouch for its condition) suggests that Carroll was already pointing to the figurative regard we have for animals rather than to their animality. Whether the presence of animals in literature written with children in mind is a historical constant or a further instance of our inevitable presentism, the fact remains that the genre we know today as children's literature contains the largest density of animal characters in all of world literature. This might reflect a peculiar view of childhood in which children are little more than animals, or perhaps it is an attempt to disavow our animal selves by mocking, infantilizing, manipulating, or otherwise animating the animal as a human plaything. The development of animation in the twentieth century—a medium whose inventiveness, plasticity, and often absurd and violent narrative situations cannot be separated from the fact that its defining characteristic is the anthropomorphic representation of animals—suggests that childhood might also be thought of as that symbolic space where our paradoxical relation to animals is first established: sentimental attachment and feckless disregard.

If literary history, as I have been describing it, is intimately tied to the representation and manipulation of animals, how then can we account for the vast multiplicity of literary animals? In this book, I take a figurative approach to classification by grouping the most commonly used animal tropes into literary taxa. The taxon "Equids," for instance, includes the various iterations of the trope of the horse, the donkey, and the mule that serve as a measure of human aspiration in the context of war, conquest, chivalry, and labor. Under the category "Canids" I include literary texts that treat dogs, wolves, foxes, coyotes, and other members of the Canidae family with the aim of specifying the tropological functions to which literature submits these carnivorous and variously domesticated animals. "Songbirds" includes all species of oscines that relate to literature's view of itself as a natural song. Grouping together the different types of cats that make their way into literature, the heading "Felids" addresses the otherness of the animal through the elusive and philosophical presence of cats. "Vermin" groups all those otherwise unclassifiable animals that appear in literature as abject others (rats, cockroaches, and other vermin) and whose tropological function is one of exclusion and accountability, and is thus foundational to politics, even to animal revolutions.

Each of these taxa forms the thematic core of the chapters that follow. In using these taxa to analyze the figurative presence of animals in literature, I am also making an argument about how we should read animals in literature. I have already described some of the ways in which animals and literature are historically intertwined, like the two serpents of the caduceus. The chapters that follow expand upon these themes by linking the representation of animals to the history of their manipulation by humans. The relation I wish to trace between the history of literature and the history of that other human invention we call the animal is in no straightforward way causal, nor is it meant to be understood as "merely" figurative. The consequences of our literarization of the animal (our rendering of animals as seemingly unreal or insignificant) in and outside of literature proper are all too real and significant to ignore. Yet my contention is that only by disentangling the various strands of the literary animal (of the literarity of the animal) at the place of its greatest visibility as figure (that is, in literature) that we can begin to understand the significances of animals "out there" in the place of greatest resistance to the figurality of the animal.

As a result, this book does not examine the whole range of what one could consider literary representations of the figure of the animal: cinema, television, and the digital media do not receive the attention that they surely deserve, whereas the various institutions of literature (prose, poetry, drama) carry an inordinate and perhaps unwarranted explicatory burden, given their somewhat anachronistic standing in today's critical and cultural environment. The term "literature" as I use it throughout, moreover, does not cover, by any stretch of the imagination, all the literature produced by humans since its inception as a recognizably literary form of discourse. The use of the term is thereby limited to the limitations of the author, and thus encompasses a very reduced number of works of literature, mostly from the global north and the hemispheric west, and mostly from the last two centuries. But, while limiting the field of inquiry to literature—and a severely limited version of literature, at that—the sample of literary animals here examined is, I hope, nevertheless representative in that it offers the necessary and sufficient conditions for reading the animal, which method might now be described thus: a figural reading of figure, or, what is it like to be a trope?

## Works cited

Agamben, Giorgio. *The Open: Man and Animal*, trans. Kevin Attell. Stanford: Stanford University Press, 2004.

Aristotle. Poetics. *The Complete Works of Aristotle*. Vol. 2, ed. Jonathan Barnes. Princeton: Princeton University Press, 1984.

Bentham, Jeremy. *An Introduction to the Principles of Morals and Legislation.* Eds. J. H. Burns and H. L. A. Hart. London: Methuen, 1781.

Berger, John. "Why Look at Animals?" In *About Looking.* New York: Vintage, 1992.

Borges, Jorge Luis. "John Wilkins Analytical Language." *Collected Fictions*, ed. and trans. Eliot Weinberger. New York: Penguin, 1999. 229–32.

Darwin, Charles. *On the Origin of Species.* Cambridge: Harvard University Press, 1964.

Deleuze, Gilles and Félix Guattari. *A Thousand Plateaus*, trans. Brin Massumi. Minneapolis: University of Minnesota Press, 1987.

Derrida, Jacques. *The Animal That Therefore I Am*, ed. Marie-Louise Mallet, trans. David Wills. New York: Fordham University Press, 2008.

Derrida, Jacques. *The Beast and the Sovereign* Vol. 1, trans. Geoffrey Bennington. Chicago: University of Chicago Press, 2009.

Foucault, Michel. *The Order of Things.* New York: Vintage, 1970.

Foucault, Michel. *The History of Sexuality: An Introduction*, trans. Robert Hurley. Vol. 1. New York: Vintage, 1978.

Giller, Geoffrey. "Are We Any Closer to Knowing How Many Species There Are on Earth?" *Scientific American*, April 8, 2014: www.scientificamerican.com/article/are-we-any-closer-to-knowing-how-many-species-there-are-on-earth/

Hacking, Ian. "Making Up People." In *Reconstructing Individualism.* Eds. Thomas Heller, Morton Sosna and David E. Wellbery. Stanford: Stanford University Press, 1986: 222–36.

Hacking, Ian. *The Taming of Chance.* Cambridge: Cambridge University Press, 1990.

Horkheimer, Max and T. W. Adorno. *Dialectic of Enlightenment*, trans. Edmund Jephcott. Stanford: Stanford University Press, 2002.

Kafka, Franz. *The Metamorphosis*, trans. and ed. Stanley Corngold. New York: W. W. Norton, 1966.

Kant, Immanuel. *Lectures on Ethics*, trans. Louis Infield. New York: Hackett, 1980.

Kete, Kathleen. *The Beast in the Boudoir.* Berkeley: University of California Press, 1995.

Kolbert, Elizabeth. "The Big Kill." *New Yorker.* Dec. 22, 2014.

Lakoff, George and Mark Johnson. *Metaphors We Live By.* Chicago: University of Chicago Press, 2003.

MacIntyre, Alisdair. *Dependent Rational Animals.* Peru, IL: Open Court, 2001.

Marx, Karl. "The Eighteenth Brumaire of Louis Bonaparte." In *Later Political Writings*, trans. Terrell Carver. Cambridge: Cambridge University Press, 1996: 31–127.

Midgley, Mary. *Animals and Why They Matter.* Athens: University of Georgia Press, 1983.

Nussbaum, Martha. "'Beyond Compassion and Humanity': Justice for Non-Human Animals." *In Animal Rights: Current Debates and New Directions.* Eds. Cass Sunstein and Martha Nussbaum. Oxford: Oxford University Press, 2005: 299–320.

Rader, Karen. *Making Mice*. Princeton: Princeton University Press, 2004.

Regan, Tom. *The Case for Animal Rights*. Berkeley: University of California Press, 2004.

Ritvo, Harriet. *The Animal Estate*. Cambridge: Harvard University Press, 1989.

Serpell, James. "People in Disguise." In *Thinking with Animals*. Eds. Lorraine Daston and Gregg Mitman. New York: Columbia University Press, 2005: 121–136.

Singer, Peter. *Animal Liberation*. New York: Ecco, 1975.

Soper, Kate. *What is Nature?* Oxford: Blackwell, 1995.

Velasquez-Manoff, Moises. "Should You Fear the Pizzly Bear?" *New York Times Magazine*. August 14, 2014: www.nytimes.com/2014/08/17/magazine/should-you-fear-the-pizzly-bear.html

Wang, Michael. "Heavy Breeding." *Cabinet* 45, 2012: 19–23.

Wittgenstein, Ludwig. *Philosophical Investigations*. 3rd Ed, trans. G. E. M. Anscombe. London: Basil Blackwell, 1968.

Wolfe, Cary. *Animal Rites*. Chicago: University of Chicago Press, 2003.

# 2    Equids (might and right)

Near the beginning of Dickens's *Hard Times* (1854), Thomas Gradgrind, a retired hardware merchant who acts as school governor, asks Sissy Jupe, one of the students at his school, to define a horse. Sissy has lived with horses all her life since her father "belongs to the horse-riding" (4), as she tells Mr. Gradgrind, a man so full of facts that he would presumably not fail to know a horse from his elbow. Yet, Sissy is unable to produce an adequate answer. Bitzer, one of Sissy's classmates who is trained in facts, facts, facts, defines it thus: "Quadruped. Graminivorous. Forty teeth, namely twenty-four grinders, four eye-teeth, and twelve incisive. Sheds coat in the spring; in marshy countries, shed hoofs, too. Hoofs hard, but requiring to be shod with iron. Age known by marks in mouth" (5). Satisfied with this answer, Gradgrind goes on to ask the school children if one ought to paper a room with representations of horses. Horses do not "in fact" walk up and down the sides of rooms and therefore, he says, pictures of horses must not be used to paper walls. On his way home, he is surprised to find his children, the "metallurgical Louise" and the "mathematical Tom," trying to catch a glimpse of the equestrian spectacle staged by "Sleary's Horse-riding," the circus where the Jupes work. Louisa, who is "tired of everything," says that they just wanted to know what it was like. They too are trying to define a horse.

*Hard Times* has been traditionally read as an industrial novel (albeit one that tends to side with management rather than labor) or as a novel on education (one that attacks the utilitarian devotion to facts over the cultivation of fancy), but what if we were to think of it as a novel about horses? It might then be read as an attempt to find different ways of defining a horse. At the end of the novel, Bitzer is held captive in a carriage by the actions of a dog and a horse that, trained to dance by Sissy's father, prevents him from catching Tom Gradgrind, who, trained on facts by his own father, has become a bank robber and is about to flee the country. "And if my horthe," as Sleary memorably puts it, "ever thtirth from that thpot where he beginth a danthing, till the morning—I don't know him!—Tharp'th the word!" (290). Sleary's "horthe" may be a graminivorous quadruped but it is also a stalwart and "tharp" performer whose actions save the day.

The industrial setting of these scenes (Coketown and then Liverpool) suggests that part of the challenge of defining a horse for Dickens and his characters has to do with the changing fortunes of the horse in the latter half of the nineteenth century as society came to rely less and less on its instrumental value. For centuries, horses had been the hallmark of human civilization: humans had been able to travel, fight, haul, and build in ways that surpassed their own natural abilities by harnessing the power of the horse. By the middle of the nineteenth century, however, horses were beginning to be replaced by the steam engine. The train, the most visible symbol of steam power in the nineteenth century, was appropriately dubbed the "iron horse." Today, horses are no longer used in industrialized societies for transport, agriculture, war, and industry, their historical significance having only been retained in the ghostly figure of the "horsepower," the unit of power championed by our fossil-fueled modernity.

Literature, as this chapter will endeavor to show, has preserved in its own history the legacy of the horse. Perhaps most commonly associated with classical epics, novels of high adventure, and coming-of-age stories for girls, the horse has nevertheless appeared as a character in all forms of literature from its very beginnings. It is also the only animal after which a major literary genre, and indeed a whole era, is named—the *cheval* (horse in French) of the chivalric romance in the age of chivalry. Indeed, the history of literature as a whole could be read, like Dickens's novel, as an attempt to define the role of the horse in human culture. In this chapter, I look at the two most important manifestations of the horse in literature: the warhorse and the laboring horse. As we shall see, the definition of political power (might) and social responsibility (right) are at stake in the historical development of these two literary tropes, and form the thematic core of the equine text.

## Warhorses

Before warriors rode horses to battle, they rode in them; or, rather, in one very special horse: the so-called Trojan horse, which, like philosophy, was really a Greek invention. The story tells of how the Greeks were able to deceive the Trojans by hiding inside a wooden horse they claimed to have built in honor of the goddess Athena before returning home. The Trojans, persuaded that the Greeks had left their shores in defeat, brought the horse inside their citadel as a trophy for their triumph, which they proceeded to celebrate with catastrophic consequences as the Greek warriors emerged from the horse to crash the party. Homer does not mention the wooden horse in the *Iliad*, but Odysseus's role in the defeat of the Trojans is mentioned in the *Odyssey* when Meneláos tells Telemachos, who is looking for news of his father, that he, Odysseus, prevented the Greeks from betraying themselves when they were hiding inside the womb of the wooden horse by making them realize that it was Helen who was calling their names using their wives' voices. Odysseus himself mentions the feat later in the *Odyssey* when he asks Demódokos, the blind minstrel, to "sing that wooden horse Epeios built, inspired by Athena" (VIII, 526–7) and weeps when the minstrel reminds him of the culminating episode in the ten-year war. Euripides's play *The Trojan Women* opens with Poseidon's description of Epeios's invention, calling it the "Wooden Horse, which hid the secret spears within" (2013, 82).

In the Latin tradition, the story of the Trojan horse appears in Virgil's *Aeneid*, told from the perspective of the Trojans. Aeneas, recently arrived at Carthage, tells Queen Dido of his seven-year voyage in search of Italy, the Trojans' ancestral home. In his narrative, he refers to the wooden horse as a "steed of monstrous height" (*montis equum*) and as a "deadly engine" (*fatalis machina*) that, against the better judgment of those who can reason free of the influence of meddlesome gods, was hauled within the city walls. The Greeks, "inside the womb" (*inclusos utero*), climbed out as soon as Sinon, the soldier who had convinced the Trojans that the Greeks were heading home, secretly opened the wooden enclosure (*pinea furtim laxat claustra Sinon*).

These iterations of the story of the Trojan horse, which should henceforth be referred to as the Trojan mare, not only suggest that one should always look a gift horse in the womb, but also that the horse as we know it is the product of human ingenuity. Inspired by Athena, Epeios builds a wooden figure that already represented a "deadly machine" to the extent that ever since humans managed to turn an imposing and graceful quadruped into an instrument of war, real horses were deadly animals; and, to the degree that the Trojan horse stands as a symbol of deception as an essential aspect of the art of warfare—the idea of building the horse is attributed to the "cunning" and "sly" Odysseus, whose adventures after the siege of Troy make him the very symbol of ingenuity—it also suggests that deception, a uniquely human attribute, is what allows humans to break, mount, and train horses. (Monty Python in *Monty Python and the Holy Grail* make this point when, after the French have used animals to attack them—catapulting cows, dogs, deer, pigs, etc.—the horseless Knights of the Round Table decide to build a wooden rabbit to help them enter the castle. Before the French seize hold of the Trojan rabbit outside the castle gates, however, the knights realize that they have forgotten to climb inside.) The Trojan horse stands as the larger-than-life symbol of the human triumph over nature and, to the extent that it was only built in literature, of the importance of singing of this triumph *in* literature.

Homeric epics provide us with another instance of the literarity of the horse in the figure of Xanthus, the first talking horse in literature. Xanthus, one of the three horses that pull Achilles's chariot in the *Iliad* (the other two are Balius and Pedasos), is granted human speech after he is chastised by Achilles, who is grieving over the death of his friend Patroclus. Xanthus tells Achilles that Patroclus was slain by a god and prophesies that a god will also kill Achilles, before the Furies, as Chapman's translation renders it, "stopp'd his voice" (XIX, 403). Xanthus and Balius are immortal horses, not only because they have endured in the *Iliad* for many centuries, but also because, in the *Iliad*, they are described as divine creatures, born of Zephyr and the Harpy Podarge.

The horse of the Homeric epic occupies a special place in human history, represented as an animal essential to the waging of war among humans, both as a laboring combatant and as a symbol of the victory of a group of humans and their gods over another group of humans and their gods. The literary figuration of the horse as an instrument of war (a "deadly engine") corresponds to the exalted place horses have held among domesticated species, and the prestige that this special place lends to the epic as a genre. But the horse also appears in antiquity in already fantastical forms, which suggests as well that the horse is a symbol of human aspiration and imagination. Consider Pegasus, the winged horse. Hesiod, our first source for the story of Pegasus, tells us that he was the offspring of Poseidon, the god of horses, and Medusa, from whose severed head he emerged:

> When Perseus cut her head off from her neck, great Chrysaor and the horse Pegasus sprang forth; the latter receives his name from being born beside the waters [*pegae*] of Ocean, the former from holding a golden [*chrysos*] sword [*aor*] in his hands.
>
> (2006, 25–27)

Bellerophon, Apollodorus tells us, rode the winged horse when he slayed the Chimera. And what about the centaur? This half-human, half-horse hybrid is not only a great warrior but also a wise teacher: Chiron, perhaps the most famous centaur, is associated with hunting and medicine. He is said to have tutored Hercules and Achilles, to whom he bequeathed a powerful spear made of ash that Homer, in Pope's translation, describes as the "death of heroes and the dread of fields" (XIX, 425).

The horse can thus be said to play two complementary roles in antiquity: it is an instrument of war and a symbol of human ingenuity and imagination. The horse makes humans bigger, faster, and more menacing in war, and, as the example of Trojan horse suggests, stands as a symbol of humans' ability to harness nature or, what amounts to the same thing, as a symbol for politics. (From this perspective, Aristotle's famous definition of the human as a political animal—*zoon politikon*—may well need to be adapted to define the horse as the political animal of the political animal, a figurative association perhaps best captured in the equestrian statue, the status symbol of status symbols.) Indeed, the domestication of the horse is one of the key features of human civilization, whose history can be charted by the changing relation obtaining between horse and human. This relation enjoys its most overdetermined cultural moment in the passage from antiquity to modernity. The relation between knight and horse, as Susan Crane notes, is "the most densely represented of all cross-species interactions" in the Middle Ages (2013, 137). To be sure, the horse is a crucial historical actor in Medieval Europe, but it is also a rhetorical repository for the cultural values espoused in the so-called age of chivalry. Before turning to the *cheval* of chivalry, however, it is instructive to first examine an imaginary equid in order to appreciate the discursive importance of the horse in the literary culture of the Middle Ages.

The unicorn, an animal that has only ever existed in literature, functions as a sort of symbolic relay between the horse of antiquity and that of the Medieval period. It carries the mythical weight of Pegasus, but operates in a recognizably Christian world for which it comes to symbolize the values of a devout yet belligerent culture. By the seventeenth century, as Boria Sax remarks, the educated classes no longer believed in the existence of the unicorn, but the unicorn, that unusual horse whose single horn was endowed with untold powers, nevertheless occupied a special place in the Medieval imagination, his capture having become an "exceptionally intricate allegory of the birth, Passion and execution of Christ" (2013, 7). This religious allegory can be traced back to the early theologians. It appears in a popular treatise called *Physiologus*, probably written by Didymus the Blind of Alexandria in the second century, where its capture is described using Christian iconography. The unicorn cannot be captured, according to this allegory, unless it poses its head on the lap of a virgin, after which it can be peacefully led away. The story of the unicorn and the virgin, however, was condemned as heresy in 496 by Pope Gelasius I, who had *Physiologus* placed on the church's list of forbidden books. The unicorn nevertheless reappeared in medieval bestiaries, where it enjoyed a symbolic second life as an allegorical vehicle for chivalric practices. A knight, like a unicorn, was supposed to be fierce and unyielding in battle yet gentle and devoted to his lady, whom he served blindly if somewhat mysteriously. The so-called "Unicorn Tapestries" (1495–1505) hanging in the Cloisters in upper Manhattan depict a series of scenes in which the capture of a unicorn parallels the death and resurrection of Christ. In one panel, a maiden and a group of hunters surround a captured unicorn whose slain body is made to resemble Christ's body with a necklace of holly standing in for a crown of thorns. In another, the unicorn, shown penned in a field of flowers, comes to embody the resurrected body of Christ, now willingly accepting the bonds of love. Sax (2013) argues that the complexity of the allegorical relay that joins the fantastical with the religious in the figure of the unicorn forms part of a complex symbolic reorganization of religion at a time in which the question of religious devotion and affiliation was fraught with danger.

It is against this background that the role of the horse in Medieval literature must be read. The first thing to note is that Medieval literature is unimaginable without the horse. The role of the horse in Medieval Europe's most important literary genre, the chivalric romance, consists, as its name implies, in nothing less than a structural necessity. The close bond obtaining between horse and horseman (*caballero, chevalier, Ritter*, knight) informs the culture of chivalry operating in the Middle Ages as well as the literature that emerges during this period. Crane analyzes two aspects of this bond: the technology of war that gave rise to a compact fighting unit in the mounted knight and the human/animal relation that subtended this war machine and which bestowed upon the horse a form of subjectivity. We see this to some extent in Homer's treatment of Achilles's horses, but the horses in the *Iliad* engage in battle by pulling the chariot on which the hero rides. In the Medieval imaginary, the horse, ridden by the knight, has become a physical prosthesis that, along with armor and weapons, creates a formidable fighting assemblage designed for what Medievalists call "mounted shock combat" (Crane 2013, 139).

At the same time, Medieval tales of chivalry (*chansons de geste*) very often personalize and personify the horse: El Cid's Babieca,

Charlemagne's Tencendur, Roland's Veillantif, Bevis's Arondel, Gawain's Gringolet. These horses are not only fearsome combatants in their own right; they are also the most noble of knightly companions. Here is Babieca in *Poema de Mio Cid* [*The Poem of the Cid*] (ca.1200) (1987):

> Por nombre el cavallo Bavieca cavalga,/ fizo una corrida, ésta fue tan estraña,/ quando ovo corrido, todos se maravillavan,/ d'és día se preçió Bavieca en quant grant fue España.
>
> (Anon. 1987, lines 1589–1592)

> [And he leaped upon him and ran a course so marvellous that all wondered, and from that day Babieca was held to be worth all Spain.]
>
> (Anon. 1879, 90)

In this telling, the horse is worthy of praise not only for its evident poise; it is a veritable national treasure that enabled the Cid to reclaim Spain, or at least part of it, for Christendom. The horse is not only the mount of a redoubtable hero. It is itself heroic, combining the most prized attributes of the knight—bravery, honor, nobility, loyalty—with the unique characteristics of the warhorse: strength and speed but also the repertoire of the, as it were, unbridled behaviors associated with stallions, including rearing, kicking, and biting (Crane 2013, 143). The Medieval warhorse, moreover, follows the affective logic of the culture of chivalry. Arondel, for instance, proves its loyalty to its master when it recognizes Bevis after seven years' absence: "Bevis went up to the horse; then the horse saw and knew him. He stood completely still until Bevis caught hold of the stirrup. Bevis threw himself into the saddle; thereby that maiden well knew him" (cited in Crane 2013, 156). The scene thus represents a double recognition: the horse recognizes Bevis and, once Bevis mounts Arondel, Josian, the "maiden" to which the passage refers, recognizes Bevis. The horse's recognition is instinctual or "animal" while the maiden's is social: Bevis is a knight only to the extent that he is mounted on a horse; without the horse, he is only a pilgrim.

The idealized horse of the age of chivalry has no better counterpart than Don Quixote's Rocinante, the first modern horse in literature. Rocinante, who is first introduced as a "rocín" (a workhorse or hack), is made to bear the burden of Don Quixote's mad attempt to recapture the lost art of chivalry, of which he has gained a profound if idiosyncratic knowledge from the many books of chivalry he has read. The act of naming the horse with which he hopes to embark on his knightly adventures is, therefore, a matter of careful consideration. It takes him four days:

> Y así, después de muchos nombres que formó, borró y quitó, añadió, deshizo y tornó a hacer en su memoria e imaginación, al fin le vino a llamar Rocinante: nombre, a su parecer, alto, sonoro y significativo de lo que había sido cuando fue rocín, antes de lo que ahora era, que era antes y primero de todos los rocines del mundo.
>
> (Cervantes 1605 [1987], 76)

> So, after many names invented, struck out and rejected, amended, cancelled and remade in his fanciful mind, he finally decided to call him Rocinante, a name which seemed to him grand and sonorous, and to express the common horse he had been before arriving at his present state: the first and foremost of all hacks in the world.
>
> (Cervantes 1605 [1950], 34)

Rocinante, a name both generic and exalted, is also a literary product, both in terms of its absent referent (Babieca, the most famous horse in the Spanish chivalric tradition) and in terms of its condition as an old workhorse, the very antithesis of El Cid's knightly horse. The rhetorical alchemy that turns a common noun (rocín) into a proper name (Rocinante) is, in horse terms, the equivalent of using a hack as a warhorse. In keeping with the deflationary irony characteristic of Cervantes's novel, the leveling effect material reality (*rocín*) has on the idealized conventions of the chivalric romance (Babieca) is matched by the sheer flair of inventiveness (Rocinante!) that draws the most prosaic of characters, objects, events, and circumstances into Don Quixote's deranged sensorium, and thereby turns a drab existence into something at least more endurable. This process is further developed in a sonnet that appears in the prologue to the first part of *Don Quixote* in which Cervantes stages a dialogue between Babieca and Rocinante. These are the last three lines of the sestet:

> ¿Cómo me he de quejar en mi dolencia,/ si el amo y escudero o mayordomo/ son tan rocines como Rocinante?
>
> (Cervantes 1605 [1987], 68)

> [How can I complain despite my aches and pains if master and squire, or is it majordomo, are nothing but skin and bone ("rocines"), like Rocinante?]
>
> (Cervantes 1605 [1950], Prologue)

Rocinante is of course correct in calling Don Quixote and Sancho Panza "rocines" since they too are unremarkable, but, to the extent that in order to do so Cervantes must give Rocinante a voice—and a poetic voice, at that—the realistic conceit of "calling a horse a horse" is counterbalanced by the figurative act of calling humans to account as horses. In Cervantes's novel, Rocinante is guided more by concrete bodily needs than by the abstract concepts (honor, glory, and loyalty) that impel Don Quixote to take to the road. But it is not only the sheer animality of his nature that makes Rocinante the first modern horse. The fact that he is made to participate in ever more demented adventures suggests that he too is a literary invention and that, in coming in and out of the fictional realm like all the other characters in Cervantes's meta-fictional universe, he too is, like all of us, constantly straddling the human–animal divide.

In an altogether different register, Shakespeare's *Richard III* offers an otherwise similar contrast between the idealized heroes of chivalric romance and material reality, in this case through Richard's deformed body. Like Don Quixote, Richard pretends to be something he is not; unlike Don Quixote, however, Richard goes to great murderous lengths to show that he is not who he is. To be sure, Richard is a tragic rather than a comic figure, and his relation to his horse, unlike that of a knight, mad or otherwise, is one in which the bond between horse and knight is characterized by the fact of its being fatally broken. The most famous horse in Shakespeare is in fact a horse that does not exist at all. As his army is nearing defeat, Richard utters these famous last words: "A horse, a horse! My kingdom for a horse!" (5.iv.9). That he utters them twice does not, for all that, provide him with a horse, and it is its absence that best reflects his political situation. Indeed, the absence of a referent for "horse" in his last words tells us more about his political fate than the many murders he has committed in order to gain ascendancy over the house of York. Richard's desperate cry for a horse rings hollow not only because he is lost but also because in equating "kingdom" with "horse" he is already invoking a past in which, like the figure of the Trojan horse suggests, the horse was a symbol of both power and deceit. Without a horse, Richard cannot be recognized as a knight the way Bevis was recognized as a knight by Josian, and thus much less as the king. Historians agree that Richard's reign brought an end to the Middle Ages, an age whose emblem, as his last words so pathetically illustrate, had left the political stage.

The modern European warhorse, conceptualized by Cervantes and Shakespeare as an empty signifier, had already been reinvented during the period that separates Babieca from Rocinante. A new horse, the American horse, had entered the scene to bear the burden of a wholly different symbolic order. First brought to the new world by the Spanish *conquistadores*, the horse would become the symbol of a new economic and political order in the Americas. The Spaniards, who had made use of the chivalric discourse of warfare during the Reconquista, the medieval wars in which they recaptured the Iberian Peninsula from Arab rule, redeployed their rhetoric to stage the conquest of the New World, which put to use a technology of war that was centered on the horse. Bernal Díaz del Castillo opens his history of the conquest of Mexico (completed in 1521) with a catalogue of the 16 horses Hernán Cortés purchased in Cuba before launching his campaign on the mainland, assessing each one in terms of its fighting ability. Here is one example: "Alonzo Hernández Puertocarrero: a gray mare, a very good charger which Cortés bought for him with his gold buttons" (Díaz del Castillo 1844, 25). But in a military campaign that was by some accounts perceived by the vanquished as the feat of angry gods who now appeared in unfamiliar disguise, the horse was as much a symbolic weapon as it was an instrument of war. In his memoirs, Díaz de Castillo describes the reaction of a Native American contingent when they first encountered a horse during a military engagement:

> The Indians, who had never seen any horses before, could not think otherwise than that horse and rider were one body. Quite astounded at this to them so novel a sight, they quitted the plain and retreated to a rising ground
>
> (1844, 76)

This encounter suggests that Native Americans accurately read the compact fighting machine devised by Medieval knights as a unit even if they had no means to oppose it in combat. While the Spanish victory over the native Mesoamerican peoples has been plausibly ascribed to disease, political cunning, technological superiority, gunpowder, and local superstition, the use of the horse in the war effort and its sheer strangeness must also be counted as decisive factors in a contest in which the invading army was heavily outnumbered. Even though the fossil record shows that equids had once lived in the New World—they became extinct at the end of the Pleistocene, approximately 12,000 years ago—their reintroduction into the Mesoamerican biomes with the landing of Cortés in Veracruz in 1519 created the conditions of possibility for a different sort of conquest. During the Spanish colonization of the Americas, and subsequently among gauchos and cowboys alike, the horse became an essential work and war instrument in the conquest of an ever receding frontier. In the space of a few generations, it also became a wild animal once again as feral or abandoned horses took splendidly to their new habitat, thereby staging their own Reconquista.

There is perhaps no better treatment of the new horse as it emerges within the imperial nexus than Jonathan Swift's Houyhnhnms in Part IV of *Gulliver's Travels* (1726). The last and, for Gulliver, the very best of the Utopian lands he had the opportunity or ill luck to visit, the country of the Houyhnhnms is populated by both horses (Houyhnhnms) and humans (Yahoos). Unlike the other lands Gulliver describes, the country of the Houyhnhnms does not represent a dramatic change of scale as does, say, Lilliput, where humans are six inches tall; rather, to the extent that it is a land governed by horses, it is a radical reversal of the social roles played by humans and animals alike. The Houyhnhnms live a peaceful, simple, and wise life in contrast to the Yahoos, who are, by Gulliver's own estimation, disagreeable and contemptible animals. The behavior of the horses is "so orderly and rational, so acute and judicious" that at first Gulliver thinks they must be magicians. As he learns their language and gets to know their culture, Gulliver realizes that, unlike the Yahoos, Houyhnhnms don't lie, don't covet possessions, and don't eat meat; they cultivate reason, friendship, benevolence, decency, and civility (Swift 1726 [2001], 246). Houyhnhnms, whose name means "The Perfection of Nature" (217), are puzzled by the Yahoo world Gulliver describes, especially, and unsurprisingly, the custom of castrating horses, and remain skeptical about Gulliver's motives for wanting to stay. In the end, Gulliver must leave the country of the Houyhnhnms because, no matter how reasonable, civilized, white, and hairless he is, he is still a Yahoo and it goes against reason and against nature to have a Yahoo living among the Houyhnhnms. Swift's Yahoos are not only racialized—they are described as "abominable" savages with "flat and broad" faces, depressed nose, large lips, and wide mouth—they are also described as animals that eat "Ass's Flesh" and draw a "Sledge" to carry Houyhnhnms as horses might draw a carriage in England (213). Indeed, as he prepares to leave, Gulliver builds a canoe that is covered with the hide of Yahoos. When he returns home to England, he realizes that he has grown intolerant of humans and can only endure life by spending "four Hours every Day" (246) conversing with his horses. To be sure, Gulliver's tale, in keeping with the reverse mimesis typical of Utopian literature, presents a poor picture of human society. But, to the extent that Swift's satire is meant to disqualify or deflate Utopian thought by using horses (a species that must have been considered by Swift to be patently unreasonable since his satire is premised on the reversal of categories) as an example of good government (or, better, governmentality, to use Michel Foucault's term to designate the ability to govern oneself according to a broadly applicable social and political logic), the text also suggests that the imperial project of which Gulliver is a mere agent represents also a new social order in which the relation between horse and human will need to be renegotiated. The Houyhnhnms' enslavement of the Yahoos, whose "Capacities never reach [...] higher than to draw or carry Burdens" (244), indicates that this renegotiation also entails the animalization of humans; the making-horse of humans by other humans.

Indeed, the renegotiation of the human–horse relation forms part of the wide-ranging social and political processes we have come to associate with industrial modernity. The transformation of the warhorse into a laboring horse in the equine text, as we shall see, is one clear manifestation of this renegotiation. Therefore, before examining the trope of the laboring horse, we must look at the last great appearance of the warhorse in realism's representations of the Napoleonic wars. Collectively, the novels by Stendhal, Thackeray, and Dumas that treat this period may be read as a sort of paean to the warhorse at a time when the horse was being transformed into an industrial laborer. In Leo Tolstoy's *War and Peace* (1869), the historical reconstruction of Napoleon's Russian campaign shows the warhorse as a structure of feeling (to use Raymond Williams's term) that defines the horse–human relation as a social relation in process. This structure of feeling, as my analysis of Tolstoy's great short story "Strider" (also known as "Kohlstomer") will show, is transformed into a relation of production by the late nineteenth century. In contrast, Tolstoy's reconstruction of the Napoleonic warhorse in *War and Peace* offers us a glimpse into one of the last moments in which the horse could still be considered a world-historical player. (The figure of the racehorse in contemporary culture fills, however inadequately, the symbolic void: a naturally gifted if selectively bred horse that displays all the behaviors of the thoroughly trained, disciplined warhorse – Secretariat as the Babieca of the Jockey Club.)

In one of its many storylines, Tolstoy's novel follows Nikolai Rostov's military career as a hussar in Russia's imperial army; it is a career that can be traced by the horses he rides. His first taste of combat riding on Rook is disastrous:

> There was warm blood under his arm. "No, I am wounded and the horse is killed." Rook tried to rise on his forelegs but fell back, pinning his rider's leg. Blood was flowing from his head; he struggled but could not rise.

(Bk. II, Ch. IX)

At the battle of Austerlitz, Rostov, now riding Bedouin, is almost knocked over by a Horse Guard: "The heavy black horse, sixteen hands high, shied, throwing back its ears; but the pockmarked Guardsman drove his huge spurs in violently, and the horse, flourishing its tail and extending its neck, galloped on yet faster" (Bk. III, Ch. XVII). Rostov, however, eventually becomes a skilled cavalryman and, four years after Austerlitz, he once again charges the French army, though now riding a Donets horse:

> With the same feeling with which he had galloped across the path of a wolf, Rostov gave rein to his Donets horse and galloped to intersect the path of the dragoons' disordered lines. One Uhlan stopped, another who was on foot flung himself to the ground to avoid being knocked over, and a riderless horse fell in among the hussars. Nearly all the French dragoons were galloping back. Rostov, picking out one on a gray horse, dashed after him.
>
> (Bk. IX, Ch. XV)

This scene, which proves pivotal in Rostov's military career, is both a commanding performance of horsemanship, symbolically framed by a previous scene in which he rides across the path of a wolf that is finally captured by a pack of hunting dogs, and a moment of self-reflection in which, faced with the prospect of killing the enemy as though he were a hunted wolf, Rostov finally understands the futility of war. The novel has been tracking Rostov's transformation from the somewhat reckless and inexperienced hussar of his early campaigns to the formidable warrior who must nevertheless accept the incongruity of war and peace.

But this transformation is not only personal; it is also world-historical, as this description of Napoleon at Tilsit shows:

> He was riding a very fine thoroughbred gray Arab horse with a crimson gold-embroidered saddlecloth. On approaching Alexander he raised his hat, and as he did so, Rostov, with his cavalryman's eye, could not help noticing that Napoleon did not sit well or firmly in the saddle.
>
> (Bk. V, Ch. XXI)

The portrayal of the great general as an indifferent horseman is in keeping with Tolstoy's general view of history. In one of the novel's epilogues, Tolstoy argues that historical events are not principally caused by individual agents, no matter how heroic; rather, they are driven by forces that put into play many different factors. Tolstoy does not explicitly mention the horse as one of these factors in his theory of history, but history as he unfolds it in the pages of a crowded and eventful novel whose scenes contain more horses than perhaps any other work of literature is unimaginable without the contributions of the warhorse. That Tolstoy's horses in *War and Peace* are mostly anonymous is all the more reason for considering them as historical agents of the sort he has in mind. But in the symbolic battlefield of the equine text, their anonymity might also suggest to us that the horse will henceforth cease to be a historical agent in the conduct of war.

Napoleon's horse is no Babieca, not even a squalid Rocinante: it is a nameless show horse in a world without heroes. It marks an abrupt shift in the horse–human relation from a world-historical structure of feeling to one that, though no less historical, will now be premised on the anonymous labor of the workhorse. It might be an exaggeration to claim that The Enlightenment transformed the aristocratic warhorse into the proletarian workhorse, but it is nevertheless suggestive to consider that it is not until the nineteenth century that the horse is portrayed as an engine of work rather than a "deadly engine" of the sort the Trojan horse commemorates in its outsized dimensions. Dickens's definition of the horse as a "graminivorous quadruped" marks the transition of the horse from a deadly to an industrial engine. The horse does not of course disappear entirely from the theater of war, but its role is increasingly subservient to the heavily mechanized armies of modern warfare. In the harrowing war scenes of Louis Ferdinand Céline's *Voyage au bout de la nuit* [*Journey to the End of the Night*] (1932), a semi-autobiographical account of World War I and its aftermath from the point of view of a misanthrope, horses, along with the men who ride them, are used as cannon fodder. The horse, in this context, cannot be said to perform a heroic historical role; it now shares the fate of the laboring classes as the alienated subject of an ideological struggle whose victors are known in advance.

## Laboring horses

In antiquity, the laboring horse is not a horse at all, but a donkey. The image we still hold of donkeys as stubborn, vain, and foolish comes to us from Aesop's fables (C6 BCE), in which the donkey, routinely tricked by horses, foxes, lions, and dogs, is portrayed as a beast of burden more deserving of beatings than caresses. In one fable, an ass wears the skin of a lion; in another, an ass wishes to be treated as a lap dog; in another, a mule thinks it has been sired by a horse only to find that it has a donkey for a father; in yet another, an ass wants to outsmart his master by wading deep into a river to dissolve the load of salt he carries only to find that, on his next trip, his master has loaded him with sponges. In the Aesopian tradition, the donkey carries the moral burden of a category mistake: the donkey ought to realize that a lowly equid is only fit to work.

In Apuleius's *The Golden Ass* (C2), the only Latin novel to have survived in its entirety, the sort of category mistake that donkeys are liable to commit becomes the structural principle around which the narrative is organized. Apuleius's narrative conceit consists in transforming Lucius, a young traveler who is keen on discovering the secrets of magic, into the "plain ass" that he demonstrably has already shown himself to be by being tricked into believing that he has killed three thieves when in reality he has merely stabbed three wine bladders. No sooner does he realize that he has accidentally transformed himself into a donkey ("my mouth long and my nostrils wide, my lips hanging down, and mine ears exceedingly increased with bristles": 1971, 136) rather than into the bird he wished to be (*non avem me sed asinum video*) than he becomes aware of the abuses and indignities to which he will now be exposed: his lover Fotis becomes disenchanted with his enlarged features (*natura crescebat*); his own horse pushes him away from the food he himself had fed it; and then he is beaten by the stable boy for trying to eat it. Eager to break the spell that has transformed him into an ass, he tries desperately to find a rose he can eat, but circumstances always seem to conspire against him as he is passed from one unseemly owner to the next until he is finally released by the goddess of wisdom Isis, to whose service, now as human again, he will devote the rest of his life.

Lucius's story, which offers a narrative blueprint for subsequent episodic adventure stories that have the road as its chronotope—Mikhail Bakhtin's term for the structural principle whereby stories come to be organized according to a specific temporal and spatial matrix—relates, like the picaresque, a socially leveling experience, which, in this case, also involves seeing life from the point of view of an animal. From the perspective of a mule, a donkey, or a horse, the chronotope of the road may appear to be paved with uneventful drudgery, but, in the equine text, traveling serves to expose the cruelty of human–animal relations in the context of a corrupt social order in which thieves, slaves, and irate lovers all tend to act like animals of a more dangerous, if outwardly less foolish, nature than the ass.

The sad fortunes of the ass inform Shakespeare's characterization of Bottom in *A Midsummer Night's Dream* (1600), which, like that of Lucius in Apuleius's novel, is premised on a misdirected magic spell. In Shakespeare's play, Titania, under a spell by her husband, the fairy king Oberon, falls in love with Bottom the weaver, who, under a separate spell by Robin Goodfellow (Puck), now wears an ass's head. As one of the "rude mechanicals" (III.ii.9), the amateur actors who are staging the play within the play, Bottom is already portrayed as a somewhat stubborn and foolish ass before he becomes one. Not only is his name associated with labor, he believes his friends are just performing a prank when they run away from him, not realizing that he has been transformed into an ass: "I see their knavery: this is to make an ass of me; to fright me, if they could" (III.i.26–27). The unsuspecting role Bottom plays as an ass in the play's elaborate romantic plot, moreover, suggests that the characterization of the ass as a clown, rather than that of Bottom as an ass, is what makes Titania's love for him incongruent, a category mistake in a play in which fairies, humans, and animals inhabit a dreamscape that is Athenian only in its setting.

Cervantes does not give Sancho Panza's ass a proper name in *Don Quixote* (1605 [Vol. 1], 1615 [Vol. 2]). Sancho refers to it as *"rucio"* ("gray one"), a word that sounds like a deformed and perhaps lesser version of the name of Don Quixote's less than fresh and shining horse, Rocinante. He also refers to it as a *"jumento"* (donkey) and as an *"asno pardo"* (gray ass), generic names for the donkey and its typical color. In one episode, Sancho's ass is stolen in the middle of the night. When he finally recovers it, he says, referring first to the thief:

> Gines, you thief! Let go my jewel! Let go my life! Don't rob me of my comfort! Let go of my ass! Let go of my treasure! Get out, you bastard! Get away, you thief! Give up what isn't yours!
>
> (266)

This scene, which Cervantes added in the third edition of the first part of *Don Quixote,* makes clear that the donkey is not only Sancho's most prized possession: it is also a beloved companion. The narrator says as much when he tells us that Sancho, upon recovering him, "kissed him as if he had been a human being" (266). The ass, of course, remains unmoved even as it passively accepts Sancho's caresses. The story of Sancho and his impassive *rucio* suggests that the chronotope of the road, which must now be identified historically with a novelistic paradigm that places everyday characters in real social relations rather than in the idealized chivalric conventions of the hero, was always shaped by the animals that make travel possible. (Indeed, equids are as integral to the classic chronotope of the road as are cars, trucks, and motorcycles to the American road picture.)

To be sure, the anonymity or generic character of Sancho's *rucio* is in keeping with the ironic reversals that structure Cervantes's novel, which is uniquely and exemplarily premised on the principle of the category mistake. But it is also informed by the Christian iconography related to the figure of the donkey. In the gospels, to name one important instance, Jesus enters Jerusalem mounted on an ass: "Go into the village opposite you, and immediately you will find an ass tied, and a colt with her; untie them and bring them to me" (Matthew 21.2). In Mark and Luke, Jesus's disciples cover the colt with their garments so he can mount it. The presence of the colt not only confirms the prophecy of the king's triumphant entry into Jerusalem as it appears in Zechariah—"triumphant and victorious is he,/ humble and riding on an ass,/ on a colt the foal of an ass" (9.9)—it also makes an implicit distinction between the ass (and the colt of an ass, at that) and the horse, which is described as an instrument of war. It would of course be a category mistake to equate Sancho with Jesus, but the characterization of Sancho (whose name is almost as generic as his donkey's) as the earthy, commonsensical, and witty foil to Don Quixote's sad but high-minded knight puts us in mind of another important trope associated with the donkey: a figure of humility that inspires social equality.

It is precisely this aspect of donkey lore that Coleridge addresses in his 1794 poem "To a Young Ass." Like the donkey of the gospels, Coleridge's donkey is a foal. The poem opens with an apostrophe: "Poor little Foal of an oppressèd race!/ I love the languid patience of thy face;/ And oft with gentle hand I give thee bread,/ And clap thy ragged coat, and pat thy head" (Coleridge 1950, 1–4). Like the hand that, in feeding and caressing him, deems the donkey an animal worthy of gentle attention, the poet extends consideration to the donkey by addressing him using the dignified "thy." Poetic attention, however, is not limited to personification; it entails an altogether new conception of subjecthood. The poet wonders why the foal, "unlike the nature of things young" (7), should look so despondent, as though it were already imagining its "future fate" of misery, pain, and starvation. Or perhaps the foal is sad to see its mother chained to a tree around which no grass grows, an image the poet immediately associates with the fate of its master, who lives "[h]alf famish'd in a land of Luxury" (22). These conjectures lead to the poem's second apostrophe: "I hail thee *Brother* – spite of the fool's scorn!" (26). The performative construction of the apostrophe together with its emphasis on "Brother" suggest a reference to the abolitionists' motto, "Am I not a Man and a Brother," widely associated at the time of the poem's publication with the Wedgwood cameo showing an African man in chains. With this reference, Coleridge, who had already won a prize at Cambridge for the poem "Greek Ode on the Slave Trade" (1792), is not only expanding the simile with which he opens the poem and by means of which we are meant to consider the ass as a member of an "oppressèd race" (1); he is also suggesting that the ass's slavery is itself of a categorical order in which our treatment of it derives from a stereotype: "spite of the fool's scorn" (26). The poem ends with an extended Utopian fantasy in which the ass would be able to "frisk about" (32) like a lamb or a kitten and his "dissonant harsh bray" (34) would be "more musically sweet" (33) than fashionable songs. Here, as elsewhere in Coleridge, this Utopia is named "Pantisocracy" and constitutes a realm of equality in which antagonisms are reversed and where rats and terriers, mice and cats, poets and asses can coexist in "Mirth."

To extend the principle of equality to animals may have seemed anathema to Coleridge's contemporaries, who were well poised, at least since Swift (see above), to view the government of animals by animals through the lens of satire. But the Romantics' attempt to rectify a long tradition of categorical mistakes that had led humans to view nature in instrumental terms alone coincided with a concerted political effort to reverse the wrongs visited upon the most "oppressèd" of humans and beasts alike. It was Jeremy Bentham who, in 1781, had put it most succinctly by arguing that it was not reason but suffering that allied humans and animals: "...the question is not, Can they *reason*? nor, Can they *talk*? but, Can they *suffer*?" (see Chapter 1, in this volume). Whatever the cultural appeal of Romanticism's investments in animal Pantisocracy, growing concern for the welfare of animals gave rise to a veritable social movement whose aim was to ameliorate the suffering of laboring animals, and to abolish cruel cultural practices such as bear baiting, cock fighting, rat baiting, and other blood sports. The Society for the Prevention of Cruelty to Animals (SPCA), explicitly created in 1824 to extend the reach of Martin's Act, which was passed by both houses of Parliament in 1822 to "prevent cruel and improper treatment of Cattle," combined enforcement, propaganda, and lobbying efforts to defend suffering animals. The RSPCA, as it came to be known after Victoria allowed the society to affix "Royal" to its name in 1840, published descriptions of animal cruelty as well as accounts of the legal cases brought against perpetrators. The most appalling cases, as Harriet Ritvo notes, were "often associated with the most routine economic activities" (1987, 137). The actions of the

RSPCA were thus disproportionately directed at the lower classes, with horses and draft animals unsurprisingly counting as the most frequently cited victims: from 1857 to 1860, according to Ritvo, 84 percent of the total convictions and 60 percent of the narrative reports published by the RSPCA involved horses (138).

It is against this background that we must read what is perhaps the most famous, and was certainly the most popular, equine text of the nineteenth century: Anna Sewell's *Black Beauty* (1877). The novel, which appealed to a public already alert to the sufferings of animals, was endorsed by the RSPCA itself, which described it as "one of the best books recently published in support of our principles. The literary merit is excellent" (Sewell 1877 [2012], xiv). To be sure, Sewell's novel is a work of advocacy, portraying the cruelty with which horses were routinely treated and addressing her portrayal of cruelty to those who worked with horses. Its rhetoric of cruelty, like that of much animal rights discourse of the nineteenth century, relies on a parallelism that likens animal oppression to slavery. But it is also, as the RSPCA's reviewer suggests, a novel written with "literary merit" in mind. *Black Beauty*'s most significant literary innovation is not that it is written from the perspective of a horse; rather, it is that the story of the horse is written as a Bildungsroman. As a fictional autobiography, a variation on the Bildungsroman especially popular in Britain (think of Charlotte Brontë's *Jane Eyre* (1847), Dickens's *David Copperfield* (1849–50) and *Great Expectations* (1860–61), and Thackeray's *The History of Henry Esmond* (1852), among others), *Black Beauty* is a retrospective account of the events and circumstances that have led to the present in which the novel is written and to a place generically, and in this case explicitly, called "home": "My troubles are over, and I am at home; and often before I am quite awake, I fancy I am a still in the orchard at Birtwick, standing with my old friends under the apple trees" (Sewell 1877 [2012], 162). Indeed, like the great novels of the genre, the story of *Black Beauty* is the story of a compromise between individuality and socialization: in this case, the compromise is between the horse's nature and the human needs to which it is submitted.

The novel begins with two scenes of instruction. The first involves Black Beauty's mother, who chastises him for engaging in rough play with the other colts on the meadow:

> The colts who live here are very good colts, but they are cart-horse colts, and of course, they have not learned manners. You have been well bred and well born; your father has a great name on these parts…I hope you will grow up gentle and good, and never learn

bad ways; do your work with a good will, lift your feet up well when you trot, and never bite or kick even in play.

(9–10)

The second involves the "master," who chastises Dick the ploughboy for throwing sticks and stones to the galloping horses. These two scenes, ethically parallel only in the horse's imaginary, set up the parameters within which the story of Black Beauty's Bildung will proceed: the gradual "humanization" of Black Beauty as he learns the value of obedience and hard work, and the collective "humanization" of horse owners in general as they become more enlightened with respect to the treatment of horses. Each of these two processes of "humanization" follows its own narrative logic, creating two didactic series that finally merge at the site, and in the figure, of "home."

For Black Beauty, the didactic series involves learning to live with a bit in the mouth—"Those who have never had a bit in their mouths cannot think how bad it feels...it is very bad! yes, very bad!" (14–15)— iron shoes, a collar, a bridle with blinkers, a saddle, and a crupper. After some time, he stops complaining about these "humanizing" prostheses— "Now, I am not complaining, for I know it must be so" (23)—but soon he learns about "bearing reins," a device invented to hold up a horse's head: "Day by day, hole by hole our bearing reins were shortened, and instead of looking forward with pleasure to having my harness put on as I used to do, I began to dread it" (73). The bearing rein, an instrument designed for aesthetic reasons alone, becomes the most damning evidence in the novel's argument against the cruel treatment of horses. It makes Black Beauty "foam at the mouth" both in the literal sense as well as in the sense of indignant protest: "But it is just as unnatural for horses as for men, to foam at the mouth. It is a sure sign of something wrong, and generally proceeds from suffering" (76). But suffering comes in many guises, and to the injury of bearing the rein is added the insult of undignified work. After becoming a "job-horse," a horse hired for rent, Black Beauty is subjected to many "ignorant drivers" who hold the reins too tightly or not tightly enough, and careless drivers who neglect to keep an eye on the road. Indeed, as Black Beauty is passed from one owner to the next, his story becomes something of a sociological assessment of a representative cross section of horse owners in different walks of life. Black Beauty's process of socialization can thus be said to entail not only the prosthetic assemblage of horse tack; it also consists in becoming acquainted with different types of humans and learning to tell the good from the bad horse person.

Furthermore, it is in tracking the collective, rather than the individual, education of the horse person that the novel develops its second didactic series. Black Beauty's owners vary in terms of class and gender as well as in degrees of skill and kindness. One of his favorite masters, Jerry Barker, who drives a cab in London, is not only a good driver ("as good a driver as I had known"); he is also considerate: "he took as much thought for his horses as he did for himself" (108). But Black Beauty's attentiveness to the family and its precarious economic situation suggests that he too has as "much thought" for his owner as he does for himself, which means, in effect, that the narrative becomes increasingly concerned with identifying horse owners of strong moral character. While a gentleman waits in Jerry's cab outside a store, he notices that, across the street, a carter is brutally beating his horses. The gentleman confronts the offender—"If you don't stop that directly, I'll have you summoned"—and then proceeds to declare his philosophy: "My doctrine is this, that if we see cruelty or wrong that we have the power to stop, and do nothing, we make our selves sharers in the guilt" (127). Making a distinction between good and bad horse owners, as this scene suggests, not only devolves upon the horse that is being treated but to the public at large who benefit from horse labor. At the end of the novel, Black Beauty ends up in a farm, tended by a kind man who, old like Black Beauty himself, is willing to let him rest.

Black Beauty is not the only story to describe human folly from the perspective of a horse. Tolstoy's "Strider" or "Kohlstomer" (1885), which he started before *War and Peace* but did not finish until after the novel was published, tells the life story of a piebald gelding and the human owners who ostracize him on account of the unusual color of his coat from an oblique point of view. Viktor Shklovsky (1990) has called this perspectival effect "ostraniene" or "enstrangement" to suggest the effect an odd or unusual point of view has on the objects being described. By way of example, Shklovsky cites the way Tolstoy uses Strider's point of view to describe the institution of property as though it were being perceived for the first time:

> I became convinced that it was with respect to everything – not only where we horses were concerned – that the concept of *my own* had no other foundation than that low, bestial instinct that they themselves call the sense or right of ownership.
>
> (1990, 87)

To be sure, the fact that the story is chiefly, though not exclusively, narrated from the horse's perspective accounts for the effect of "enstrangement," but, to the extent that Strider is already estranged from the humans who own and tend to him as well as from other horses—he has been gelded to prevent him from having offspring with piebald coats—the effect of enstrangement is made all the more acute since his perspective makes *both* humans and horses alike newly "strange" to the reader. Remarkably, this double perspective is maintained even when the story continues from a perspective that has been established for Strider but which is no longer focalized through him. Social estrangement and aesthetic enstrangement both contribute to make Tolstoy's story a meditation on the very limits of anthropocentrism.

Strider's story begins in old age, when he is already in a state of decrepitude, his forelegs "bowed," his forehead "sunken and rough," his worn teeth mere "yellow stumps," the tail bone "almost bald" (1885 [2005], 72). Yet, Strider still shows signs that he must have been a remarkable horse in his youth:

> There really was something majestic about that horse, even in that terrible combination of hideous decrepitude that his coloured patches only served to emphasize with the supremely self-confident manner typical of creatures serenely aware of their own beauty and strength.
> (72–3)

We find out what makes Strider "majestic" over the course of five nights as he tells the horses gathered around him the story of his life. Though of first-rate pedigree, Strider is immediately disliked by his owner, a Count, who sees in the piebald's coat a less than flattering reflection of his purebred stable. He is first gelded and then denied the dignity of work—"All I wanted was the chance to show them my readiness and liking for hard work!" (88)—before finally being sold when he is seen to be faster than the Count's favorite horse. He tells the other horses, who seem to know of him by reputation, about his favorite owner, a "handsome, happy, and rich" hussar, and his coachman, Feofan, who run him ragged and give him "too much to drink," which ruins his legs. "I sacrificed half my life and all my best qualities working for them," he says, adding: "But in spite of that these were the best days of my life" (92). Strider is hurt when the hussar, chasing his estranged mistress over terrible roads, cruelly beats him in order to make him run faster. Now crippled, he is sold to an old lady.

His story ends ignominiously back at the paddock when his beloved hussar, whom he recognizes immediately as he enters the stables, fails to recognize him. The hussar, who is now "fat and bald, with a large moustache and side whiskers," has lost his fortune and taken to drink, which has made him exist in a "state of fear and trembling" (98–9). His decline parallels Strider's own, yet the hussar's is clearly of his own making while Strider's is entirely attributable to the way he has been treated by his various owners. Without knowing that Strider is in the stables, the hussar tells his hosts the story of how Strider beat a famous horse at the racetrack, but the story is so embellished that it sounds like a lie to audience and storyteller alike. Strider eventually becomes infected with mange and has to be sacrificed: "There was a stab of pain, he shuddered, kicked out with one leg, but then checked himself and waited for what would follow. What followed was that something liquid streamed down his neck and chest" (105). His body is abandoned in a gully, where dogs, crows, kites, and wolves eat his flesh. In contrast, when the hussar dies, a forgotten and defeated man, his corpse, dressed in uniform, is of no use to anyone.

In closing with these deaths, that of an old and misused horse and of a decadent hussar who never needed a warhorse, the story also closes an important equine epoch. No longer an exalted war machine nor yet a noble laborer, the horse has become something of an anachronism, a figure of the past as such. The death of the horse as a trope of conquest and labor, of might and right, is aptly captured by Émile Zola in the denouement to his novel *La Bête humaine* (1890). The novel, set in the French railroad system, traces the parallel development of two "human beasts," Jacques Lantier, an engineer with a hereditary predisposition to murderous violence, and La Lison, the train he drives, which is often described as a horse, a man-made, or human, beast. At the end of the novel, Jacques, increasingly unhinged, drives the train, running at full speed, into the horse-drawn carriage that has been placed on the tracks by his one-time love interest. The spectacular train wreck that results is described in these terms:

> La Lison toppled over to her left on to the dray, as though disemboweled; while the blocks of stone had split asunder exploding the fragments as though shattered by a quarry blast, and of the five horses, four were dragged along, killed on the instant. The tail of the train, the remaining six carriages which were all intact, had come to rest without ever leaving the rails…. like a monstrous mare gored by some formidable horn, La Lison lay with her wheels in the air, her connecting-rods twisted, her cylinders broken, and her valves and eccentrics all smashed, a horrible wound gaping at the sky and from which her soul continued to seep with a furious hiss of impotent despair. And just beside her was the horse which had not died, lying there with both its forelegs gone and, like the

engine, losing its entrails through a rent in its belly. By the look of its head straining stiffly upwards in a spasm of extreme pain, it could be seen to give one last terrible whinny, of which no sound reached the ear above the roar of the dying engine.

(Zola 1890 [2009], 289–90)

The dying engine is also the dying of the horse as a "deadly engine" and as a working machine as technology makes the horse obsolete, and the train, the car, and the airplane supplant it as a means of transport. In Zola's dramatic, if not quite epic, simile, the trope of the horse dies along with the horses that derail the train, no longer a rhetorically efficacious vehicle for the attributes of nobility, grace, and hard work for which horses were once prized.

It is not that horses cease to appear in twentieth- and twenty-first-century literature. The American Western, after all, is one of the dominant narrative forms of the first half of the twentieth century, and the horse is a staple of young adult literature. But the so-called "horse operas" of Hollywood cinema are already oddly archaic remnants of a culture all but liberated from the backwardness of the horse-drawn carriage, the pony express, and the Sheriff's posse, and the stories of *Flicka, National Velvet, Red Pony,* and *Black Stallion,* like the adolescents who read them, represent the inchoate stirrings of a culture that anticipates leaving its past behind, as though the horses of youth made possible the conquest of future frontiers without horses and served as mild, if imperfect, reminders of a past that would make such futures possible. Indeed, the relative dearth of the trope of the horse in contemporary literature speaks to our sense that the horse has been amply defined, or, at any rate, that we no longer need to define it, in order to feel conversant in a culture that has left it behind, proving that you can take a horse to the text, but you cannot make me read it.

The demise of the equine text, like that of the equids that appear in the last few texts I have discussed, is as dramatic as it is inevitable. Yet, its long history suggests that the invention of the horse is of a piece with that of the literature that represents it. I now turn, by way of conclusion, to Juan Ramón Jiménez's *Platero y yo* (1906–16), a text that features a donkey rather than a horse. An elegiac poem in prose, Jiménez's text is a lyrical reconstruction of the poet's hometown of Moguer in Andalucía, now in decline, hence its subtitle: "Elegía andaluza" ("An Andalusian Elegy"). But it can also be read as an elegy to the equine text itself. Accompanied by Platero, a "small, downy, smooth" donkey, the poet describes the scenes, people, and events of the small town over a period of one year, from spring to spring, in a series of 138 fragments. In an early fragment, Platero is seen to carry no burden other than "white butterflies"; in another, he is likened to the school boys who make fun of him; in yet another, the poet promises to give him a proper burial in lieu of sending him to the slaughterhouse. Platero, in short, is less a donkey than the poet's almost human companion and confidante.

The poem proceeds in a series of didactic moments in which the poet teaches the donkey about nature, thus reversing, or returning, the Romantic *topos* in which the poet learns from nature about himself. "I shall teach you about the flowers and the stars," the poet promises in one fragment, and tells Platero in another all about the returning swallows: "The swallows are here already, Platero, yet one can scarcely hear them as in other years, when on the very day of their arrival they greeted and investigated everything, chattering without pause in their fluted trills" (Jiménez 1956, 33). In one fragment, he tells Platero what he would experience were he able to see the town from the rooftops; in another, he describes what the empty cistern looks like from the inside; in yet a third, he shows him a photograph of his dog Lord. These episodes are examples of the poet's attempt to offer Platero a new way of looking in a reciprocal movement that mirrors the way Platero has presumably been able to offer the poet a new perspective on the otherwise familiar aspects of his own town. In a fragment aptly titled "Friendship," the poet describes this reciprocity as a species of filial or perhaps even romantic love:

> He is so like me that I have come to believe that he dreams my very dreams...Platero has given himself to me like a passionate young girl. He protests at nothing. I know that I am his happiness. He even flees from other donkeys and from men.
>
> (67)

This entirely earnest and passionate love between man and donkey suggests that, at least in poetry, the human–animal divide is less stable and certainly less dogmatic than it purports to be outside of literature. Words, the tropes that have traditionally made the donkey the object of satire, become the subject of a fragment titled "Donkeyography" (the Spanish "Asnografía" more closely suggests the theme of asininity that is developed in the fragment), in which the poet corrects a dictionary entry that refers ironically to the donkey by writing in the margin that the term "Donkeyography" must refer to the "imbeciles" who write ironically about donkeys in dictionaries. This definition of the donkey, unlike the definition of the horse Gradgrind demands of his pupils, is absurd not only because it defines the donkey according to its cultural status as a foolish and stubborn animal; it is absurd because for the poet the donkey cannot be defined. Platero represents the possibility of relating to the animal other for its own sake on the basis of respect, affect, and empathy. Recollected in the poem's closing fragments, Platero's death ends a natural cycle that also ends the poem. It is an uneventful death, save for the delicate presence of butterflies, which suggest, as an overt imagery of metaphorical language itself, that Platero lives on in the poem. Platero, who has served to convey the poet's past, now only carries the figurative burden of the poetry that would convey his own life into posterity. Now buried under his favorite tree, Platero and the "yo" that accompanies him in the poem's title become one as a poetic subject that, changing less and remembered better, will remain with us for donkey's years.

## Works cited

Anon. *The Poem of the Cid*, trans. John Ormsby. London: Longmans, Green, and Co., 1879.

Anon. *Poema de Mio Cid*. Fifth ed., ed. Ian Michael. Clásicos Castalia. Madrid: Castalia, 1987.

Apuleius. *The Golden Ass*, trans. W. Adlington and S. Gaselee. Loeb Classical Library. Cambridge: Harvard University Press, 1971.

Bakhtin, M. M. *The Dialogic Imagination*, trans. Caryl Emerson and Michael Holquist. Austin: University of Texas Press, 1981.

Bentham, Jeremy. *An Introduction to the Principles of Morals and Legislation* (1781). Eds. J. H. Burns and H. L. A. Hart. London: Methuen, 1982.

Cèline, Louis Ferdinand. *Voyage to the End of the Night*, trans. Ralph Manheim. New York: New Directions, 1983.

Cervantes, Miguel de. *Don Quixote*, trans. J. M. Cohen. London: Penguin, 1950.

Cervantes, Miguel de. *El ingenioso hidalgo Don Quijote de la Mancha I*. Fifth ed., ed. Luis Andrés Murillo. Clásicos Castalia. Madrid: Castalia, 1987.

Coleridge, S. T. "To a Young Ass." In *The Portable Coleridge*. ed. I. A. Richards. London: Penguin, 1950.

Crane, Susan. *Animal Encounters*. Philadelphia: University of Pennsylvania Press, 2013.

Díaz del Castillo, Bernal. *The Memoirs of Conquistador Bernal Díaz de Castillo*, trans. John Ingram Lockhart. London: J Hachard and Son, 1844.

Dickens, Charles. *Hard Times*. World's Classics. Oxford: Oxford University Press, 1991.

Euripides. *The Trojan Women*, trans. Richard Lattimore. In *Euripides III*. Third ed., eds. Mark Griffith and Glenn W. Most. Chicago: University of Chicago Press, 2013.

Hesiod. *Theogony, Works and Days, Testimonia,* ed. and trans. Glenn W. Most. Loeb Classical Library. Cambridge: Harvard University Press, 2006.

Homer. *The Illiad,* trans. Richard Lattimore. Chicago: University of Chicago Press, 1950.

Homer. *The Odyssey,* trans. Robert Fagles. London: Penguin, 1997.

Jiménez, Juan Ramón. *Platero and I,* trans. William and Mary Roberts. Oxford: Dolphin, 1956.

Jiménez, Juan Ramón. *Platero y yo,* ed. Michael P. Predmore. Madrid: Cátedra, 1978.

Ritvo, Harriet. *The Animal Estate: The English and Other Creatures in the Victorian Age.* Cambridge: Harvard University Press, 1987.

Sax, Boria. *Imaginary Animals.* London: Reaktion Books, 2013.

Sewell, Anna. *Black Beauty.* World's Classics. Oxford: Oxford University Press, 2012.

Shakespeare, William. *The Oxford Shakespeare. The Compete Works,* Second Ed. Oxford: Oxford University Press, 2005.

Shklovsky. Viktor. *Theory of Prose,* trans. Benjamin Sher. Normal, IL: Dalkey Archives, 1990.

Swift, Jonathan. *Gulliver's Travels.* Penguin Classics. London: Penguin, 2001.

Tolstoy, Leo. *War and Peace,* trans. Louise and Aylmer Maude. World's Classics. Oxford: Oxford University Press, 1983.

Tolstoy, Leo. "Strider." In *Master and Man and Other Stories,* trans. Ronald Wilks and Paul Foote. Penguin Classics. London: Penguin, 2005.

Virgil. *The Aeneid.* Robert Fitzgerald. New York: Vintage, 1990.

Zola, Émile. *La Bête humaine,* trans. Roger Pearson. World's Classics. Oxford: Oxford University Press, 2009.

# 3    Canids (companionship, cunning, domestication)

In 2012, there were approximately 60 million dogs in the European Union;[1] 83 million in the United States;[2] and 36 million in Brazil. Pet ownership among the middle classes is a relatively recent phenomenon in China, yet there are already 27 million dogs in Chinese households.[3] India has the fastest growing dog population in the world, with a growth rate of 58.1 percent from 2007 to 2012.[4] These figures suggest that dogs, like modern appliances, are a constant of consumer culture, embodying, through the trope of domesticity, the aspirational ethos of middle-class prosperity. From among the extraordinary variety of dog breeds that humans have domesticated and selectively invented over time, dog owners are able to choose the size, color, appearance, personality, and attributes of a dog that best fits their idea of themselves as social actors. You need not be a hunter to purchase a Labrador Retriever, who, according to the American Kennel Club, is a "friendly, active, outgoing" dog with the "temperament to be a family companion."[5] Nor need you be particularly active or smart to get a Poodle, who is, which is perhaps why he has "an air of distinction and dignity peculiar to himself."[6] If you own sheep, you might consider a Border Collie, a "remarkably smart workaholic" who is not "adverse to a good cuddle."[7] Allergic to dog hair? Why not try a Mexican Xoloitzcuintli, who, besides being hairless, is "calm, tranquil, aloof, and attentive."[8] Most dog breeds, moreover, seem to embody national traits, so if you feel like expressing the German in you, you can opt for a Pointer, a Pinscher, or a Shepherd. Or perhaps that mutt resignedly eyeing you from a cage in your local dog shelter embodies your cherished democratic ideals. In every case, these walking, breathing, and occasionally irascible animals have become personifications of human social conventions, many of which not only tend to repress their animal natures, but, in doing so, also minimize the animality of the human that breeds them.

This admittedly cynical view of dog ownership ignores the many virtues of canine companionship, virtues that have been extolled in the suburban household as well as in the hospital ward. Yet, the scale of dog ownership and the various forms it takes make us pause to wonder about the function of pet keeping in a culture increasingly abstracted from nature. To be sure, the peculiar character of modern dog ownership owes some of its pathos to the historical role dogs have played in human societies since antiquity. In ancient Greece, the dog was already a cultural symbol of fidelity and courage, and, for philosophy, a standard-bearer of a form of natural living that rebelled against the artifice of social conventions. The Cynics—the term comes from the Greek "kunikos," doglike or churlish—were known as the "dog philosophers," and Diogenes, one of the founders of Cynic philosophy, was known as the "Dog." Living in a tub in the streets of Athens, Diogenes would perform in public what most people today would only do in private, following no schedule, no order, no prescribed routine. Today, the cynic is someone who is commonly understood to be distrustful or incredulous toward sincerity and human goodness, but, in ancient Greece, the Cynic (capital C) was a practical philosopher who led a life of poverty and hardship the better to make a virtue of satirizing the folly of social conventions. Diogenes taught that the right way of life was to have the simplest possible needs and to satisfy them in the most direct way, without shame. But the Cynics' ethos not only embraced self-sufficiency; it was premised on a form of self-mastery that was born of a healthy contempt for one's own pleasures and pains, and, especially, born of impatience with the conventions and hierarchies of a corrupt society. Nature was the great leveling force for the Cynics, who maintained that it was only by being close to nature, and thus unmindful of the precepts of convention, etiquette, and religion, that one could live a virtuous life. Yet, the Cynic, as the example of Diogenes makes clear, is no hermit; the Cynic lives in the streets of the city, performing by means of example an important critical function. In taking the dog as their symbol, the Cynics took a stance against culture, but like dogs themselves, without for all that abandoning culture. After the Cynics, the dog comes to stand in for the presence and power of nature *within* civilization.

Nothing could be farther from the Cynics, then, than the conventions that rule dog ownership today, however unsurprising their presence in culture would be for them. Indeed, dogs tend to personify human artifice and, in doing so, they also tend to naturalize it since they are the privileged non-humans who allow humans to measure the distance that separates them from the animal world, as if the process had no history of its own. The familiar trope of the dog as "man's best friend" expresses the close ties that have bound dogs to humans ever since dogs and their lupine ancestors began to attach themselves to human social groups many thousands of years ago. But the trope also tends to suppress with its proverb-like force a changing history of relations between dogs and their human owners, for over time humans have used dogs in a great variety of endeavors, many of which were, and indeed continue to be, less than friendly. That the dog in the trope plays the role of the "best friend" seems to shield "man" from the necessity of reciprocity, or at least to allow him to adopt the somewhat cynical stance of expecting devotion from a being toward whom one need not act as a friend. Indeed, the changing history of dog–human relations can be tracked by following, as though one were following a scent, the presence of dogs in literature, which from this perspective can be understood to act as both the medium and the means whereby nature is naturalized. The familiar trope of the dog as man's best friend, as it turns out, is familiar less for its prevalence in literature than for the fact that dogs are a familiar presence outside of literature. The representation of dogs in literature is relatively sparse, as though dogs were the necessary but anonymous figures that make literary history "literary" in any meaningful sense; that is, as a human product that suppresses nature *in* and *for* civilization. Romulus and Remus may have been nourished by a wolf, but the wolf, for all that, remains outside the Rome they subsequently built, save as the very symbol of the distance that separates humans and the cities they build from the realm of Nature.

The canid text, as this chapter will endeavor to show, is thus both familiar and strange, reflecting the paradoxical role of canids in society as the companions, guardians, and laborers that make possible the naturalization of civilization and, at the same time, as the natural cynics (the dog-like dogs) that reflect back to humans the folly of "natural" conventions.

## You've got a friend in me

In Book XVII of Homer's *Odyssey*, Odysseus returns to Ithaka disguised as an old beggar. As he approaches his palace accompanied by Eumaios, the loyal swineherd with whom he has come to his own palace, he notices a dog lying on a heap of dung. Argos, the dog, recognizes him immediately:

> Now, as he perceived that Odysseus had come close to him, he
> wagged his tail, and laid both his ears back; only he now no longer

had the strength to move any closer to his master, who watching him from a distance, without Eumaios noticing, secretly wiped a tear away...

(Homer 1991, 301–305)

The scene, one among several scenes of recognition that stage Odysseus's long delayed homecoming, is significant in that it shows the legitimacy of Odysseus's claims on his household in spite of his long absence. But the scene is also one of mutual recognition: not only has Argos recognized Odysseus in spite of his disguise; Odysseus has also recognized Argos, a dog he had known only as a puppy, and who, now neglected, abandoned, and tick-infected, is also something of a beggar. Argos and Odysseus, that is, are both "distasteful," the meaning of the name "Odysseus" as given to him by his grandfather Autolykos (XIX, 409). When Odysseus asks Eumaios if he knows anything about the dog, Eumaios tells him that Argos was once a formidable hunter—"Never could a wild animal, in the profound depths of the forest, escape, once he pursued. He was very clever at tracking" (315–317)—but has now fallen on "bad times." The description of Argos as a "clever" hunter suggests that, also in this regard, he is an extension of Odysseus, who is repeatedly described as "resourceful" and "clever." Odysseus and Argos thus mirror each other, warriors now come to resemble beggars, each on the outside looking in to the household they once reigned.

This form of mirroring, however, differs significantly from the way Odysseus and Telemachos, his son, resemble each other in an earlier scene in which Telemachos comes to Eumaios's shelter. Orchestrated by Athene, the encounter between father and son is announced by the reaction of Eumaios's dogs: "Eumaios," Odysseus tells him, "someone is on his way here who is truly/ one of yours, or else well known, since the dogs are not barking/ but fawning about him, and I can hear the thud of his footsteps" (XVI, 8–10). Dogs are able to distinguish between friend and foe and thus can be said to be animals of recognition. Eumaios's dogs recognize Telemachos but not Odysseus. When Odysseus first comes to Eumaios's shelter, his "wild-baying" dogs run to him with "a great outcry" until Eumaios controls them: "Old sir, the dogs were suddenly on you and would have savaged you/ badly; so you would have covered me with shame" (XIV, 37–38). Eumaios's dogs, probably too young to remember Odysseus, nevertheless recognize Telemachos, which in turn allows Odysseus to recognize his own son. When Athene appears to Odysseus, Eumaios's dogs are intimidated: "Odysseus saw her and the dogs did; they were not barking, but cowered away, whimpering, to the other side of the shelter" (XVI, 162–163). In these crucial scenes, dogs symbolize the idea of home, acting as both members and guardians of the household and, like humans, subject to the power of the gods. When Athene transforms Odysseus back into a recognizable form and he is finally free to tell Telemachos that he is in fact his father, Odysseus's reaction is similar in kind, if to a much greater degree, to the reaction he has when he sees Argos, with "tears running down his cheeks." In both cases, recognition signals the end of "long-suffering" Odysseus's odyssey.

Argos, having waited for his master for twenty years, finally dies upon seeing him: "But the doom of dark death now closed over the dog, Argos,/ when after nineteen years had gone by, he had seen Odysseus" (XVII, 326–327). Argos's death touchingly expresses his loyalty to Odysseus, and, by extension, that of all those who still love him, including Penelope, who has been long besieged by "haughty," "arrogant," and "insolent" suitors while she awaits Odysseus's return. But it is also a scene of selfless sacrifice since Argos dies before his own recognition of Odysseus, "he wagged his tail, and laid both his ears back," might reveal to the others that Odysseus is "one of yours," much like Eumaios's dogs revealed to Odysseus that Telemachos was coming by the fact that they were "fawning about him" rather than barking and baying. In addition, the fact that the mutual recognition of master and dog, both now resembling beggars who, as such, are unrecognizable to others, occurs at the very threshold of Odysseus's palace also suggests that it represents an entry into the elaborately staged homecoming whose first phase, as we saw above, involved revealing himself to his son Telemachos. The scene of Argos's death foreshadows a further phase of this process since it reproduces in a minor key another scene of recognition that involves Odysseus's nurse Eurykleia. Still disguised as a beggar, Odysseus has persuaded Penelope to have the old nurse wash his feet and, as she does so, she recognizes him by the scar on his thigh: "She came up close and washed her lord, and at once she recognized/ that scar, which once the boar with his white tusk had inflicted/ on him, when he went to Parnassos, to Autolykos and his children" (XIX, 392–394). This scene of recognition, interrupted by a long excursus that describes the hunt, is similar to Argos's recognition of Odysseus in that Eurykleia is compelled to keep his identity secret so that Odysseus can carry out his plan to get rid of the suitors.

Erich Auerbach does not mention Argos in his magisterial reading of Odysseus's scar, but the scene of mutual recognition pet and master stage at the threshold of the palace as well as the dog's death are very much in keeping with Auerbach's description of the Homeric style as a style that "knows only a foreground, only a uniformly illuminated, uniformly objective present" (1974, 7). The role of Argos and the other dogs may not be as determinant as that of Telemachos and Eurykleia in the description of Odysseus's homecoming, but it is a role that is nevertheless significant because the proximity of animals tell us something about Odysseus's "natural" authority over the land, and about his legitimacy as the king of Ithaka. It also tells us about two complementary roles dogs tend to play in human culture: as guardians able to discriminate friend from foe, and as mirrors upon which humans recognize themselves as human. In occupying the "uniformly illuminated" foreground, Argos is thus not only recognizing Odysseus; he also makes us recognize him as the custodian of the literary realm as such since he is the first dog to ever bear a proper name in literature.

This Homeric scene of recognition provides the deep background to a short text by philosopher Emmanuel Levinas titled "The Name of a Dog, or Natural Rights," in which he writes about his experience as a prisoner of war in Nazi Germany and the humanizing presence of Bobby, a dog that wanders outside the camp.

> One day, he [a dog] came to meet this rabble as we returned under guard from work. He survived in some wild patch in the region of the camp. But we called him Bobby, an exotic name, as one does with a cherished dog. He would appear at morning assembly and was waiting for us as we returned, jumping up and down and barking in delight. For him, there was no doubt that we were men.
>
> (1990, 153)

While the Nazis treat Levinas and the other prisoners of war (all Jewish soldiers wearing French uniforms) as a "gang of apes" and the prisoners themselves feel as if they "were no longer part of the world," Bobby makes no distinction between free and imprisoned, Jew and non-Jew, human and non-human. But in invoking the story of Bobby (whose "exotic name" recalls that of an American GI), Levinas is making a distinction between different types of dogs. On the one hand, there are dogs that belong to "allegories" that convey conventional or clichéd canine attributes (miserable dogs, servile dogs, rabid dogs, etc.) and whose existence is framed by the structures of home, family, and nation. (A dog like Argos, whom Levinas cites without naming him, belongs to this category.) On the other, there are dogs that are just dogs—"... the dog is a dog. Literally a dog!" (152)—and have certain "natural" rights "beyond all scruples" to transform the "flesh that is torn by beasts in the field" (Exodus 22:31) into "good flesh." (Bobby belongs to this category.) For Levinas, Bobby is the "last Kantian in Nazi Germany" (153) because he recognizes the prisoners as humans, which, in the context of the Holocaust, becomes a moral rather than a "natural" stance. Levinas suggests that, unlike Argos, Bobby does not recognize the prisoners as belonging to a specific "Ithaca" (the traditional trope for "home") since they are in fact "nowhere." Even though he names Bobby, Levinas is at pains to insist that Bobby is "literally a dog" rather than an allegory or an allegorized dog in order to create a categorical distance between the rhetorical mechanisms whereby the Nazis transformed humans into animals ("a gang of apes"), and the ethical risks entailed in claiming that to humanize animals is tantamount to animalizing humans. Yet, the personification of Bobby as the "last Kantian in Nazi Germany" is precisely to take "the name of a dog in the figurative sense" (152). The question Levinas's text raises, then, is not so much about whether we should read dogs literally or figuratively (can we really tell the difference?), but rather about whether we read them well or not. The recognition of Odysseus by Argos and of Argos by Odysseus is a touching reminder of a living relation whose terms are already rhetorical, even as they are established by means of ears, tails, and tears. The story of Bobby's recognition traces the lineaments of a relation between an animal and a group of humans whose conditions of possibility are overdetermined by circumstances under which the very fate of relation has been circumscribed by a rhetorical operation that condemns people to "being 'signifiers without a signified'" (153); that is, to being people without rhetoric. To similarly deprive dogs of rhetoric is thus also to condemn them to the same fate as the Jews. Levinas is right to be cynical about the allegorization of the figure of the dog (it is of a piece with the dehumanization or animalization of the human), but, in maintaining a "natural" hierarchy between dogs and humans, he is also arrogating to himself the "right" to provide a "signifier" for a dog — "I am thinking of Bobby," (151) — without thereby also granting him the right to a "signified." Man's best friend, indeed.

## Mondo cane

Cervantes's exemplary 1613 novella "El coloquio de los perros" ("The Dialogue of the Dogs") begins with a moment of self-reflection in which two dogs, Cipión (Scipio) and Berganza, wonder at their ability to talk and reason, having often heard that dogs are in fact capable of neither. The two dogs then go on to enumerate the different tropes through which dogs have been described: "Lo que yo he oído alabar y encarecer es nuestra mucha memoria, el agradecimiento y gran fidelidad nuestra; tanto que nos suelen pintar por símbolo de la amistad" (Cervantes 1613 [1944], 659). ["People go on and on about our strong memories, our sense of gratitude, our great fidelity – so much so that artists sometimes use us as symbols of friendship" (1613 [2008], 24).] They are baffled by their ability to speak and consider that it must be an omen, yet decide to make the most of it since they have always had a yearning to speak.

Berganza is the first of the dogs to recount his life, promising that Cipión will get a chance to recount his own adventures before the night is over. In the comic exchanges between the two dogs that ensue, we find out that Berganza was born in Seville near a slaughterhouse where he learned firsthand about humans' cruelty and pettiness. As Berganza begins to tell Cipión his life story, the dogs soon realize that the bafflement caused by their ability to speak matches that which is caused by their inability to understand the things they have heard humans say and the things humans have made them do. In the course of his life, Berganza has been employed in a variety of endeavors by a number of different owners who, collectively, form a representative cross section of early modern Spanish society. In the tradition of the picaresque, Berganza makes his way in the world by outsmarting the humans who try to take advantage of him, and using wit and canine wiles to ingratiate himself to those of whom *he* might take advantage. The dog's reflections thus present a *"cuadro de costumbres,"* or sketch of types and scenes, that offers insight into social conventions, cultural habits, and human foibles, and, in doing so from the point of view of a dog, also provides an oblique perspective on aspects of human–animal relations that make human endeavors all the more puzzling.

But Berganza's tale is also an occasion to reflect upon the art of storytelling itself as the dogs' newfound ability to talk allows them to use the considerable discursive resources they have assimilated from humans, and thus to explore the rich rhetorical repertoire of their time and place, as well as the literary tradition they, perhaps unwittingly, inhabit. In one episode, Berganza tells Cipión about his experiences working as a sheep dog, noting how surprised he was to discover that the shepherding life is nothing like the *"felicísima vida"* (happiest life) led by the love-struck characters found in pastoral literature. Berganza's shepherds are coarse, petty, and dishonest and display rather vulgar musical taste. Some of them even kill sheep from their own flock while pretending, shepherds in wolves' clothing, that a wolf has been stalking their pastures. In another episode, Berganza and Cipión discuss the relative merits of using Latin phrases when speaking in the vernacular. Berganza claims that Latin, which he learned when he acted as companion to a student attending class with the Jesuits, can be used to good effect in conversation if it is not used merely to pretend to have knowledge of Latin before those who have none. Cipión, in contrast, argues that it is much worse to know Latin and to then use it before those who would not know it such as cobblers and tailors. But when Berganza subsequently uses a Latin proverb— *"Habet bovem in lingua"* ["He has an ox in his tongue"]—to illustrate one of his adventures, it is unclear whether he should be counted among those who show off their knowledge gratuitously, or those who pretend to know Latin to make others feel inadequate. Cipión naturally chides him for using Latin, but, in chiding Berganza, Cipión himself illustrates an earlier objection to his friend's propensity to gossip since it opens them up to the charge of being Cynics, or *"perros murmuradores"* ("gossiping dogs").

Indeed, as the two dogs continue to exchange witty opinions about humans and their different habits of speech, it becomes increasingly clear that a considerable part of the affective charge of the dialogue rests on their newfound ability to gossip about a world they know well but about which they have always had to *"morderse la lengua"* (bite their tongue, or remain silent). It is as though they had found release for their pent-up frustrations at being mere dogs in their ability to speak, which is more profitably invested in speaking the language of those who would treat them as dogs than in pretending to be above their condition, and to speak philosophically of their subservient condition as silent *"símbolo[s] de la amistad"* ("symbols of friendship"). Or, at least this is the attitude expressed by Berganza. Fearing that he will not get a chance to tell his own tale before sunrise, Cipión urges Berganza to follow rhetorical decorum and discursive economy in advancing his tale. Berganza's story, however, keeps getting longer and more elaborate as he uses what discursive occasions Cipión presents him to reflect on the act of storytelling rather than on the story itself. In the end, Cipión never gets to tell his own story, acting throughout as a restless yet enabling listener who, in objecting to Berganza's dawdling, in effect encourages his digressions.

None is perhaps as revealing of the effect the dialogue has on our conception of the role of dogs, and certainly none is longer, than the tale of Camacha, the witch who is said to have had the ability to turn men into animals. The story begins when Berganza, now a dazzling performing dog known as *"el perro sabio"* ("the learned dog"), is approached by Cañizares, a witch trained by Camacha but now repentant and reformed. Cañizares claims that Berganza is in fact the son of yet another witch, Montiela, who, under a spell conjured by the jealous Camacha, once gave birth to two puppies. Making a reference to Apuleius's *Golden Ass* (see Chapter 2), Cañizares tells Berganza, whom she calls Montiel, that, unlike the ass in the Latin tale, there is nothing he can actively do to break the spell; he has to wait patiently until Camacha's enigmatic prophecies come true. Farfetched and implausible though it may seem to the dogs, Cañizares's story would at least explain why Berganza and Cipión have been able to talk to each other. Camacha's prophecies must then become the object of literary analysis, Cipión suggesting that perhaps they should be interpreted allegorically. But no matter how the prophecies are read, they remain inconclusive and the dogs have no choice but to believe that they are in fact dogs living a dream rather than humans trapped in canine bodies.

Cervantes uses the picaresque adventures of a pair of dogs (or, in fact, only one dog) to offer an unvarnished portrait of a rich and complex society peopled by a great variety of characters and types. But the originality of Cervantes's narrative conceit rests on the fact that this portrait is painted from a canine perspective in which the dogs are both speaking *as* dogs (that is, as exploited animals that in their abjection act as proxies for marginalized humans) and also *for* dogs since in revealing the corrupt, petty, and ultimately bizarre world of humans they are also drawing attention, like the Cynics, to the unnatural world humans have created for themselves. This form of mirroring differs from the dynamics of recognition we find in the Homeric text in that Berganza and Cipión do not primordially act as mirrors in which humans recognize themselves, or become recognizable, as humans; rather, they act as uncanny mirrors in which humans, in perceiving that dogs act like humans, see themselves as the dogs they have become, in the pejorative sense of being uncivilized and inhuman. Cervantes's self-conscious treatment of traditional stereotypes concerning dogs complicates the socially fraught comedy traditionally associated with the figure of the *pícaro* by literalizing his social condition as a fate fit only for a dog; the cynic has become a Cynic. Indeed, Cervantes's representation of the humanized Berganza and Cipión makes us reconsider the very origins of the picaresque genre. After Cervantes, we can no longer think of Lazarillo, Guzmán, and el Buscón—the most famous *pícaros* in the tradition—as anything other than the dogs they always were, less by design or temperament than through abuse, abjection, and violent neglect. From this perspective, the figure of the *pícaro* can be seen to belong to the longstanding Aesopian tradition of the wily canid that we tend to associate with urbane foxes rather than urban dogs; a tradition to which I now turn.

# The vulpine epic

To say that Wile E. Coyote, the Warner Brothers cartoon character created by Chuck Jones, does not live up to his name is not only to remark on the rather obvious fact that he is an ineffectual predator, perpetually eating the Road Runner's dust rather the bird itself. It is also to suggest that his corporate identity, the middle initial signaling a form of branding similar to that of the ACME products he invariably uses to disastrous effect, would seem to imply a form of ruthlessness belied by his characterization as an eager but hardly clever company man who will never reach the acme of his profession. In either case, Wile E. Coyote's lack of guile, wiles, and cunning suggests nothing so much as a category mistake since among the canids it is typically the fox, rather than the coyote, who bears the representational stigma of the clever thief. In being neither clever nor particularly vulpine, Wile E. Coyote thus comes to represent a lapsed *pícaro*, a trickster tragically condemned to fall prey to his own tricks. The deflationary rhetorical economy of the Road Runner cartoons—poor Wile E. Coyote can't even lay claim to the title of the very cartoons in which he virtually monopolizes the screen—is based on the failed attempt to attain epic status: dehydrated boulders, jet-propelled roller skates, build-it-yourself missiles, invisible paint, and the many other ACME products he employs are mere accessories in a career of dogged determination and can-do spirit whose aspirations to a form of super-heroism remains painfully unattainable.

Indeed, Wile E. Coyote represents the ironic modern reversal of a tradition in which canids are represented as intelligent and somewhat devious beings capable of outwitting even the most feared of beasts. In some Native American traditions, the coyote is portrayed as a trickster, a figure at times endowed with magical powers that enable him to be creative and thus social and, at others, considered to be a deceptive creature who, on account of his untrustworthiness, is ostracized from the group to which he once belonged. Anthropologist Claude Lévi-Strauss argues that in North American tales the coyote, portrayed as a carrion eater, functions as a mediating figure between carnivores and herbivores, between life and death (1963, 224–25). Like the *pícaro* of the picaresque, the wily canid is a mediating figure, representing human folly by being both cultured and natural.

The most famous literary example of the clever canine in the European tradition is Reynard the Fox, a character whose own complex literary genealogy can be traced back to those Aesopian fables that show the fox to be a crafty and unscrupulous animal whose charm and verbal gifts more than make up for his small size while protecting him from those who covet his prized tail. The fable of the fox and the crow, for instance, shows the sly fox getting the better of a crow who has just stolen a piece of cheese by the use of flattery. The fox praises the crow's beautiful feathers and magnificent wings and pleads with him to sing him a song. The crow is of course flattered and, in emitting his ugly caw, he drops the cheese he had been holding. In La Fontaine's rendering of the fable, the fox himself offers the story's moral lesson:

Mon bon Monsieur,/ Apprenez que tout flatteur/ Vit aux dépens de celui qui l'écoute:/ Cette leçon vaut bien un fromage, sans doute.

[You see? Be edified:/ Flatterers thrive on fools' credulity./ The lesson's worth a cheese, don't you agree?" (2007, 6)

To be sure, the moral suggests that you should not trust those who flatter you, but, to the extent that the fable is about a thief stealing from another thief, it also illustrates the fox's superlative cunning. Other Aesopian tales describe the fox's comeuppance, as in the fable of the fox and the grapes. Unable to attain the desired fruit that hangs just out of his reach, the fox concludes that the grapes he covets must be sour. Sour grapes, indeed, suggest that the clever fox is also a sore loser, though the instances of defeat for the fox are rare in the Aesopian universe. More often, the fox is made to pay for his desire to make fun of others by becoming the butt of a joke of his own making, as in the fable about the fox's tail. Having lost his tail in a trap, a fox tells the other members of his skulk that their tails are overrated, dirty, and superfluous, and should therefore be removed. They tell him to turn around to let them see his tailless rump, which immediately comes to bear the brunt of their mockery. (A tale, incidentally, that can be thought of as the source text of R. W. Fassbinder's 1975 film *Fox and His Friends*.)

The ambiguity of the fox's moral standing in the fables is not exceptional among the Aesopian fauna: it is not always clear whether animal attributes offer moral lessons, or whether moral lessons make use of animal attributes to illustrate widely held precepts. But it is also true that the specific qualities associated with the fox—cunning, mockery, pride, arrogance, and charm—are hardly commendable as models of social behavior, which makes them ineluctably fascinating as well as eminently narratable, to use D.A. Miller's clever term. It is thus not surprising that the fox occupied a prominent position in the religious culture of the West nor that he would become the subject of a widely disseminated early modern text whose roots may well be found in the Aesopian tradition but whose representational ambitions were entirely epic in scope. The beast epic *The Historye of Reynart the Foxe*, translated into English from the French and published by

William Caxton in 1481 but in fact dating back to the twelfth century, tells the story of Reynard, a fox who has managed to antagonize the whole animal kingdom by lying, cheating, and stealing his way to relative prosperity. But the text's characterization of Reynard already tells us something about how other animals regard him, as well as about how we should understand his deceptive character and thus about how we ought to judge him. Reynard lives in Maleperduys, a labyrinthine castle full of holes, nooks, and passages that, like a fox's den (or "earth"), is designed to deceive, elude, and frustrate his many enemies. Reynard's own name, moreover, betrays the slyness we have come to associate with the literary species of the fox since the French word for fox, "renard," comes from Reynard, the character, in a form of reverse antonomasia that replaces the older Latinate name for fox in French, "goupil," a name that, like that of the proper name associated with Shakespeare's Scottish play, was considered to be of ill omen. In using the French word for fox, however, the translation repeats its generic name, which amounts to calling him Fox the fox. Like the Linnaean Latin binomial used centuries later to classify the fox, *Vulpes vulpes*, Reynard's double name, Fox the fox, which is something like an embodied antonomasia, places him as both the member of a set (cunning foxes, say) and a subset (especially cunning foxes), but, in addition, it also individualizes him as the one and only fox, the fox of foxes, the specimen that represents the species.

When Reynard is initially summoned to King Noble's palace where all the animals are assembled, he demurs: he knows he is almost universally reviled and might run the risk of being lynched. So, at any rate, we gather from the many inflammatory comments made about him in court by the wolf he has cuckolded, the cock whose offspring he has eaten, the dog whose meat he has stolen, and so on. The bear, who has been sent by the lion king to fetch the fox, returns empty-handed, as does the cat who follows him. Reynard finally arrives in court to face his accusers accompanied by the badger, his nephew, to whom he has confessed his sins. Once in court, Reynard defends himself as best he can from the long litany of crimes he is said to have committed, but the king remains unswayed and condemns him to death. The clever Reynard, however, tells the king that he has an enormous treasure, part of a war chest created by the other animals in their effort to depose the king. The king asks Reynard to take him to the treasure, but Reynard tells him that he has a previous engagement in Rome with the Pope and can only offer a set of (incredibly complicated) directions to get to the treasure. Reynard has no intention of going to Rome, of course, and he instead goes home, where, having convinced a hare to follow him on the grounds that a carnivore and a herbivore pose no threat to each other, he proceeds to kill him and feed him to his family. Reynard is then summoned back to court to answer for his crime and, once again, narrowly escapes death by flattering the king and feigning ignorance of his crimes. He is subsequently challenged by the wolf to a duel, to which Reynard agrees, not without first preparing himself for battle by following the counsel of his aunt, the ape. The contest is violent and drawn out, but Reynard is eventually victorious, winning by fighting in a less than honorable manner and finishing off the wolf by violently "twisting" his testicles. The king is impressed by this display of courage and makes Reynard a peer of the kingdom.

The narrative's reliance on Aesopian fables in order to make the animals and their familiar attributes intelligible is in keeping with the episodic structure of the beast epic, but it also tells us something about Reynard's own methods for escaping punishment since it is mostly his verbal skills, his ability to tell stories, that save him. We know full well that he is telling lies—and it is conceivable that the king himself knows he is lying—but there is nevertheless something compelling about his tales that makes up for their assault on our gullibility. That Reynard's ability to trick those who by rights should overpower him—an ability assimilated in the subsequent history of the canine text in reference to the figure of the *pícaro*—should be seen as an admirable quality in itself speaks as much to the sheer inventiveness of his discourse as to the fact that it is an ability that transcends rank and social position. If Reynard can not only trick a hare into entering his burrow but also convince a king to acquit him, who is to say that any other animal, provided he uses his wits, cannot similarly prevail? The sad truth, however, is that the other animals are too venal, greedy, and corrupt to notice that they are incapable of using wit and reason to get what they want. Indeed, Reynard's ability to trick the other animals rests on another ability: his ability to read their weaknesses and limitations. To be sure, there is something redemptive about Reynard's ability to expose frauds and contradict the sanctimoniousness of the powerful, but there is also something caustic and disturbing about his discourse that would seem to make redemption hardly an adequate moral framework in which to read him. Unlike the Cynic, Reynard does not advocate for a natural way of life; nature, in this vulpine epic, is already beyond redemption, not because it is unjust but because it is amoral.

The dynamics of recognition in the vulpine epic can be said to proceed through a form of displaced or belated mirroring. According to James Simpson, a tripartite structure of recognition characterizes the Reynardian story: an initial moment of recognition in which animals are seen to act like humans, followed by a moment in which animals are understood to act like the animals they are, and, finally, a moment in which humans are revealed to be like animals (Simpson 2011, 197–8). This likeness-difference-likeness sequence informs the canine picaresque of the early modern period, adding poignancy to the human mirroring we find in Berganza and Cipión and, in a literalization of the third stage, providing dramatic ballast for another vulpine text that does away entirely with animal characters, Ben Jonson's *Volpone* (1605–6). Indeed, Jonson's comedy is thoroughly informed by the Reynardian tradition of the vulpine epic, even as it operates within a moral universe in which a degree of order, in the form of poetic justice, is achieved. The play's protagonist, Volpone (sly fox, in Italian), sets out to dupe three fortune hunters, Voltore (vulture), Corbaccio (crow), and Corvino (raven), with the aid of his parasitic servant Mosca (fly). That the fortune hunters bear the names of carrion eaters—and thus act as mediators between life and death, according to Lévi-Strauss's schema—suggests that we are meant to take the simile likening humans to animals literally. The cunning and deceitful Volpone is like a fox to the precise degree that he is able to embody the literary figuration of the fox—that is, to be Reynard—and to do so literally. Indeed, the play's elaborate staging involves intricate play-acting as Volpone dons disguises and performs various roles in order to deceive those who seek to prey on him so as to dispossess them of their own fortunes. But Volpone's performance, which we might attribute to his vulpinariness, in fact becomes a generalized phenomenon as his own deviousness seems to leave others with no recourse but to put on an act, most signally Mosca, who surprises his master by plotting to keep Volpone's fortune for himself. This conceit allows Jonson's comedy to satirize avarice as a form of "rare punishment" to itself since no one is spared from the fox's wiles, least of all the big fox himself. But the dizzying reversals and ironic interruptions on which the drama is built also tend to naturalize avarice since, in the end, the world the play inhabits will continue to be guided by avarice, even if those whom the play reveals to have been playing confidence games end up being punished. In equating human vices to "beasts," the play suggests that immoral human actions may be contained but, because they are instinctual, are ultimately ineradicable.

Indeed, one is left to wonder if fox-hunting, a widely practiced yet useless sport, is not in itself a cultural response to this moral dilemma, as though the elaborate ritual of riding to hounds were a form of cultural retribution for the moral paradox posed by the fox. In Anthony Trollope's *The Eustace Diamonds* (1871), for instance, Lizzie Greystock, a conniving hunter of fortunes intent on keeping the diamonds her infirm late husband has bequeathed to her, even though she has no permanent claim on them, joins the chase for what seems to be no more than another attempt to pretend that she is a rightful member of the hunting party. In the novel's hunting scene, however, it becomes clear that she is hunting for an entirely different quarry in the form of Lucinda Roanoke, her American rival, in the violent though engrossing pursuit of a suitable husband that is being allegorized in the hunt. The vices symbolized by the figure of the fox come to be naturalized in this tale of social cunning and upward mobility in which the fox itself plays an almost invisible role. The vulpine epic thus offers a significant counternarrative to the benign tale of recognition and domestication that characterizes the dog tale. Dogs are a "companion species," to use Donna Haraway's suggestive phrase, in part because we share our otherness with them in a domestic space, along with the microorganisms, habits, and affects that transit between both species. Foxes, in contrast, exist at the further edges of domestication, remaining wild as a species, even as they are routinely hunted for sport, which makes the fox a symbolically rich site for staging the encounter between nature and civilization.

Late in Wes Anderson's film *Fantastic Mr. Fox* (2009), which is based on Roald Dahl's story of the same name, we see Mr. Fox (whose name, incidentally is "Foxy" Fox, repeating, like Reynard, the common noun for fox as antonomasia) riding on a motorbike with his son Ash, his nephew Kristofferson, and his friend Kylie, an opossum. Mr. Fox stops on the side of the road when he notices a black wolf on a distant ridge. Thinking that the wolf is not likely to speak English or Latin, Mr. Fox calls out to him in French, asking him if he thinks the coming winter will be harsh. The wolf does not initially respond, but then lifts a fist in a gesture of acknowledgement (perhaps as an echo of the symbol of black power in the 1960s) before turning his back on the curious foxes. "What a beautiful creature," Mr. Fox says as he sheds a tear, and then adds: "Wish him luck, boys." The scene, staged as an encounter between nature and civilization, encapsulates the dramatic conflict at the center of Anderson's film. Mr. Fox is a suburban family fox who has promised his wife to give up stealing for the more decorous though certainly less appetizing job of writing for the local newspaper. No matter how earnestly he tries to adapt to his new life, however, he still has a yen for the hunt, and, with the help of his friend Kylie, he plots to steal poultry and produce from the three farms that operate near his new home. When his wife, Mrs. Fox, finally catches on, she asks him why he has been lying to her; he answers simply: "Because I am a wild animal." Mr. Fox, a modern embodiment of Reynardian cunning, is nevertheless less concerned with exploiting the vanity and avarice of those around him—though Boggis, Bunce, and Bean, the three farmers he victimizes are certainly morally corrupt—than in ascertaining what it means nowadays to be a fox: "How can a fox ever be happy without, you'll forgive the expression, a chicken in its teeth?" Foxy loses his tail in one encounter with the farmers, yet retains his "pure wild animal craziness" in the face of ever encroaching human development, a state of affairs neatly captured by the bevy of bulldozers, earth movers, and explosives the farmers use to attack his burrow.

Nothing less than the fate of wild animals, indeed of the very notion of wildness, is at stake in Mr. Fox's quest to deceive the farmers. Wilderness, which is not quite equivalent to wildness, may well be a human invention, as William Cronon has argued, but, from the perspective of animals that live in the midst of this invention, the prospect of heeding the call of the wild, as Mr. Fox modestly does, has been compromised by the very forces that would want to tame it: farmers weary of poachers, developers eager to transform the landscape, the suburban ethos of preserving nature as the condition of possibility for prosperous human community. The wild wolf that appears at the end of the movie is not wild because it fails to recognize the signs of civilization (to know Latin, say); it is wild, as his lifted fist suggests, because he resists the notion of wilderness that would render it, like Mr. Fox, a civilized creature. Mr. Fox, of course, is under no illusions and, even if the wild wolf tugs at his instincts, he realizes that his place is on the grocery store's linoleum floor upon which, at the end of the film, he is able to celebrate the fact that he is a survivor.

Mr. Fox, like the vulpine literary tradition from which he emerges, occupies a "middle ground," Cronon's term for the negotiated coexistence of humans and non-humans on carefully managed land. This position, a middle ground between nature and civilization, finds its discursive vehicle in the toast Mr. Fox gives to his friends when they first find themselves trapped in the sewer system into which they have been flushed by the farmers: "Wild animals, with true natures and pure talents. Wild animals with scientific-sounding Latin names that mean something about our DNA. Wild animals each with his own strengths and weaknesses due to his or her species." To toast wildness of course is also to reabsorb it into civilized discourse, which in the case of Mr. Fox means using animal cunning to outsmart the humans who have ensnared them. The anarchist credo Mr. Fox echoes here neatly captures the vulpine double bind, since the substitution of "species" for "abilities" suggests a social order ruled by nature rather than convention. Less taxonomic schema than casting call, the Latinate binomials Mr. Fox uses to name his friends—*Lutra lutra* (otter), *Meles meles* (badger), *Castor fiber* (beaver), and, of course, *Vulpus vulpus* (Foxy fox)—may well describe their "strengths and weaknesses," but they also enable him to allocate practical roles and assign tasks in his elaborate plot against the farmers. Anderson's use of clay figures and stop-motion animation in *Fantastic Mr. Fox* is, in this regard, entirely appropriate since the visual plasticity of this representational mode makes evident the very fact of manipulation, which can be thought of as the fox's "true nature" and "pure talent." The vulpine epic, as Anderson's film so cunningly illustrates, outsmarts its readers by showing us that the animality of animals is not the obverse of civilization but its *raison d'être*. Civilization, in this reading, is that compensatory effort made by slow, brainy primates with little fur and unremarkable sense perception to make do in a world full of wild animals whose "pure talents" we both fear and secretly covet.

## Marking territory

It is something of a critical commonplace to say that Jack London's *The Call of the Wild* (1903) and *White Fang* (1906) are mirror images of each other, the former tracing a dog's progressive transformation into a wild wolf, and the latter a wild wolf's gradual domestication into a dog. The symmetries are misleading, however, not least because Buck and White Fang, the canine protagonists of these stories, are from the outset implicated in the circuits traced by humans in the Yukon, both during the Klondike gold rush contrived by the white descendants of Europeans, and for centuries before that in the settlement patterns and extensive trading routes of the First Nations. The mirroring at play in London's tales therefore has less to do with crossing the nature–culture divide than with showing how nature and culture are already imbricated in the passage from civilization to what the texts variously call the "primitive," the "primordial," the "savage," and, of course, the "wild." London styled himself a "naturalist" after French novelist Émile Zola, and, like Zola before him, he endeavored to show the effects the environment has on individuals with specific hereditary traits. Yet, unlike Zola, London chose to trace this form of biological determinism in animals rather than in humans, which is one reason why his anthropomorphic tales seem to be both allegorical and realistic at once, offering cautionary Darwinian parables of survival in a world that is indifferent to the fate of the individual, and showing in painstaking detail how this world actually works. Indeed, the environmental pressures that "call" Buck to the wild and socialize White Fang are both natural and cultural, with human and non-human animals shaping each other under circumstances that cannot in any simple way be called entirely natural, nor, for that matter, entirely cultural. Whether we view this form of determinism as dogmatic, asinine, or brutally honest matters less for our purposes than the fact that in London's tales, animals are granted a degree of moral stature unusual in literary history in that, unlike, say, the animals in classic fables, Buck and White Fang never have to relinquish instinctual behavior. We may condemn human actions in the name of morality even if, like Zola, we believe that we are biologically predetermined to conduct such actions, but it is much harder to judge animal behavior on the grounds of moral inadequacy even when, like London, we believe that there exists something like canine subjectivity. Moral imperatives, in any case, are suspended in London's naturalism, and a new model of embodied instinct is made possible by the literary focalization of animal endeavors.

Natureculture, the term Donna Haraway (2007) uses to designate the varied ways in which humans and non-humans are engaged in a constant process of mutual becoming, perhaps offers a better rubric under which to examine Buck's and White Fang's metamorphoses than the categorical distinction implied by phrases such as "the call of the wild" or "the call of kind," which suggest a threshold that ought to be crossed or a summons towards difference that must be heeded. Before proceeding to the Yukon, however, it will be important to sharpen our sense of what Haraway means by the term natureculture to avoid the temptation of erasing difference altogether when we read London's tales of human–animal relations *in extremis*. In Haraway's reading of Gilles Deleuze and Félix Guattari's "1730: Becoming-Intense, Becoming-Animal, Becoming-Imperceptible," an important text in animal studies, she notes with some regret that, in spite of the authors' productive formulation of the concept of becoming as an appealing alternative to hierarchical and patrilineal thinking, they make a troubling distinction between dogs as Oedipal pets and wolves as members of a pack. For Deleuze and Guattari, the process of "becoming-animal" occurs not among individuals but at the level of the pack; not through heredity but through contagion. In their provocative description of becoming, Deleuze and Guattari are admittedly dismissive of pets, of "the little cat or dog owned by an elderly woman who honors and cherishes it" (1972, 244), yet it is also a bit reductive to suggest, as Haraway does, that their description does not enlighten us about "real" animals because they do not take pets seriously. Their description of "becoming-animal" gives us a valuable way of thinking about animals in terms that go against the grain of London's "naturalism" since it is not the individual (the pet, the "little person," the specimen) that instantiates the human–animal interface but the group, with its own internal differences, functions, patterns, etc. If we are to subscribe to the notion of natureculture, a notion that can serve us well as a thematic guide to London's tales, it is only by thinking of it in terms of the narratives' larger movements. Indeed, London's tales can be read as narratives of territorialization in which the culture–nature divide is a moving border both within the pack, and at the point of contact of between packs: dogs, wolves, Europeans, and Amerindians marking continually changing territories in the yet-to-be established map of the Yukon. In this sense, the tales can be said to be thoroughly political since they offer a pragmatic account of "mutual inclusion," one of Brian Massumi's propositions regarding animal politics (2014, 49).

*The Call of the Wild* begins with a political act. Buck, Judge Miller's favorite dog, is stolen by Manuel, a Mexican farmhand addicted to the Chinese lottery, and then sold to the first in a long line of unscrupulous men that extends from California to the Yukon, where big, laboring dogs are needed to prospect for gold. Buck first learns to obey the "primitive law" (12) of the club by a dog-breaker who sells him to a French-Canadian government courier, and then the law of the fang when he witnesses a dog from his sled team being torn apart by a hungry pack of huskies. These laws are territorial in that they demarcate a naturecultural region within which Buck must find his way as he begins to adapt to the toilsome labor of pulling a sled under trying conditions in the Yukon. But these laws are also disciplinary in that they produce a new being: he becomes a "new dog, utterly transformed by the harness" (19), and though the text calls this process of transformation a form of "decivilization" (22), he remains beholden to the "law of club and fang" (15, 21) which suggests that Buck's coercion is also a form of "subjectivation" in the Foucauldian sense. Indeed, as he becomes used to his new life he also discovers his "dominant primordial beast," which drives him to confront, subvert, bully, and ultimately overpower Spitz, the lead-dog. The "dominant primordial beast" (36) may refer in London's telling to a "decivilized" animal-within-the-animal, but it is also a highly socialized one since the struggle for supremacy is political. Furthermore, it is a struggle that is not only focused on the political organization of the pack; the sled team, a functioning human–animal system, must periodically fend off the famished huskies "from some Indian village" (52) that lay siege to their supplies, and the sundry wolves that follow them as they toil through the snow and ice. The team itself changes as it makes its way through the Yukon with different humans and different animals constantly reconfiguring the system. A particularly cruel and incompetent trio of humans, for instance, almost kills the whole pack. Buck's transformation, in short, is of a piece with a politics of mutual inclusion in which humans and animals alike are implicated in a state of natureculture.

Buck is finally able to escape from the social structure of the sled-team—a failed or flawed political organization to the extent that it cannot guarantee his future—to enter into another form of naturecultural sociality when he meets John Thornton. Thornton, who is a gold prospector, not only becomes his protector; he also becomes the object of his love. Together, they travel throughout the Yukon, prospecting for gold, and, in doing so, marking a contingent and fluid territory that gives shape to their love. This amorous territorialization seems to function well until they find gold and settle down, for, no matter how "feverish" and "burning" (61) his love for Thornton becomes, Buck is summoned by a "primordial law" that beckons "out of the depths of Time" (75). Seized by "irresistible impulses" (76), he is drawn to a wolf, who becomes his "brother" (78) and with whom he wanders away from humans for a few days, marking a "wild" (78) territory similar to the one he has mapped with Thornton in that it is a crosshatch of mutual dependency, but also different in that it is a natureculture principally constituted by canids. Buck's affective ties to Thornton are not yet completely torn, though, and he eventually returns to camp. The make-up text does not endure, however, and Buck's instincts are once again aroused when a moose happens by. Somehow compelled to go after it, Buck tracks it for four days until he is able to kill it. Returning to camp, he finds that Thornton and his partners are dead, killed by the Yeehats, a native tribe into whose territory the gold prospectors have unwittingly entered. Buck attacks the Yeehats, exacting revenge for Thornton's death, and, at the same time, breaking the last tether that binds him to the human community. He joins a pack of wolves and howls with them at the moon, as though voicing for the first time the "call of the wild." Unlike the sled-team, this new social structure is politically viable since it is able to guarantee Buck's future: a few years after Buck's "return" to the wild, the Yeehats notice that the wolves of the pack now show "splashes of brown on head and muzzle" (86).

White Fang, the canine protagonist of *White Fang*, could well be thought of as one of Buck's offspring. His mother is a red she-wolf that, as the narrative begins, is leading a pack of wolves as they follow a sled-team along the "trail of meat." This chase scene suggests that the narrative energy of *White Fang*, like that of *The Call of the Wild*, is directed at the effort of mapping a series of territories marked by the interaction between humans and animals, as though the very borders that make up natureculture were configured by the wide-ranging encounters—violent, instrumental, predatory, economic, affective, serendipitous, perhaps even divine—that occur among mutually inclusive species that find themselves face to face in the world. White Fang, to whom the texts first refers as the "gray cub," is captured by the same group of Native Americans who had once captured and domesticated his mother, the red she-wolf, whom the Native Americans call Kiche. From the young wolf's perspective, humans are superior "man-animals" whose power is "inconceivable" and "beyond the natural" and whose ability to "change the very face of the world" makes them terrible and "god-like" (164, 166). White Fang and Kiche both render their allegiance to these "makers of fire" and subsequently enter into a form of bondage whose logic is more economic than affective. Indeed, the wolves' new territory is mapped not so much by meat as by barter, mother and pup having been separated when Gray Beaver, the Native American who has tamed the wolves, trades Kiche to Three Eagles. As the seasons change and the tribe moves on to new hunting grounds, moving on what the text calls the "trail of the gods," White Fang, now harnessed and pulling a sled, comes to realize that the world is "fierce and brutal" and "without warmth" and that his only duty is to the "law of property" (London 2009, 192, 194). The territory, marked by beatings, blood, and occasional food, comes to encompass White Fang's experience of the world as he grows into adulthood, molded by "his heredity and his environment" (200).

White Fang's first encounter with the descendants of Europeans in Fort Yukon during the Klondike gold rush, however, changes the shape of his territory since he perceives them—it is a "feeling" rather than a reasoned argument—to be "a superior race of gods" to the Native Americans among whom he has lived. He also encounters the dogs the prospectors have brought north with them, who, though atavistically inclined to fight him—they have an "inherited memory" of an "ancient feud"—are routinely killed by the friendless wolf. One of the "white gods" who people the town—a "monstrosity" by the name of Beauty Smith who has been molded by drudgery and cowardice—notices White Fang's fighting prowess and buys him from Gray Beaver in exchange for whiskey. This "mad god" begins to exhibit White Fang as "The Fighting Wolf" along the Yukon River, turning him, by virtue of the "plasticity of his clay," into a feared "professional fighter" with "terrible ferocity" (224). While Fang's socialization thus rests on his ability, coveted by humans, to display his wildness by engaging in civilized combat; that is, in combat with no use value to the animal. During one particularly brutal fight against an English bulldog, perhaps ironically named Cherokee, in which White Fang is nearly killed, he meets Weedon Scott, a human who will change his life. Through patience, affection, and a soft touch, Scott and Matt, a "dog-musher" who works with Scott, transform White Fang into a docile dog whose own feelings change from "like" to "love" as he realizes that "his god" loves him, and that his only purpose is to make him the leader of his sled team. Affect, rather than violence, disciplines White Fang, which suggests that the process of subjectivation whereby the wolf becomes the dog also entails sentimentalization, a literary process that abstracts the wolf into the literary trope of the dog. Indeed, when Scott decides to return to California with White Fang, the narrative calls this process the "long trail," a territorialized rite of passage at the end of which the wolf comes into civilizing contact with a domesticated Collie. That Weedon's father is a judge also suggests that this new sentimentalized territory, which the text calls "god's domain," is thoroughly regulated, and that White Fang's domestication will depend on his ability to abide the law, an ability he puts on full display when he helps capture an escaped convict.

White Fang's territorialization is thus a thoroughly political act, and, to the extent that he enters into a legalized or regulated domain much like the one Buck is forced to leave at the beginning of *The Call of the Wild* (Buck's first owner is also a judge), it is also an economic one in which becoming (wild, domesticated, lawful, outlawed, savage, civilized, etc.) is an endless proliferating process that creates not one but many naturecultures. Indeed, London's *The Call of the Wild* and *White Fang* can be said to show the political landscape of turn-of-the-century North America as it comes to be configured by the complex entanglements of humans and non-humans under laws whose varied application forms mutually inclusive territories. Buck and White Fang are molded by complex environments in which biological, physical, economic, and affective forces give shape to changing territories. London's tales may seem too deterministic for the modern reader, but in offering a view of human–animal relations from the perspective of the animal, they also tend to blur the nature–culture divide they seemingly police. Put differently, the passage London's stories seem to trace between dog and wolf is also a passage created by multiple histories, both natural and cultural, that complicate our account of the "wild" as the obverse of civilization. The narrative construction of this passage, moreover, occurs through the persistent trope of "the trail," as though the territories mapped by the stories were not in fact marked by a rigid border between nature and culture, but rather existed as mutually inclusive zones through which humans and animals passed, continually reconfiguring packs, teams, tribes, and families.

Far from blurring difference, this process of mutual implication is in fact premised on the existence of difference. In nature, as Darwin showed, difference is the very engine of evolution; whether it should also constitute the logic of culture is of course a question that lies at the heart of politics and which these texts can only pose.

## Strange little people in disguise

In an essay aptly titled "People in Disguise," James Serpell argues that the question of anthropomorphism, commonly broached among scientists intent on establishing empirical grounds for interpreting animal behavior that avoid the attribution of human predicates to their objects of study, can also be invoked to describe the "transformative force" that has shaped the morphology and the behavior of our non-human companions and, through them, our own health and affective wellbeing (2005, 123). In this telling, anthropomorphism accounts for humans' ability to domesticate other animals by projecting our thoughts, feelings, attitudes, and beliefs onto other species, an otherwise anomalous activity from an evolutionary perspective since no natural advantage seems to be gained at first blush from keeping pets. The view that pets are parasitical on human societies, deriving sustenance by exploiting our gullibility but offering nothing in return (Serpell cites the so-called "cute response" that makes us baby our pets), or else appendages in the pathologically asocial existence of modern humans, cannot account for the fact that pets are so prevalent as to suggest that they are less an afterthought than consciously acquired companions eminently disposed to enrich our lives. But one need not be a Cynic to suggest that this salutary practice is also made possible by the fact that in domesticating animals as pets, we are also shaping them according to our preferences and necessities. Some of the ways in which we shape our pets by means of grooming, training, and clothing them seem to cause no harm, but other practices that come under the rubric of what Serpell calls "anthropocentric selection"—selective breeding that favors traits that correspond to human states of being—can result in physically disabled and psychically handicapped breeds. The English bulldog, for instance, is now so physically deformed that it has difficulty breathing and walks on stunted limbs (129). The benefits of pet ownership still outweigh its drawbacks, Serpell argues, but if we continue to practice "anthropocentric selection" without repairing on the damage we can cause, he warns, we may end up with hybrid monstrosities for pets, "no longer animals so much as strange little people in disguise" (132).

There is perhaps no better text to analyze the anthropocentric logic of pet keeping than Virginia Woolf's *Flush* (1933), the biographical account of Elizabeth Barrett Browning's cocker spaniel. Woolf does not take as her model autobiographical animal tales such as Anna Sewell's popular *Black Beauty* (1877); instead, she adapts a traditional impersonal, third-person narrative voice to encompass the world view of a dog. Using what may be characterized as a form of cross-species ventriloquism, or free indirect discourse *obligé* (FIDO), Woolf focalizes her tale through the impressions, feelings, and opinions of Flush without for all that giving the dog a voice nor, strictly speaking, a point of view. Woolf bases her loving portrait of Flush partly on her own spaniel Pinka, but also draws on Elizabeth Barrett Browning's correspondence to flesh out her portrait. The text is constructed as a memoir (this is the word Woolf herself uses to describe her text in its opening sentence), but it is narrated in the third person. Whether the text's almost exclusive attention to Flush amounts to a caninocentric view of the world is not always clear however, since the narrative of Flush's life follows a human, or anthropocentric biographical arc. Indeed, Flush is presented at the outset as the product of "anthropocentric selection" in that his pedigree is first linked to the "Royal Houses of Bourbon, Hapsburg, and Hohenzollern," then equated to his breeder, one Dr. Mitford, who is "a mongrel man unfitted to carry on his kind" (Woolf 1933 [1983], 9), and then finally described, absent any proof to the contrary, as a "pure-bred Cocker of the red variety marked by all the characteristic excellences of his kind" (10). These "characteristic excellences" include being "by nature sympathetic," and in the case of Flush, this attribute manifests itself in "an even excessive appreciation of human emotion" (11).

Yet, even as this excessive attention to human emotion appears to be anthropocentric in the telling, the text allows Flush to delight in his own caninity, as in this passage that describes his behavior as he walks through the grass:

> What a variety of smells interwoven in subtlest combination thrilled his nostrils; strong smells of earth, sweet smells of flowers; nameless smells of leaf and bramble; sour smells as they crossed the road; pungent smells as they entered the bean field.
>
> (12)

He then smells a "sharper, stronger, more lacerating" smell, a smell that "ripped across his brain stirring a thousand instincts, releasing a million memories" (12). The lyricism of the passage suggests intimate proximity to the dog's sensory experience, but this experience is not for all that rendered in the form of "stream-of-consciousness," Woolf's signature style. Flush thus remains at an ontological remove from the narrative's center of consciousness, a discursive situation that surely corresponds to the structure of traditional biography in which biographer and the subject of biography are kept categorically distinct, but it also suggests more generally that dogs, no matter what their "characteristic excellences," are socialized as the unquestioning subjects of human affection, towards which their sensory impressions are directed. Put differently, if Woolf's modernist aesthetics tend to problematize the very legitimacy of address—the self is a "wedge-shaped core of darkness," as she memorably writes in *To the Lighthouse* (1927 [1981], 62)—the fact that Flush is characterized as a fully embodied presence means that he has been granted a form of subjectivity, via FIDO, that remains virtually unaffected by the often debilitating if sobering insights of acute self-reflexivity.

The point of this somewhat abstract excursus into modernist representational aesthetics is not so much to draw attention to the limitations of canine biography; it is, rather, to suggest that the representation of Flush as a fully sentient being with claims to subjectivity corresponds to the manner in which we have invented dogs as "little people." Indeed, Woolf's *Flush* can be read as the chronicle of such invention. When Flush is given to "England's foremost poetess, the brilliant, the doomed, the adored Elizabeth Barrett," the gift is understood to be "a fitting token of the disinterested friendship" that exists between Miss Mitford and Miss Barrett, but it soon becomes clear that this "token" is "fitting" not least because Flush will serve as an uncanny mirror image to Miss Barrett herself: "There was a likeness between them. As they gazed at each other each felt: Here am I – and then each felt: But how different!" (Woolf 1933 [1983], 23). This is both a poetic as a well as a social encounter since while each seems to shape the other as though engaged in a sort of canine *poiesis* (the Greek term for creation), the process is a thoroughly socialized one that involves situating the confined domestic space they share within the larger social world. Indeed, as Flush begins to get used to city life and encounters a great variety of dogs in his walks, he realizes that dogs, like humans, exist in highly structured societies organized on the principle of difference: "Flush knew before the summer had passed that there is no equality among dogs: there are high dogs and low dogs" (32). Rather than a reason for anger or dejection, the existence of social hierarchies is for Flush an occasion to come to terms with his own social position: "No sooner had Flush got home than he examined himself carefully in the looking-glass. Heaven be praised, he was a dog of birth and breeding!" (32). Miss Barrett thinks he might be a philosopher, as he gazes intently at himself in the mirror, but the narrator suggests he is simply an aristocrat.

This is a far cry from the Homeric dynamics of recognition in which humans recognize themselves as human by virtue of being recognized by dogs as their masters. In gazing at himself in the mirror, Flush is recognizing himself as the "little person" he already is in the eyes of her owner and, for that matter, of all the dog-owning Londoners through whom dogs attain social identity. That the price Flush must pay for such identity is the suppression of "the most violent instincts of his nature" is more than compensated for by the fact that a special bond, "an uncomfortable yet thrilling tightness," has developed between dog and human. Flush, like the invalid Miss Barrett, is soon confined to a single bedroom and no longer seeks to escape into the open. Both are "chained to the sofa" (35). The effect of this mirroring extends into Miss Barrett's writing since, though Flush is at a loss as to what the black smudges that she produces with a stick on a page might mean, he longs for "a time when he too should black paper as she did" (39). Alarm bells are usually set off when this form of mimetic behavior occurs among human flat mates, but dogs, as the example of Flush amply illustrates, are routinely taught to imitate their owners, even when the intention is not explicitly to create mirror images of themselves. Dogs may look just like their owners only in the cultural imaginary—consider the opening of Disney's *101 Dalmatians* (1961) as the cultural benchmark for this form of mimetic doubling—but there is in any case little doubt that the "imitation game" holds great benefits for humans. James Serpell and others have noted that dogs are not only excellent companions for the infirm; they also aid in the process of healing. Also, to the extent that dogs no longer exist in the "wild," dogs too benefit from their ability to adapt to the exigencies of human confinement.

The relation established between Miss Barrett and Flush is thus one of happy codependence, even if the love they feel for each other is not exactly reciprocated: "She loved Flush, and Flush was worthy of her love" (49). The bedroom they share, however, soon becomes a bit more crowded as, first, letters from a mysterious correspondent that tend to agitate Miss Barrett begin to arrive, and, then, the "hooded man" who has written them arrives in person. Robert Browning's arrival turns Flush's blissful "firelit cave" into a "dark and damp" cave where everything has changed and Flush himself has turned into a lonely, whiny, and ignored dog who is no longer the sole object of Miss Barrett's affections: "Flush, poor Flush could feel nothing of what she felt" (57). Indeed, Flush only feels "an intense dislike for

Mr. Browning" (61). As Miss Barrett's condition improves under the influence of Mr. Browning, Flush himself reverts back to a state in which he dreams of hares and foxes, as though he were still a puppy in the country. When he finally senses that a change is coming and fears, his jealousy "inflamed," that he might lose Miss Barrett, he finally attacks Mr. Browning in an effort to reclaim her attentions. Mr. Browning seems not to take notice of his bite, which hurts less than Miss Barrett's rebuke. This sequence is repeated once more with the same result. The somewhat Oedipal conceit of this triangulated desire between two humans and a dog is finally resolved when Flush decides to eat the cakes Mr. Browning had once brought for him but which he had ignored: "[T]hings are not simple but complex. If he bit Mr. Browning he bit her too. Hatred is not hatred; hatred is also love" (69).

Two further events serve to settle the affective dynamics of this particular triangle. First, Flush is stolen by a band of dog robbers and held captive for five days and, then, once Miss Barrett secretly becomes Mrs. Browning, he moves to Italy with the couple. Both events change Flush's admittedly limited conception of society: the first exposes him to the cruelty and coarseness of human society; the second, to the cruelty and coarseness of canine society: "He was the only pure-bred cocker spaniel in the whole of Pisa" (113). In Italy, Mrs. Browning undergoes a miraculous transformation, recovering her health, becoming active once again, and, eventually, giving birth to a child; and Flush is transformed as well. Now best of friends with Mr. Browning, Flush learns to live in the democratic dog world of Pisa: "All dogs were his brothers" (117). Most important, however, he finds love:

> Now Flush knew what men can never know – love pure, love simple, love entire; love that brings no train of care in its wake; that has no shame; no remorse; that is here, that is gone, as the bee on the flower is here and is gone.
>
> (119)

Flush not only mirrors the Brownings' conjugal bliss, he actually multiplies it, since he proves to be no snob when it comes to finding partners. When the Brownings welcome their child into the world, Flush initially feels the sting of jealousy and neglect, but he learns to live with the child. Now older, Flush has certainly grown wiser, but, in doing so, he has also become increasingly human: "His flesh was veined with human passions; he knew all grades of jealousy, anger, and despair" (133). Upon the family's return to England, Flush, now in old age, dies. In thus attaining closure, Flush's biographical arc suggests that his life was not only a life of companionship, helping Elizabeth Barrett Browning cope with her infirmities, but also a life that incorporated all the human passions. We might do worse than name this story a "lapdog romance," a genre whose affective charge, poetic energy, and narrative displacements must now be equated with the all too familiar transformations we incite in our pets. Flush's story is the story of how we create "strange little people in disguise."

The canine text is the chronicle of that peculiar territorialization whereby we domesticate wild wolves and cunning foxes the better to recognize ourselves as "civilized," "intelligent," "god-like," or merely Cynical. From the mutual recognition of humans and dogs in Homer and the picaresque to the uncanny mirroring effect of the vulpine epic and the lapdog romance, this form of territorialization blurs the strict division we postulate between human and non-human, even if, in blurring it, we have often reaffirmed it. In reading the canine tropes that the history of literature has employed as something more than a representation of companion species, we are also reading literature's employment of these tropes as one of the features that makes literature recognizable *as* literature. For all we know, talking dogs and toasting foxes are the stuff of literature, but they are also, for all that, a persistent presence in literature that makes us reconsider the differences that separate us, not so as to eliminate differences, but rather so as to multiply them, as each of the canine texts I have cited here do in their imaginative entanglements with wolves, foxes, and dogs.

## Notes

1  Figures obtained from "Facts and Figures 2014," a document published by the European Pet Food Industry Federation (FEDAF) and available at: www.fediaf.org/facts-figures/

2  See website of the American Pet Products Association. Available at: www. americanpetproducts.org

3  See "China's Skyrocketing (Pet) Population," Christina Larson. *Bloomberg Business*, August 21, 2014. Available at: www.bloomberg.com/bw/articles/2014-08-21/chinas-skyrocketing-pet-population

4  See "The Dog Economy is Global – but What is the World's True Canine Capital?," Theresa Bradley and Ritchie King. *The Atlantic*, Nov. 13, 2012. Available at: www.theatlantic.com/business/archive/2012/11/the-dog-economy-is-global-but-what-is-the-worlds-true-canine-capital/265155/

5  See American Kennel Club. Labrador Retriever. Available at: www.akc. org/dog-breeds/labrador-retriever/

6  See American Kennel Club. Poodle. Available at: www.akc.org/dog-breeds/poodle/

7  See American Kennel Club. Border Collie. Available at: www.akc.org/dog-breeds/border-collie/

8  See American Kennel Club. Mexican Xoloitzcuintli. Available at: www. akc.org/dog-breeds/xoloitzcuintli/

## Works cited

Anderson, Wes. *Fantastic Mr. Fox*. Twentieth-Century Fox, 2009.

Auerbach, Erich. *Mimesis: The Representation of Reality in Western Literature*, trans. Willard R Trask. Princeton: Princeton University Press, 1974.

Cervantes, Miguel de. *Novelas Ejemplares*. Madrid: Aguilar, 1944.

Cervantes, Miguel de. *The Dialogue of the Dogs*, trans. David Kipen. Brooklyn: Melville House, 2008.

Cronon, William. "The Trouble with Wilderness; or, Getting Back to the Wrong Nature." In *Uncommon Ground: Rethinking the Human Place in Nature*. Ed. William Cronon. New York: W. W. Norton, 1995: 69–90.

Deleuze, Gilles and Félix Guattari. *A Thousand Plateaus: Capitalism and Schizophrenia*, trans. Brian Massumi. Minneapolis: University of Minnesota Press, 1972.

Haraway, Donna. *The Companion Species Manifesto*. Chicago: Prickly Paradigm Press, 2003.

Haraway, Donna. *When Species Meet*. Minneapolis: University of Minnesota Press, 2007.

Homer. *The Odyssey of Homer*, trans. Richard Lattimore. New York: Harper Perennial, 1991.

Jonson, Ben. *Volpone and Other Plays*. Ed. Michael Jamieson. Penguin Classics. London: Penguin, 2004.

La Fontaine, Jean de. *The Complete Fables*, trans. Norman R. Shapiro. Urbana: University of Illinois Press, 2007.

Lévi-Strauss, Claude. *Structural Anthropology*, trans. Claire Jacobson and Brooke Grundfest Schoepf. New York: Basic Books, 1963.

Levinas, Emmanuel. "The Name of a Dog, or Natural Rights." In *Difficult Freedom*, trans. Seán Head. Baltimore: Johns Hopkins University Press, 1990.

London, Jack. *The Call of the Wild, White Fang, and Other Stories*. Eds. Earle Labor and Robert C. Leitz, III. Oxford World's Classics. Oxford: Oxford University Press, 2009.

Massumi, Brian. *What Animals Teach Us about Politics*. Durham: Duke University Press, 2014.

Miller, D. A. *Narrative and Its Discontents*. Princeton: Princeton University Press, 1989.

Serpell, James A. "People in Disguise: Anthropomorphism and the Human-Pet Relationship." In *Talking with Animals: New Perspectives on Anthropomorphism*. Eds. Lorraine Daston and Gregg Mitman. New York: Columbia University Press, 2005: 121–136.

Sewell, Anna. *Black Beauty*. World's Classics. Oxford: Oxford University Press, 2012.

Simpson, James. "'And that was litel nede': Poetry's Need in Robert Henryson's *Fables* and *Testament of Cresseid*." In *Medieval Latin and Middle English Literature*. Eds. Christopher Cannon and Maura Nolan. Cambridge: D. S. Brewer, 2011: 193–210.

Simpson, James, trans. *Reynard the Fox*. New York: Liveright, 2015.

Trollope, Anthony. *The Eustace Diamonds*. World's Classics. Oxford: Oxford University Press, 1871.

Woolf, Virginia. *To the Lighthouse*. New York: Harcourt, 1981.

Woolf, Virginia. *Flush*. New York: Harcourt, 1983.

# 4   Songbirds
## (poetry and environment)

If such a thing as a naturally occurring literature were to exist (and who are we to say that it does not?), it would undoubtedly be the song of birds. Scientists tell us that songbirds, or oscines, as they term them, emit songs that are so distinctive that members of the same species can identify each other by repeating vocal patterns whose frequencies, pitch, and repertoire encode a language of whose multiple functions the demarcation of territory and the enactment of sexual selection are only the most conspicuous. Indeed, birdsongs constitute a language, or set of languages, whose complexity humans can merely fathom. Poets have said something similar for a long time, but they have said it in ways that resemble the songs they are describing, for, in writing of nightingales or robins or crows, poets also emit songs that single them out to other poets, who are the only ones to fancy they can fathom this particular form of language. This is one of poetry's favorite conceits and perhaps its foundational premise.

A long tradition of oscine poetry subtends the literary tradition as a whole, but no period better exemplifies the poetic appeal of songbirds and birdsongs than Romanticism. Virtually every Romantic poet wrote on songbirds and, in doing so, entered into dialogue with other poets about the very nature of poetry, a question at the very heart of the project of Romanticism. The genealogical tree of Romanticism has many roots, but it is in Britain, with the poetry of William Wordsworth, Samuel Taylor Coleridge, John Keats, Percy Bysshe Shelley, Charlotte Smith, John Clare, and many others who perched on this same tree, that, at the turn of the nineteenth century, literature took on as its own calling the search for answers to the most urgent issues of the day in the contemplation of nature. Nature for the Romantics was never only a source of beauty, nor only a passive repository of ancient wisdom; nature transformed the very working of the mind by emitting an enigmatic call that could only be returned, after a period of tranquil recollection, in the equally perplexing form of poetry. The songbird was thus an emblematic figure for the poet's practice of engaging in reciprocal song with nature and, yet, was also itself a part of nature, becoming for the poet an occasion for imagining what it would be like to be a bird in flight; an occasion, that is, for imagining imagination.

Nature was then as it is now endangered, and poetry was conceived of as a part of nature's living memory as well as a memorial to its future disappearance. Nature is always remembered in Romantic poetry, but to say that the songbird augurs its own demise is premature. The genealogical tree of Romanticism, as I suggested above, has many roots that can be traced back through the oscine tropes of antiquity and the Middle Ages to their recuperation in the Renaissance. But it is also a tall and many-branched tree that extends through different literary traditions into the present. Edgar Allan Poe, Pablo Neruda, Wallace Stevens, Paul Muldoon, and many other poets perch on the branches of Romanticism and sing of birds as to nature's singers. The birds change, of course, as does the song, but the Romantic trope for poetry migrates across the world *in* poetry. Indeed, the persistence of the oscine lyric would seem to belie the songbirds' elusiveness, yet, as Twitter reminds us in no more than 140 characters a tweet, birdsong is everywhere in culture.

It is nevertheless a sad truth that songbird populations are rapidly disappearing across the planet, prey to rapid deforestation, excessive pesticide use, and global warming. In *Silence of the Songbirds*, Bridget Stutchbury argues that it is usually at their southern wintering grounds that environmental degradation most dramatically affects songbird populations. But the devastation of songbirds' southern habitats, of course, is not the sole culprit in the decline of their populations. The consumption of sun-dried coffee in the more prosperous north, for instance, accounts for much of the deforestation of Central American biomes, and the wind farms and electric towers that have increasingly become permanent features of the landscape in developed countries kill large numbers of migrating songbirds. Northern habitats are also suffering under various environmental pressures, of course, and predators such as cats, squirrels, and invasive cowbirds account for the death of many songbirds. The decline in songbird populations is not only devastating to those who love poetry and music. Songbirds play an essential role in plant pollination and insect ecology, and their loss therefore has a ripple effect on biodiversity across the globe. Indeed, it is no hyperbole to say that the future of our planet depends on these migratory birds. Poetry is one way in which songbirds speak to us about their plight, and it is to poetry that we must turn to save them. "'Hope,'" wrote Emily Dickinson, "is the thing with feathers" (1961, 254).

The oscine lyric is thus doubly poetic: poetic in the sense that the songbird as a trope comes to symbolize poetry and poets, and poetic in the sense that it augurs a future for us all. The Romantic legacy is rich in oscine song and, because the songbird always calls on us to attend to nature, it is also at the root of our renewed impulse to think of nature differently, to think of it as the place of songbirds. In what follows these twin Romantic legacies, poetry and the environment, will guide my reading of a set, or perhaps a flock, of beautiful and stirring songbird lyrics.

## A nightingale in the hand...

In the European lyric tradition, no songbird is more prominent than the nightingale. No doubt this has to do with the fact that the nightingale (*Luscinia megarhynchos*) is a beautiful singer that sings at night, as well as in the day, but it also has to do with the double symbolism of mourning and melancholia that has attached to it from antiquity. In Book VI of Ovid's *The Metamorphoses*, the nightingale appears in the myth of Philomela, which tells the story of a brutal rape. Tereus, the King of Thrace, rapes Philomela when she is on her way to visit her sister Procne, to whom he is married. Afraid that Philomela might talk, Tereus cuts off her tongue and abandons her in a cabin in the woods. Thus violently silenced, Philomela embroiders a tapestry representing the rape and sends it to Procne. The sisters exact revenge upon Tereus by killing his son and serving him for dinner. Tereus then attacks the sisters, but, before he can strike, Zeus transforms Philomela into a nightingale. It is to this myth that poets allude when they use the name Philomela or Philomel to refer to a nightingale, even though the myth is misleading on two counts: the song of the nightingale is hardly a sorrowful song and it is the male, rather than the female, that sings it. Moreover, subsequent representations of the nightingale, though often based on the legend of the rape of Philomela, do further violence to the significance of the story since the nightingale, which is most often personified as a female voice singing without being seen, develops as one of the predominant symbols of romantic love in Western literature.

In Sonnet 102 (1609 [2005]), for instance, Shakespeare uses the figure of Philomel to depict a lover's reticence in expressing his love to his lover. Philomel appears in the second quatrain:

My love is strengthened, though more weak in seeming;
I love not less, though less the show appear;
That love is merchandized, whose rich esteeming,
The owner's tongue doth publish every where.
5   Our love was new, and then but in the spring,
When I was wont to greet it with my lays;
As Philomel in summer's front doth sing,
And stops his pipe in growth of riper days:
Not that the summer is less pleasant now
10  Than when her mournful hymns did hush the night,
But that wild music burthens every bough,
And sweets grown common lose their dear delight.
Therefore like her, I sometime hold my tongue:
Because I would not dull you with my song.

The poet has already sung his lover's praises when they were first in love, and, though now stronger than before, the poet's love might be "merchandized" if it is "published" at every opportunity. Like the nightingale, whose song "hush[es]" the night in early summer, the poet holds his tongue in "riper days." The poet does not want to express his love again, for, just like the "wild music" of other birds "burthens" the boughs on which they perch in the middle of summer and thereby demean the nightingale's "mournful hymns," the poet's song would "dull" his love. In Shakespeare's sonnet, the nightingale is a symbol of love's preciousness and not of its precariousness for though the nightingale's song is seasonal, its delights are "strengthened" over time. The ambiguity of the possessive pronoun "his" in line 8, which seems to refer to "Philomel" but, given the unmistakably feminine identity of the nightingale in line 10, "her mournful hymns did hush the night," would seem to refer somewhat incongruously to "summer," suggests that the bird and the poet are already being equated and lover and loved made one. The *volta*, accomplished by the definitive "Therefore" of line 13, makes this relation of equivalence explicit as the subject of the closing couplet. In Shakespeare's sonnet, the association between the nightingale and poetic creation passes through love, for the bird's song and the poet's sonnet are both directed at love. "Our love" that opens the second quatrain is thus made all the more capacious a term and enduring an experience by incorporating the figure of Philomel, for Philomel, like the poet's love, is a lasting reference to and for love, even if the bird, which is not named "nightingale" in the body of the sonnet, departs.

Shakespeare's reference to "my lays" in line 6, moreover, suggests that the sonnet itself is part of a longer tradition, and perhaps even situates the action of the poem in the past. Marie de France's *Laüstic*, one of the most recognizable of her *Lais* and a masterpiece of twelfth-century French literature, is the story of a mediation. Two lovers live side by side in adjoining castles; he is an unmarried knight, she is married to his friend and neighbor. They communicate with each other through facing windows but cannot ever be together "completely for their pleasure" because the lady's husband closely guards her. The lady gets up at night to talk with her lover across the open windows, but she gets up so often that her husband begins to get upset and questions her about what she does at night.

> "My lord," the lady answered him,
> "there is no joy in this world
> 85  like hearing the nightingale sing.
> That's why I stand there.
> It sounds so sweet at night
> That it gives me great pleasure;
> It delights me so and I so desire it
> 90  I cannot close my eyes."

The nightingale here is both a symbol of love and its object since, in the lady's telling, it is the nightingale, rather than the lover, that she desires. The lady gets up in the middle of the night to talk to her lover, of course, and would presumably continue to do so even in the absence of the nightingale. The lady's husband, however, seems to take her at her word and orders his servants to ensnare the bird. "When they had caught the nightingale,/ they brought it, still alive, to the lord" (lines 101–102). He takes the captured bird before his lady and, in a surprising act of cruelty, breaks its neck and tosses the body to his lady: "her shift was stained with blood,/ a little, on her breast" (lines 118–119).

The dead nightingale, now a symbol of the lady's broken heart, comes to stand in for the loss of love, the ambiguous "a little" suggesting that the lady is still circumspect about her love for the knight next door, or for love itself. Since she can no longer go to the window at night, she must find a way to tell her lover that she was not "pretending" (line 131). She wraps the bird in a piece of embroidered silk and sends it to her lover, charging the servant who delivers it with relating the story of the nightingale's demise at the hand of her husband. The knight listens carefully to the sad tale and decides to encase the nightingale in a golden casket set with stones, which he will henceforth carry "with him always" (line 156). The transformation of the nightingale from a bird whose song inspires the lovers to an ornate tribute to the lovers' unconsummated love suggests that, though it is introduced as merely a ruse to placate the husband's anger at the lady's absence from his bed, it also acts as a mediator for the lovers, for, though lost, love becomes itself a work of art. The nightingale's gilded entombment, then, makes possible an impossible love by memorializing it. Furthermore, that the nightingale, or Laüstic, gives its name to Marie de France's *lai* suggests that it is a doubly encased work of art. The work of mourning in the *lai* is thus performed through art, which bears witness to the love that once existed, though especially to its bereavement.

In Milton's Sonnet I, "O Nightingale!" (1645), the song of the nightingale, which fills a lover's heart with hope, is favorably compared to that of the cuckoo, whose song is both shallow and rude. "Thy liquid notes that close the eye of Day,/ First heard before the shallow Cuckoo's bill,/Portend success in love…" (lines 5–7). But Milton also suggests that the nightingale has two "mates," Love and the Muse, which means that for him it is as much a figure for poetic composition as it is for romantic inspiration: "Whether the Muse, or Love call thee his mate,/ Both of them I serve, and of their train am I" (lines 12–14). The double valence of the nightingale, only implicit in Shakespeare, becomes in Milton an explicit attribute, recalling Philomela's tapestry even as her story hardly illustrates how Love calls her (or the nightingale she becomes) his mate. That the sonnet ends with the subject pronoun "I," however, suggests that the nightingale, to the extent that it too forms part of the same "train" as the poet, is also a symbol for the poet himself, or, at any rate, becomes one after the sonnet since the opening apostrophe, "O Nightingale," turns into the final "am I" only after the composition of the sonnet has been accomplished. After all, the sonnet, like the nightingale's song, the "heart dost fill" with its "liquid notes." The striking "Now" of the *volta* in Milton's Petrarchan schema maintains this correspondence as a living function of song, a performative event rather than a constative description.

In both Shakespeare and Milton, the exacting formal characteristics of the sonnet offer an apt aesthetic correlate to the nightingale's song. In Quevedo's *décima* "Al Ruiseñor" (#208 in Blecua, 1999), the nightingale becomes a symbol for poetic tropes themselves:

| | | |
|---|---|---|
| | Flor con voz, volante flor, | Vocal flower, flying flower, |
| | Silbo alado, voz pintada, | Winged whistle, painted voice, |
| | Lira de pluma animada | Animated lyre of feathers |
| | Y ramillete cantor; | And singing posy; |
| 5 | Di, átomo volador, | Tell me, flying atom, |
| | florido acento de pluma, | Flowery accent of feathers, |

|                                   |                              |
| --------------------------------- | ---------------------------- |
| Bella organizada suma             | Pretty organized sum         |
| De lo hermoso y lo suave          | Of the beautiful and the soft |
| ¿cómo cabe en sola un ave         | How can so much music        |
| 10   cuanto el contrapunto suma?  | Fit into a single bird?      |

The nightingale is a "singing flower," a "flying flower," a "singing posy," a "feathered lyre," a "flowery accent of feathers." The self-consciously excessive rhetorical construction of the nightingale as both flower and musical instrument in this poem might lead us to regard the nightingale as nothing but an over-determined poetic trope for poetry itself since all three tropes commonly refer to poetry. Yet, to the extent that the poet apostrophizes the nightingale with the imperative *Di*, the rhetorical construction could also be considered to be the nightingale's own doing. The correspondence thus created could therefore be construed, as Milton construes it in his own sonnet, as one of equivalence between poet and nightingale. But, if the poem is read as the answer given to the question posed in the last two verses, a question which could be paraphrased as "how can so much music fit into a single bird?," then the excessive rhetoric could only be said to "fit" (*cabe*) in the bird itself, as though the poem were the very bird it describes without once naming it. The ambiguity between the literal and the rhetorical meaning of the question is captured in the word *contrapunto* or counterpoint, which can never amount to a fixed *suma* or sum, as the repetition of the word in lines 7 and 10 implies. The referents of bird and poem, and for that matter of "flower" and of "musical instrument," are suspended in the form of the question since it is impossible to say at the end of the *décima* whether the bird is a poem, or the flower a bird, or the poem an instrument of song. The poem, in sum, is impossible to sum and the bird in the poem, as the bird that sings at night, remains elusive.

It would be tempting, though excessive, to say that the trope of the nightingale evolves over the course of European literary history from its origins in the myth of Philomela through its iterations as art object, poet, and poem to develop into a trope for trope itself. To be sure, the nightingale remains a powerful rhetorical resource for the treatment of love and art in the lyric, but the trope does not for all that follow a chronological pattern of evolutionary development. As a mythopoeic symbol, the nightingale is as elusive as the bird itself is for the poet who tries to capture it in the lyric. As it comes to be assimilated into Romantic poetry, the nightingale retains some of its symbolic aura, but the means of capturing it change as it is de-idealized and re-symbolized as a figure for nature itself. Though Romantic poets will invoke the myth of Philomela, the invocation will most frequently appear as just that: an invocation that prevents us from understanding the bird itself as it appears in nature.

Charlotte Smith's triad of nightingale sonnets, Sonnet III: "To a Nightingale" (1784), Sonnet VII: "On the Departure of the Nightingale" (1786), and Sonnet LV: "The Return of the Nightingale" (1791), constitute an attempt, still somewhat tempered by the bird's evocative power, to describe the bird as it really is. In Sonnet III, the nightingale is apostrophized in entirely conventional terms: the "[p]oor, melancholy bird" that opens the first quatrain becomes a poet, a martyr, and a songstress in subsequent verses. Smith's attention to the particularity of the bird's place in nature through the figures of "little breast," "dewy eve," "thy nest," and, in line 10, the seemingly straightforward "now released in woodlands wild to rove" suggests that she is also being attentive to the difference between convention and realism, or, put differently, between allegory and reference.

Similarly, in Sonnet VII, the poet bids adieu to the bird and its song after its seasonal residence:

> Sweet poet of the woods – a long adieu!
> Farewell, soft minstrel of the early year!
> Ah! 'twill be long ere thou shalt sing anew,
> And pour thy music on "the night's dull ear."
> 5   Whether on Spring thy wandering flights await,
> Or whether silent in our groves you dwell,
> The pensive muse shall own thee for her mate,
> And still protect the song she loves so well.
> With cautious step, the love-lorn youth shall glide
> 10   Through the lone brake that shades thy mossy nest;
> And shepherd girls, from eyes profane shall hide
> The gentle bird, who sings of pity best:
> For still thy voice shall soft affections move,
> And still be dear to sorrow, and to love!

The poem's central conceit is not new: poetry, the "pensive muse," will preserve the nightingale's song after it departs on its "wandering flights." The nightingale's song inspires love, sorrow, and pity in those who listen to it, whether in the remembered form of a poem or by remembering its song from the presence of its "mossy nest." But this poem, too, situates the bird in its natural habitat, its "woods," where it sings protected by poetry, or perhaps by love's natural reticence (after all, it is personified in "shepherd girls"), from "profane" eyes. The

notable rhyme between "adieu" and "anew," which is punctuated by
the "Ah!" of the third line, plausibly echoes the "sweet" poet's song. But
it also instantiates the bird's departure (adieu!) and anticipates its return
(anew) in a cyclical pattern that is repeated in the conceit of youthful
love's "cautious step." "For" in the sonnet's *volta* in line 13 introduces
as a matter of course the "soft affection" for which the bird may now
also come to stand, as though the iteration of its song, as well as its
migratory returns, signaled nothing so much as the natural cycles that
alter as they repeat the very life processes it heralds in the "early year."

By the time Smith writes Sonnet LV: "The Return of the Nightingale,"
the natural environment predominates, even if the characterization
of the bird as a symbol of love persists as does its association with
"sweet" sounds:

> Borne on the warm wing of the western gale,
> How tremulously low is heard to float
> Thro' the green budding thorns that fringe the vale
> The early Nightingale's prelusive note.
> 5    'Tis Hope's instinctive power that through the grove
> Tells how benignant Heaven revives the earth;
> 'Tis the soft voice of young and timid love
> That calls these melting sounds of sweetness forth.
> With transport, once, sweet bird! I hail'd thy lay,
> 10    And bade thee welcome to our shades again,
> To charm the wandering poet›s pensive way
> And soothe the solitary lover›s pain;
> But now! – such evils in my lot combine,
> As shut my languid sense – to Hope›s dear voice and thine!

In this Sonnet, the nightingale's "prelusive note"—a song or note
that serves as a prelude—once again heralds the "budding" year, but the
song is also a reminder of prior occasions since it is a retrospective view
of its natural returns and, at the same time, of a previous song the poet
sang to the "sweet bird," an ascription Smith herself uses in Sonnet VII.
To the degree that the nightingale once symbolized the "solitary lover's
pain," it also offers a future-oriented promise of "sweetness" in the
form of "Hope." In the present of the poem, "But now!," the poet looks
upon the bird for signs of hope since it is hope's "instinctive power"
that, juxtaposed with "young and timid love," might "revive the earth."
But it is as much the bird's "preclusive note" as the poet's previous
rendering of it—"I hail'd thy lay"—that buttresses the poet's call for
hope (that makes hope hopeful) to remedy or combat "such evils in

my lot combine." The use of "lay" to refer to the bird's song is also, by extension, a reference to Smith's own poems, present and past, as well as to the nightingale's mythopoetic tradition. The poem leaves the vivid impression, however, that such revisionary readings of the nightingale as an inspiration for the "wandering poet's pensive way" may in fact be hopeless. The abrupt "once" in the middle of line 9, acting as a somewhat displaced *volta*, suggests as much. Smith's sonnets—on nightingales, to be sure, but also on a wide variety of subjects—represent an attempt to revive a form thought, since at least Samuel Johnson, to be moribund in English letters. Whether the sonnet, a poetic form "once" robust, becomes a new vehicle of hope is a question posed by the Romantics, who collectively revitalized the sonnet.

Smith's nightingale sonnets inaugurate a new cycle of returns for the oscine lyric inscribed in a new referential relation to nature among the Romantics. Coleridge's and Keats's extraordinary nightingale poems constitute the most self-conscious instances of the Romantic recuperation of the nightingale as a trope for the trope of nature. But, before examining their poems in some detail, it is worth alighting on another nightingale poem, this one written by John Clare, the Romantic poet most closely associated with rural life and its unsentimental view of nature. Like much of his poetry, Clare's "The Nightingale's Nest" (1835), is willfully unconventional in its original version, often foregoing standardized speech and grammatical construction, not to mention conventional poetic forms. The nests that frequently appear in his poems might be read as apt figures for the very form of his poems, which, unlike, say, the sonnet, revel in the relative freedom granted rhyme and syntax by the unconventional voice that pervades them. His interest in the nightingale is thus not so much guided by its mythopoetic weight as it is by its "natural" song. Otherwise unremarkable, Clare, like the nightingale, is a "natural" poet.

Clare's poem opens with a mild rebuke to the imagined nightingale of poetry: "For here I've heard her many a year –/ At morn and eve, nay, all the livelong day,/ As though she lived on song" (lines 5–7). The poet knows something about the nightingale that he could not have learned from reading poetry. It is his experience over "many a year" that makes him know, and makes him tell us, that the nightingale in fact sings throughout the day, the "As though" a finely ironic take on poetry's "livelong" conceit that the nightingale is nature's poet. He also tells us that his knowledge of the nightingale is born of curiosity for its natural way of life—a species of poetic ethology—rather than for its poetic life, which he nevertheless acknowledges in phrases such as "home of love" (line 4) that he uses to refer to its nest: "There have

I hunted like a very boy,/ Creeping on hands and knees through matted thorns/ To find her nest and see her feed her young" (lines 12–14). Having failed to catch the nightingale in her nest as a boy, he lies down to catch it in song:

> And where those crimping fern-leaves ramp among
> The hazel's under boughs, I've nestled down,
> And watched her while she sung; and her renown
> 20    Hath made me marvel that so famed a bird
> Should have no better dress than russet brown.

The use of "nestled" to describe the poet's stance as he listens to the nightingale emit its song does not immediately suggest that the poet sees himself as a nightingale, nor that he sees the nightingale as a poet. It speaks of the rather less noteworthy stance of a fellow creature that seeks to find out what it might feel to be a nightingale. That "so famed a bird" should prove to be so unremarkable is itself an unremarkable fact. The "russet brown" bird does sing in "ecstasy," with its feathers standing on end and with its mouth wide open "to release her heart/ Of its out-sobbing songs" (lines 24–25), but it does this in an act of generosity rather than in the vain pursuit of beauty: "The happiest part / Of summer's fame she shared, for so to me/ Did happy fancies shapen her employ" (lines 25–27). The poet compares the nightingale's song to that of the "emulating" thrush, but only to draw attention to the fact that the nightingale's song is seasonal rather than to denigrate the thrush, since its songs are "scarce inferior." Now in adulthood, the poet tries again to find the nightingale's nest, hidden in a "black-thorn clump," a place where "rude boys never think to look" (line 52).

After many years, the poet has finally found the nest—"Aye, as I live! her secret nest is here" (line 53)—and notes how fear has silenced the nightingale, which sees the intrusion from afar. He addresses the bird directly for the first time at the beginning of the second stanza, as though to reassure it that no harm will come to its nest and, in his retreat, to prompt her to sing again: "Sing on, sweet bird! may no worse hap befall/ Thy visions, than the fear that now deceives" (lines 67–68). But this apostrophe is itself deceptive since the surrounding woods are themselves full of the nightingale's song, and the nest itself is, like the nightingale's song, hardly self-contained:

> How curious is the nest; no other bird
> Uses such loose materials, or weaves
> Its dwelling in such spots: dead oaken leaves

Are placed without, and velvet moss within,
80 And little scraps of grass, and, scant and spare,
What scarcely seem materials, down and hair;
For from men's haunts she nothing seems to win.

The precision of the poet's description is belied by both the construction of the period, which tends to "weave" its materials in a curious and seemingly haphazard manner, and the materials themselves, which are discontinuous and "scarcely" material at all. The adjectives "scant and spare" modify the empty "what" that may or may not be filled, like the nest, by down and hair. The nesting structure of the sentence, accomplished by the subordination of its clauses and by the use of enjambment, suggests the simultaneously open and enclosed nature of the nest, which is separated from its surroundings yet made of its surrounding materials. The rhyming scheme invites comparison with the harmony of the nest's design, but this design is not the work of a poet. The nest is nature's work: "Yet nature is the builder and contrives/ Homes for her children's comfort even here" (lines 83–84). The nightingale's hidden nest is purposeful but its purposiveness, while subjective in Kantian terms, is not teleological, even though the nest's nest—the "old prickly thorn-bush" that hides it—guards the nightingale's eggs, and thus preserves and protects the "old woodland's legacy of song." The repetition of "old" in the poem's last two lines anchors its orientation towards the future but does not for all that represent a form of purposiveness with purpose. Clare's poem may be said to "nest" the trope of the nightingale in nature with the aim of capturing the poetry of the woodland, unconventional and natural, rather than the received poetry of the nightingale as a trope for poetry.

Coleridge had already attempted to reclaim the nightingale from its poetic image in "The Nightingale," a conversation poem from 1798. Like other poems included in the first edition of Coleridge and Wordsworth's *Lyrical Ballads*, Coleridge's "The Nightingale" seeks to capture the poet's state of excitement before nature and the emotions this state inspires when recollected in tranquility. In the preface to this collection, written in 1800 and revised in 1802, Wordsworth tells us that he and Coleridge chose to represent "incidents and situations from common life" in their poems, and to do so using the "language really used by men" while adding "a certain colouring of the imagination" (2013, 96–7). Coleridge's "The Nightingale" follows this program by trying to capture the language of the nightingale, not as it appears in poetry but as it occurs in nature. Coleridge states the terms of his engagement in the poem's first reference to the nightingale: "And hark!

the Nightingale begins its song,/ 'Most musical, most melancholy' bird!/ A melancholy bird? Oh! idle thought!/ In Nature there is nothing melancholy" (lines 12–15). Coleridge quotes Milton's "Il Penseroso" in these lines not so as to decry Milton, but in order to repudiate a practice common among poets, who too often project their feelings onto nature unreflectively. Only because "some night-wandering man" (line 11) has made the nightingale's song "tell back" the tale of his own melancholy, Coleridge argues, offers no reason for thinking that the nightingale's song is in fact melancholy. Poets are wont to "echo the conceit" and build rhymes accordingly instead of "surrendering" their "whole spirit" to the "influxes" of nature's shapes and sounds and "shifting elements" (lines 27–29). The alert passiveness of the poet, a Romantic trope captured most pervasively in the image of the Aeolian harp, the subject of one of Coleridge's best known poems, is the condition of possibility of poetry itself. Poetry is born of the reciprocal though somewhat asymmetrical relation between nature and the poet's mind: the poet loves nature for its own sake, its beauty having excited the imagination, which, in remembering this feeling, produces poetry whose beauty, like that of nature, will be loved. This relation is represented in many Romantic poems; in "The Nightingale" it is represented in these terms: "so his fame/ Should share in Nature's immortality,/ A venerable thing! and so his song/ Should make all Nature lovelier, and itself,/ Be loved like Nature!" (lines 30–34).

The answer to the question posed by Coleridge when he first "surrenders" to the nightingale's song—"A melancholy bird?"—is not itself a passive response nor an "idle thought" since it involves the use of reason and imagination. In contrast, "youths and maidens most poetical" who frequent "ball-rooms" and "hot theatres" instead of resting in a "mossy forest-dell" as Coleridge himself does in the poem, will revert back to the stereotypical nightingale to express their lazy sentiment in the form of "Philomela's pity-pleading strains" (line 39). Coleridge, Wordsworth, and his sister Dorothy (to whom Coleridge refers as "our Sister!") are different; they cannot "profane" (line 41) nature's song, even if they detect in the nightingale's "delicious notes" (line 45) a "love-chant" (line 47). Unlike the "meek sympathy" (line 38) of those who frequent ball-rooms and hot theaters, the poet actively seeks out "Nature's sweet voices" (line 41) in groves "Of large extent" (line 50) where the nightingales, like the three friends who attend to them, "answer and provoke each other's song" (line 58). The conversation in this "conversation" poem can thus be understood at this stage to refer to a) the conversation among the nightingales, b) the conversation among the three friends, and c) the conversation between the nightingales and the three friends; or, to use the terms the poem itself uses, between Nature and imagination. To the extent that the poem addresses the reader directly though not individually in "You may perchance behold them on the twigs" (line 66), the conversation includes you as well. But the poem also stages a fantastic scene in which a "most gentle" maid who lives "hard by the castle" near the same grove Coleridge has invited the reader to visit listens to the birds' "choral minstrelsy" (line 80) as though they were "A hundred airy harps" (line 81). This scene, which is entirely in keeping with Coleridge's role in the composition of *Lyrical Ballads*, contributing poems based on "incidents and agents in part supernatural," thus makes possible a further conversation in which the imagination, personified as a maid, is itself engaged in conversation with the nightingales, which are like "Aeolian harps" ("airy harps") in that they too are passive conduits to nature's song. In the poem's last stanza, the poet's child enters into the conversation because he too, though "capable of no articulate sound," would bid everyone listen to the nightingale's song.

In Coleridge, the nightingale becomes the thematic vehicle for a whole theory of poetry that is put into practice in the writing of a poem about a nightingale. "A poet," wrote Shelley in "A Defence of Poetry" (1821 [2002], 516):

> ...is a nightingale who sits in darkness and sings to cheer its own solitude with sweet sounds; his auditors are as men entranced by the melody of an unseen musician, who feel that they are moved and softened, yet know not whence or why.

That Shelley should refer to the poet as a "nightingale" in one of the two or three most important theoretical texts written by Romantic poets suggests that the nightingale is not only singing in and for nature in Romantic poetry; it is also singing about poetry. For the Romantics, at any rate, the nightingale is used as a trope for poetry itself, a trope that, as a trope for trope, remains as elusive as the bird itself.

John Keats's "Ode to a Nightingale" (1819), one of the most beautiful poems in the language, is perhaps the least self-conscious of the Romantic poems about nightingales, though it does not, for all that, return to their mythopoetic representation. It is a poem about what it is like for a poet to want to be a nightingale. For the poet, if not for the reader, the form of the poem and the form of the bird cannot be compared. The bird's beauty surpasses the flights of the imagination that allow the poet to contemplate what it would be like to be a nightingale. The desire to be like the bird is not an attempt to take its place, but rather to share with it in affective reciprocity its ability to sing in the "full-throated ease" of summer: "'Tis not through envy of thy happy lot,/ But being too happy in thine happiness" (lines 5–6). The comparison between the poet and the nightingale is structured by a further comparison the poem explicitly and implicitly makes between nature (the "forest" in line 24) and civilization ("here," line 38), which is a despairing, sickly place unknown to the nightingale. The poet at first wishes to overcome the distance separating him from the nightingale by using hemlock, opiates, and wine—"fade," "dissolve," and "forget" are the verbs the poet employs—but none of these can bring him closer to the experience of the nightingale. It is only poetry that offers an experience of disembodiment that can only crudely approximate the free flight of the nightingale:

> Away! Away! for I will fly to thee,
> Not charioted by Bacchus and his pards,
> But on the viewless wings of Poesy,
> Though the dull brain perplexes and retards...

As the poem advances, however, it is not only Poesy that seems to be bringing the poet closer to the experience of the nightingale but nature itself, since he now finds himself in a place with "flowers at [his] feet" (line 41); or, put more precisely, Poesy and nature seem to coincide since it is *in* poetry that the approximation to the nightingale is being staged as a passage through nature.

The poet listens for the song of the nightingale in the poem's sixth stanza and seems to do so with the ear of its poetic tradition rather than for its actual song: "Darkling I listen; and, for many a time/ I have been half in love with easeful Death" (lines 51–52). The nightingale's "ecstasy" (line 58) brings into sad relief the poet's pain so that its song comes to resemble a requiem. Mourning and melancholia, however, turn out to be but passing intimations since the nightingale is eternal: "Thou wast not born for death, immortal Bird!" (line 61). The poetic and natural histories of the nightingale are conflated and, while not exactly erasing the distance separating poet and nightingale, this conflation does bring nature closer to the "here" of civilization. The last stanza, however, rejects this reading and bids the nightingale adieu:

> Forlorn! the very word is like a bell
> To toll me back from thee to my sole self!
> Adieu! the fancy cannot cheat so well
> As she is fam'd to do, deceiving elf.

75    Adieu! adieu! thy plaintive anthem fades
      Past near meadows, over the still stream,
      Up the hill-side; and now 'tis buried deep
      In the next valley-glades;
      Was it a vision, or a waking dream?
80    Fled is that music: – Do I wake or do I sleep?

The first word of the last stanza, "Forlorn!," repeats the last word of
the seventh stanza, suggesting that it is the poet's own word that acts like
a "bell" to bring him back from reverie to himself, or "sole self," which
seems to repeat or echo "thy soul" of line 57 with which he addresses the
nightingale. These iterations offer hope of Poesy's ability to transport
the poet to the "soul" of the nightingale, but, since each constitutes
a change of address or reference—the first "forlorn" describes the
nightingale's song while the second the poet's reaction to it; similarly,
"soul" refers to the bird while "sole" to the poet—the repetitions also
serve to mark the distance separating the bird from the human. The
"Adieu!" of line 73 represents both a realization and a resignation:
poetry and the imagination cannot broach the gap ("fancy cannot cheat
so well") and the bird, for it to remain a nightingale, must fly away. The
"Adieu! adieu!" of line 75, which is addressed to the nightingale, echoes
the "Away! away!" of line 31, which refers to the imagination, and, in
so echoing it, it also makes a categorical distinction between them. Yet,
to the extent that it is rendered in imagination, the poet, who is the
fixed term of the comparison since we only have access to the poem,
not the bird's song, cannot entirely be sure that he, and not the bird,
has flown away. At the end, the poet must ask: "Do I wake or sleep?"
This question, an iteration of the question formulated in the previous
line—"Was it a vision, or a waking dream?"—also represents a change
of reference since the subject "it" of the first question seems to refer to
the fleeing bird, while the second question refers to the poet himself
after the bird, or rather its music, has fled, as in "Fled is that music," the
passive voice of whose construction seems to open up an insuperable
distance between the bird and the poet. The fact that these questions
remain unanswered and unanswerable, however, seems to suspend the
conceit of the poem over this distance, as if the question implied by the
poet's desire to know what it is like to be a nightingale only generated
more questions rather than provided questions. This negative knowledge
is not useless, however, since it reaffirms the usefulness of poetry, music
that has not fled, for asking questions that might otherwise seem absurd.
      Keats's great ode represents something like the nightingale's last full-
throated song before the Romantic summer flees into the darkling valley-

glades of the Victorian imagination. The nightingale lives on, of course, but its immortality becomes a burden to the poets who dare invoke it, as many nonetheless do. In Elizabeth Barrett Browning's "Bianca among the Nightingales" (1862), for instance, the nightingales' song torments the narrative's protagonist by reminding her that her lover has left her for an English woman. Bianca, to whose love for Giulio nightingales once sung in Florence, now finds herself in England, where she has traveled in an attempt to find or steal him back. The nightingales, which have traveled in the same direction, from the "Tuscan trees that spring/ As vital flames into the blue" to the "dull round blots of foliage" (lines 57–58) that soak up the fog in England, sing the same song they sang in Florence, even as the supposed object of their song, Bianca and Giulio's love, no longer sings to them. The nightingales "torture and deride" her by reminding her of a love that is now impossible. The poem's last stanza is plaintive in its pointless incredulity:

> Giulio, my Giulio! – sing they so,
> And you be silent? Do I speak,
> And you not hear? An arm you throw
> Round some one, and I feel so weak?
> 140   Oh, owl-like birds! They sing for spite,
> They sing for hate, they sing for doom,
> They'll sing through death who sing through the night,
> They'll sing and stun me in the tomb –
> The nightingales, the nightingales!

Bianca's despair over the song of the nightingale represents an inversion of previous patterns of description regarding the nightingale. Bianca's monologue in Elizabeth Barrett Browning's poem competes with and is then overwhelmed by the song of the nightingales, now so cacophonous as to represent the death of both poet and perhaps poetry. The nightingale is not the symbol of love here, or, if it is, it is love itself that kills. It is not a symbol of nature nor of nature's music: it is the overwhelming echo of a poetic tradition whose iterations, unlike the iterations that structure the end of Keats's ode, generate despair rather than hopeful curiosity, however enigmatic. The questions posed by Bianca are rhetorical, but there is no ambiguity as to whether they should be read literally or figuratively since there is never any hope for Giulio's change of heart from the moment they are asked. The nightingales become "owl-like" not because they are wise or prescient, but because they are nocturnal, as the gloomy and ambiguous line "who sing through the night" suggests (and who is the "who," exactly?).

The nightingales' song spells doom and, as the repetition of "the nightingales, the nightingales" throughout the poem makes clear, also come to stand in for a sort of penitence.

In Barrett Browning's poem, it is unclear whether the nightingale is being attacked for its mythopoetic significance as a trope for love or for sorrow (though the latter is avidly embraced), or for its Romantic lineage as a bird whose song extends the poet's. The poem's archaisms, otherwise in keeping with Victorian revivalist enthusiasms, offer a possible, though discouraging, reading of this dilemma. Barrett Browning's obvious discomfort with the nightingale is moralistic: her story of unrequited or at least inconstant love follows the migratory pattern of the nightingale only to mock its song. Bianca, after all, is hardly "bianca" (that is, white) or innocent herself, and the bird that once symbolized eternal love now only sings of its doom. Birds, of course, sing only for their own sakes, and to blame their song for "stunning" the poet to her death is the equivalent of making the seasons responsible for one's objectionable thoughts. To be sure, the nightingale could have become a nuisance for the Victorians with its promiscuous song, but the violence to which it is subjected in Barrett Browning also suggests a degree of poetic bad faith, as if poetry, or its Romantic formulations at any rate, constituted a threat to propriety itself. To the extent that such a threat is also an invitation, the nightingale frustrates what is secretly desired. The foreign setting together with the somewhat reluctant use of gothic elements suggest that this frustration is cloaked as otherness, which makes the nightingale "owl-like" and strange.

The strangeness of the nightingale becomes the central conceit of Paul Muldoon's much wittier revisionary treatment of the bird. In "Nightingales" (1998), Muldoon abstracts the bird from its poetic tradition not by killing it to spite his poem in the manner of Barrett Browning; rather, he resituates the nightingale in unfamiliar contexts: a nineteenth-century dictionary, makeup, Japan, the floorboards of a castle. The poem is in three parts, each of which might be said to stand in for a different nightingale since the title of the poem "Nightingales" suggests a multiplicity of them. In the first part of the poem, Muldoon quotes Alfred Newton, a prominent Cambridge ornithologist of the late nineteenth century and one of the first and most vociferous advocates for the protection of birds in Great Britain. The entry on the nightingale in Newton's *Dictionary of Birds* (1894), from which Muldoon quotes, offers a detailed scientific description of the bird, as well as an overview of its poetic lineage. The nightingale's "indescribable" song, writes Newton, suggests melancholy to some listeners, and "many poets have discanted on the bird (which they nearly always make of the feminine gender) leaning its breast against a thorn and pouring forth its melody in anguish" (Newton 1894, 636). Newton betrays some sympathy regarding poetry's attempt to express the nightingale's song in syllables but will have no truck with the poets' penchant for personifying it as a sorrowful female. The Newton quotation with which Muldoon opens his poem further de-idealizes the bird, noting as it does "so winningly" that its plumage hardly matches its song. The surprising second stanza of the first part of the poem also rather winningly refers to "powdered nightingale-shit" as a source of beauty (makeup) that makes the poet fall in love. The nightingale may still be a symbol of love for the speaker, but it is a love that is not inspired nor reflected by its song, but by its shit:

> "In great contrast to the nightingale's pre-eminent voice
> is the inconspicuous coloration of its plumage,"
> as Alfred Newton so winningly puts it
>
> in his *Dictionary of Birds*. I fell in love with a host-face
> 5   that showed not the slightest blemish
> They tell me her make-up was powdered nightingale-shit.

If the first part of the poem consists of two forms in which the nightingale is misidentified (at least by poets), the second part tells of a different kind of misidentification involving the confusion of one species for another.

> They tell me the Japanese nightingale's not a nightingale
> but a Persian bulbul. Needless to say, it's the male bird
> that's noted for opening the floodgates
> 10   and pouring out its soul, particularly during nesting season.

The "They" that opens this stanza, echoing and perhaps coinciding with the "they" that appears in the previous line, suggests that, like that contained in Newton's dictionary, there is something like nightingale science or nightingale lore to whose authority one must appeal in order to disabuse poets of their misconceptions regarding the "real" nightingale. In this case, the misconception has to do with the fact that what in Japan passes for a nightingale is not really a nightingale, or at least in name it is not, since its habits, "needless to say," are those of the nightingale, which suggests both that the misconception might be common and perhaps even justified. (Newton, incidentally, suggests that the Persian bulbul is a "species of true Nightingale," 1894, 59.)

The third part of the poem shifts registers once more, the nightingale now acting as a referent to the noise the floorboards make in a Japanese castle. The presence of twittering "wedges and widgets and wooden nails" in the first line of the stanza further suggests that the description of the floorboards, of the sort one might find in a dictionary of building materials perhaps, also emits, in syllables, a sound that is otherwise "indescribable," just like the nightingale's song is for Newton "indescribable." That a phrase such as "like nightingales" needs to be used to describe the noise the floorboards make at any rate suggests as much:

> Now they tell me a network of wedges and widgets and wooden nails
> has Nijojo Castle's floorboards
> twitter "like nightingales." This twittering warned the shogunate
> of unwelcome guests. Wide boys. Would-be assassins.

With its increasingly abstract reference to multiple nightingales, Muldoon's poem deflates the bird's mythopoetic identity, not to return it to its natural habitat as the Romantics once did, but to create a new myth. The speaker may be an "unwelcome guest" in the poetic citadel of the nightingale, his own "twittering" threatening to undo, or assassinate, the work of poetry itself, which may no longer be, in any case, what we once thought it was. But, as it turns out, the speaker is also a poet, and the "they" to whom he listens may constitute a community of poets speaking to other poets. The nightingales of the title may then themselves be a misconception since they encompass a "they" that is as elusive as the birds are in this poem, in which no bird, only its referents, can speak. The nightingale, in this reading, then becomes an occasion for poetry rather than its subject; a trope for the making of tropes.

Muldoon's recasting of the nightingale as a trope whose referent changes across different cultural contexts puts us in mind of another aspect of the oscine lyric. The genealogy of the trope of the nightingale that I have been constructing here may have given the false impression that the nightingale is the only songbird to unsettle the song of poets. To make a rather obvious but perhaps necessary point, the nightingale as I have been describing it is both a European bird and a bird of European poetry; indeed, it may even be said to be the bird that symbolizes European poetry *tout court*. (According to Newton (1894), Persian poetry has many references to the bulbul, which is normally translated as "nightingale," but it is in fact another species.) No doubt this corresponds to the geographic distribution of the nightingale, but in its historical distribution as a literary trope in European poetic traditions, the universality of the bird (as a trope for love, melancholia, mourning, nature, etc.) has hardly ever been put into question. The nightingale poems I have read constitute a migratory corridor spanning western Europe, but they certainly do not represent the oscine lyric as a whole. I now turn to the Americas where different songbirds perch on the poetic imagination in order to examine the relation between poetry and environment in different climates.

## ...is worth a tapaculo, a raven, and a blackbird in the bush

Pablo Neruda writes in his memoirs, *Confieso que he vivido [I Confess that I Have Lived]* (1974), that he was inspired to write *Arte de pájaros [Art of Birds]* (1966), an illustrated book of poems about birds, when he was in Moscow in 1962. Standing in Red Square attending the public celebration of the Vostok 3 and Vostok 4 flights of the Soviet space program, which had sent two cosmonauts on opposite though simultaneous trajectories around the earth, Neruda had a sort of epiphany: "Yo me sentía muy cerca de sus alas. El oficio del poeta es, en gran parte, pajarear" [I felt very close to their wings. The poet's duty is, in large measure, to flutter] (Neruda 1974, 346; my translation). The verb "pajarear," which I've here rendered here as "flutter," involves the work of the imagination and implies daydreaming and curiosity. Used as Neruda uses it, however, "pajarear" also means "to be or to become a bird," quite literally. In the context of the occasion that serves as the inspiration for the book, "pajarear" also suggests the idea of soaring, like the cosmonauts, beyond one's own confines in order to see the world anew. To become a bird is to adopt a new perspective on the everyday. This is reflected in the very conceit of the book, which Neruda dreamed up in Moscow: a book containing poems of real and imaginary birds with illustrations by different Chilean artists. The birds he describes in the book are sometimes "pajarantes," as Neruda calls his imaginary birds, and sometimes "pajarintos," birds commonly known in Chile. The juxtaposition of these two neologisms invites us to look at birds differently, perhaps as though we had a cosmonaut's-eye view of birds.

Not all of the birds in *Arte de pájaros* are songbirds of course. Neruda lived near the ocean in Chile and many of the birds he describes are seaborne; others, like the condor, are Andean. But there is one songbird with the suggestive name of tapaculo, a name which according to some commentators refers to the fact that the tail never covers ("tapa") the bird's behind ("culo")—the name would then be an imperative to cover it—while others suggest it is an onomatopoeic rendering of its distinctive song. Two varieties exist, both of which Neruda includes in his poetic ornithology: *Scelorchilus rubecula*, also known as chucao tapaculo, and *Schelorchilus albicollis*, or white-throated tapaculo. In *Arte de Pájaros*, Neruda usefully includes the Linnaean Latinate binomials, but the poem that refers to the first is titled "Chucao," while that which refers to the second is titled "Tapaculo." In the *Journal of Researches* (1839), Darwin describes the Chucao, which he calls "Cheucau," as a "red-breasted little bird" that runs around the forest floor making strange noises that the Chilotans (he is on the island of Chiloé, off the coast of Chile) hold in superstitious fear (1839, 352). For Darwin, the tapaculo, which he calls "Tapacolo," is a "very crafty" bird because he remains motionless when frightened by a person and then tries to crawl away. Its notes, some of which Darwin likens to the "cooing of doves, others like the bubbling of water, and many defy all similes," change according to the season (330).

Neruda's ornithopoetic project in *Arte de pájaros* forms part of a larger and more general project, begun in *Canto general* (1940), of bearing poetic witness to the unique history, natural and cultural, of Chile and Latin America. The book of birds is thus a poetic inventory of bird species endemic to Chile that, in depicting birds about which few if any poems have been written, gives them poetic voice, as if to make nightingales of them all. Neruda begins "Chucao" with the bird's cry, as though the poem were itself crying: "Ay, qué grito en las soledades!" ("Oh, what a cry in these solitudes!") (line 1). The ambiguous "qué grito" could refer to the bird's voice ("what a cry") or to the poet's ("what should I cry?"). The poem follows the poet as he walks through a deserted forest near the Golfo de Reloncaví, cited in the poem's last line:

|  |  |
|---|---|
| y el chucao lanza su lanza, | And the chucao throws his spear, |
| su largo grito desbordante: | His long cry brimming over: |
| él rompe con su grito de agua | He breaks the water with his cry |
| mil años largos de silencio | A thousand long years of silence |
| 20 en que sólo cayeron hojas | During which leaves fell |
| y las raíces ocuparon | And roots occupied |
| como invasores este reino. | This realm as if they were invaders. |

The "y" at the beginning of line 16 interrupts the poet's walk as well as the flow of the poem, with the clever "lanza su lanza" ("throws his spear"; that is, its song) both denoting the double interruption and imitating its lengthened cry. Modified by the somewhat incongruous "desbordante" ("brimming"), which, though hardly incongruous or unusual in Neruda's poetics, nevertheless signals a change of register from the airborne "lanza" to the aquatic "él rompe con su grito de agua" ("He breaks the water with his cry") of the next line. It is as though the chucao's piercing cry were not only new to the poet but to the world itself since it breaks, in the form of a spear or as water, a thousand years of silence. The violent "lanzas" is echoed in the last line, since the presumably silent roots have "occupied like invaders" the forest where the chucao now dwells. In the poem's last period, the poet identifies the chucao's song with a bell ("campana de las soledades"), an arrow ("oscura felcha"), and a superhuman song ("trino sobrehumano"). The different rhetorical registers at which the chucao's song is described do not amount to similes; the song is not being compared to this disparate collection of entities. Rather, the chucao bears something like a relation of identity with all of them: the song is a bell and an arrow and divine song all at once. It is as if the song of the bird, like the bird itself, were so elusive as to require ultimately inadequate metaphoric substitutions in order to capture it. In the end, the dizzying metaphoric turns amount to positing the bird as a metaphor for metaphor itself, a "trino sobrehumano," or superhuman trill, in the sense that it is beyond human, as though language itself originated among the birds.

Edgar Allan Poe's "The Raven" (1845) offers a similar conception of the origin of language, but it casts it in completely different light, preferring foreboding Gothicism rather than natural piety to create an effect of enstrangement. In the poem, a lonely scholar (the poem does not mention his profession, but Poe describes him as a scholar in his essay "The Philosophy of Composition") tries to cheat his sorrow for his dead lover Lenore by reading books of "forgotten lore." He falls asleep and is awakened from his nap by a rapping on the door, which, upon further scrutiny, turns out to be a talkative raven. The raven enters the room and perches on a bust of Pallas the scholar has placed over the door. The bird seems to suit the scholar's despondent mood as he seeks to determine the significance of its arrival. Though the bird is already symbolically overdetermined as he enters the room—the scholar addresses it as "Ghastly grim and ancient Raven" (line 46)—its presence invites speculation. The raven utters "Nevermore" when the scholar asks for its name, but the utterance is both enigmatic and unstable, prompting further questions and entering into the language of the poem itself. At first, the scholar interprets it as the mechanical repetition of a word the raven has learned from some "unhappy master," yet it soon becomes the echo of the scholar's own "melancholy burden," which he expresses emphasizing the same word: "Never – nevermore." The utterance not only rhymes with Lenore; it also takes the place of her name, at least temporarily, since the scholar's readings were meant to render her "Nameless *here* for evermore" (line 12). The discursive status of the utterance, furthermore, is unclear since it seems to invite a referential interpretation (what or who will be "nevermore"?) but, at the same time, seems to perform the function of a speech act, in which case the semantic content is only secondary.

55 But the Raven, sitting lonely on the placid bust, spoke only
   That one word, as if his soul in that one word he did outpour.
   Nothing farther then he uttered – not a feather then he fluttered –
   Till I scarcely more than muttered "Other friends have flown before –
   On the morrow he will leave me, as my Hopes have flown before."
60 Then the bird said "Nevermore."

In this stanza, the scholar initially takes the word to be a word (rather than, say, an onomatopoeic rendering of a raven's gurgling croak or scratchy caw) that could express the raven's "soul." But then, as the scholar, talking to no one in particular, suggests that the bird, like both his friends and his hopes, will soon fly away, we get the distinct impression that it is his own soul that the raven is "outpouring." When it utters "Nevermore" again, however, it is not clear whether the bird is replying literally to his plaintive call by suggesting that it will never leave, or whether it is just repeating an utterance whose force is yet to be determined. As if to solve the puzzle, the scholar then sits before it and the bust and begins to wonder "What this grim, ungainly, ghastly, gaunt, and ominous bird of yore/ Meant in croaking 'Nevermore'" (lines 71–72).

The work of analysis, however, seems interminable since every attempt at "guessing" what the raven means is followed by further puzzlement and more "divining" until, in a maddened frenzy, the scholar himself begins to utter an enigmatic word of his own: "Lenore," which he had promised not to utter again "here," wherever "here" may be, at the beginning of the poem. The raven, however, does not change his tune and repeats "Nevermore." As though his "Lenore" had not had the desired effect (of silencing or at least perplexing the raven), he tries another word: "Prophet!," he apostrophizes. But he receives no prophecy in return and comes no closer to deciphering the meaning of "Nevermore." The scholar gets increasingly exercised by the raven's reticence and begins to shriek at it, demanding that it leave, but his words "leave," "quit," and "take thy beak from out my heart" (lines 100–101) have no force whatsoever and the raven remains perched atop the bust. Reminiscent of the enigmatic utterance "I would prefer not to" used by Melville's immovable character Bartleby, the raven's utterance drives the scholar to a sort of quiescent madness that is also a form of silence since the poem's last word "nevermore" is simply a repetition of the raven's enigmatic utterance. The scholar's "soul" at the end of the poem becomes one with the shadow cast by the raven, which is also the shadow cast by the bust of Pallas on which it is perched. To the extent that all three figures, Pallas, the "Prophet" bird, and the scholar, represent wisdom or knowledge, the fact that they appear only as shadows suggests that we can never know for certain how to interpret or act upon the utterance "Nevermore." Under normal discursive circumstances this state of affairs would be cause for alarm, but, in the context of the oscine lyric, it might also be thought of as an invitation to regard the caws and croaks of corvids as calls to shift our perspective regarding songbirds, not so as to coincide with theirs but in order to engage with their sheer strangeness from the point of view of mutual otherness. We have Poe and poetry to thank for this form of prophecy.

Wallace Stevens's "Thirteen Ways of Looking at a Blackbird" (1954) achieves some of the same effects by forcing us to reconsider how we look at birds. The poem is divided into thirteen parts of unequal length, each of which refers to one or several blackbirds such that it is never clear if the same blackbird, or blackbirds, are being described in every stanza, or whether the blackbird, or blackbirds, appearing in each stanza represent(s) a member of a set of blackbirds or the set itself. The somewhat tortured grammar of this sentence offers a glimpse of the difficulty we have in using language to describe the lives of otherwise familiar birds. Stevens makes thirteen attempts in his poem, and while each represents a "way" the poet has of looking at a blackbird, these attempts are partial and provisional. The structural features of the poem, in other words, reflect the way we tend to look at birds since it is hard, not being birds, to individualize them by simply looking at them. The blackbird or blackbirds in Stevens's poem, in any case, prompt the speaker to reflect upon the nature of perception and, in doing so, to try to determine what sort of relationships bind us to the birds we see.

In part I of the poem, the poet focuses on the eye of a blackbird, noticing its movement. The "twenty mountains" among which the poet sees the bird seeing are the equivalent of the "thirteen ways" in which the poet will see the bird as it sees the mountains, the bird's moving eye resembling the poet's eye if only by numerical association (thirteen birds, twenty mountains). This numerical logic and its implications for equating the poet with the blackbird continues into the second part, where the poet is of "three minds," corresponding to three blackbirds perching on a tree, but here the relation is explicitly metaphorical as the strong "Like a tree" (line 5) suggests. The third part, like the first and the second parts, is written in the past tense, as though the preterite set the scene for a present in which poet and blackbird have already exchanged "eyes" and "minds." In part four, the tense shifts to the present, but the rhetoric is algebraic rather than narrative: "A man and a woman/ Are one./ A man and a woman and a blackbird/ Are one" (lines 9–12). The existence of two equivalent equations suggests that the blackbird joins a union not as a nonentity, or a zero, but as an equal. The poet's "I" returns in part five, though not to describe a visual tableau, as he did in parts one and three, but to reflect upon the effect of the blackbird's song according to the poet's uncertain preferences:

> I do not know which to prefer,
> The beauty of inflections
> 15  Or the beauty of innuendoes,
> The blackbird whistling
> Or just after.

If inflections are preferable to innuendoes, then the whistling of the blackbird will be more beautiful than its aftermath. If the contrary is true, then the moment after the blackbird whistles will be more beautiful. This algorithm of beauty is entirely subjective, of course, but its logic is objectively generous since it implies that both moments are indeed beautiful. The sixth part of the poem returns to the preterite to describe the shadow of the blackbird as it crosses the frozen window (rendered somewhat in the style of Borges as "barbaric glass"), prompting, or perhaps resulting from, a mood, which is enigmatically described as an "indecipherable cause" (line 24). Part seven apostrophizes the "thin men of Haddam" (line 25), a town which, despite its biblical-sounding name, is in fact located in Connecticut. The apostrophe chastises the men who look at golden birds (that is, unreal, precious birds) and urges them to look instead about them, as the poet himself does, to see the blackbirds as they walk among the women. The poet adopts a confessional mode in the next section, giving a sound reason for why we, along with the men of Haddam, should be looking at blackbirds: "But I know, too,/ That the blackbird is involved/ In what I know" (lines 32–34). The poet may only know about "noble accents" and "inescapable rhythms," but it is precisely in this context that the blackbird contributes to his knowledge, as if poetry itself owed some of its wisdom and much of its sounds to blackbirds. The ninth part of the poem describes the bird in flight, as it traces circles out of sight. The poet's vision, as much as the bird's flight, is involved in this image, however, since it is the bird's absence that marks its presence as a "circle," a circle of involvement, as the previous section suggests. Part ten contains the famous "bawds of euphony" line (40), which has given critics much to say. Perhaps more than the bird itself might warrant since the phrase lends itself to irony as it suggests, like the "golden birds" the men of Haddam imagine, a figment of clichéd imagination; that is, of no imagination whatsoever. But the sight of blackbirds is such that even those who are poetically compromised would "cry out" sharply, like a bird perhaps. In the eleventh part, the narrative voice is cast in the third person, relating the impression made by a series of shadows on an anonymous "he" who has mistaken them for blackbirds. The "he" could in turn be plausibly mistaken for the poet, and this not only because the scene is set in Connecticut; the fear he feels as he mistakes the shadows for blackbirds "pierce[s]" him as it might only pierce he who would like to see them for what they really are, not as "ominous birds" of the sort Poe's narrator describes in "The Raven." The twelfth part of the poem, the shortest and perhaps the most moving in its haiku-like simplicity, suggests that the blackbird, like a river, is always on the move: "The river is moving/ The blackbird must be flying" (lines 48–49). The inference, derived from the flow of the river, is justified: just like we can never step twice into the same river, the blackbird, here portrayed in the singular, can be one out of any number of blackbirds. We never see the same blackbird twice. The last part of the poem—number thirteen, but not ominously so—signals the change of seasons, with the blackbird perching on a tree as the evening turns into winter. The last blackbird may have been left behind, but it is not a sorrowful bird; it just sits "In the cedar-limb" (line 54).

Stevens's poem, the culmination of the oscine lyric in its modern form, offers a powerful directive for handling our relationships to birds. We ought to look at birds, and nothing else. To see birds as poets see them is not to sentimentalize them nor to figure them as living symbols of human aspiration, nor yet to imagine what it might be like to be like them. Rather, if sentiment, figuration, and imagination be the means to regard the bird as a poetic bird, then to see birds as poets see them is to train our interest on their nature and, in doing so, to be responsive to their lives. Anthropomorphism is often regarded as a weak heuristic for speaking of animals, but we have no other way of speaking for them than by using figures that might implicate us in the task of speaking about them. For many scientists, as Eliott Sober reminds us, anthropomorphism is considered a "factual mistake and an intellectual failing," but as Sober and other philosophers have argued there is a more nuanced approach to the problem posed by the attempt to describe animal behavior using human behavior as a model. It is not that observed similarities between members of closely related species, humans and chimpanzees, say, provide strong evidence that chimpanzees are like us; it is just that such similarities do provide *some* evidence that the two species are in at least this context similar. This modest form of anthropomorphism is itself similar, though not equivalent, to what Frans de Waal has termed "anthropodenial," the mistaken reluctance on the part of humans to attribute human characteristics to non-humans. Anthropomorphism and anthropodenial, however, are somewhat unwieldy terms, inviting fascinating but perhaps needless hairsplitting on the more fundamental questions posed by the oscine lyric in all its rhetorical diversity: "¿cómo cabe?"; "Adieu! adieu!"; "qué grito"; "Nevermore"; "cry out."

Mary Midgely offers a somewhat different argument for why we cannot escape our anthropocentrism, suggesting that the term anthropomorphism is not only clumsy but also misleading since what is really at stake in these discussions is the mistake of "groundlessly attributing unsuitable human qualities" to other entities (1983, 128). She proposes the concept of "undue humanizing" as a more appropriate way of describing what we do when we describe animals using terms that tend to favor humans in advance, and which pertain to abstract thinking, consciousness, and feelings. The oscine lyric urges us to "duly humanize" the birds we see, inviting us to see birds as poets see them, for our sake, to be sure—who would want to give up poetry?—but also for theirs since to look at them is to let them be; we ought to capture them only in our poetry. It is not that poetry is better; it is that we have nothing else. Some scientists might object to this assertion, but most will recognize that birding—another way to understand Neruda's term "pajarear"—is as much a poetic duty ("oficio") as it is an environmental one. If nothing else, the oscine lyric urges us to learn to regard birds differently, from more than thirteen different perspectives, if we want to continue to involve them in what we know.

## Works cited

Barrett Browning, Elizabeth. "Bianca among the Nightingales." In *Selected Poems*. Eds. Marjorie Stone and Beverly Taylor. Peterborough: Broadview, 2009.

Clare, John. *Major Works*. Oxford World's Classics. Eds. Eric Robinson and David Powell. Oxford: Oxford University Press, 2008.

Coleridge, Samuel Taylor. *The Portable Coleridge*. Ed. I. A. Richards. New York: Penguin, 1978.

Darwin, Charles. *Journal of the Researches*. London: Henry Colburn, 1839

de Waal, Frans. "Are We in Anthropodenial?" *Discover* (July 1, 1997): 50–53.

Dickinson, Emily. "Hope is the Thing with Feathers." In *The Complete Poems of Emily Dickinson*. Ed. Thomas H. Johnson. Boston: Back Bay Books, 1961.

de France, Marie. *The Lais of Marie de France*. Eds. Robert Hanning and Joan Ferrante. Durham: Labyrinth Press, 1982.

Keats, John. "Ode to a Nightingale." In *Keats's Poetry and Prose*. Ed. Jeffery N. Cox. New York: W. W. Norton, 2008.

Midgely, Mary. *Animals and Why They Matter*. Athens: University of Georgia Press, 1983.

Milton, John. *Complete Poems and Major Prose*. Ed. Merritt Y. Hughes. Indianapolis: Hackett, 2003.

Muldoon, Paul. *Hay*. New York: Farrar Straus Giroux, 1998.

Neruda, Pablo. *Arte de pájaros*. Buenos Aires: Losada, 1966.

Neruda. Pablo. *Canto general*. Buenos Aires: Losada, 1971.

Neruda, Pablo. *Confieso que he vivido*. Barcelona: Seix Barral, 1974.

Neruda, Pablo. *Art of Birds*, trans. Austin: University of Texas Press, 1989.

Newton, Alfred. *A Dictionary of Birds*. London: Adam and Charles Black, 1894.

Ovid. *The Metamorphoses*, trans. Frank Justus Miller. Loeb Classical Library. Cambridge: Harvard University Press, 1971.

Poe, Edgar Allan. "The Raven." In *The Oxford Book of American Verse*. Ed. Richard Ellman. Oxford: Oxford University Press, 1976.

Quevedo, Francisco. *Obra Poética*. Ed. José Manuel Blecua. Madrid: Castalia, 1999.

Shakespeare, William. *The Oxford Shakespeare*. Eds. Stanley Wells and Gary Taylor. Oxford: Oxford University Press, 2005.

Shelley, P. B. "A Defence of Poetry." In *Shelley's Poetry and Prose*. Eds. Neil Fraistat and Donald H. Reiman. New York: W. W. Norton, 2002.

Sober, Elliott. "Comparative Psychology Meets Evolutionary Biology: Morgan's Canon and Cladistic Parsimony." In *Thinking with Animals: New Perspectives on Anthropomorphism,* Eds. Lorraine Daston and Gregg Mitman. New York: Columbia University Press, 2005: 85–99.

Smith, Charlotte. *The Poems of Charlotte Smith*. Ed. Stuart Curran. Oxford: Oxford University Press, 1995.

Stevens, Wallace. "Thirteen Ways of Looking at a Blackbird." In *The Palm at the End of the World*. Ed. Holly Stevens. New York: Vintage, 1990.

Stutchbury, Bridget. *Silence of Songbirds*. New York: Walker and Company, 2007.

Wordsworth, William and Samuel Taylor Coleridge. *Lyrical Ballads 1798 and 1802*. Ed. Fiona Stafford. Oxford World's Classics. Oxford: Oxford University Press, 2013.

# 5   Felids (enigma and fur)

We have lived with cats ever since the Egyptians domesticated *Felis catus* some 10,000 years ago. Cats have helped us keep our houses free of rodents, insects, and vipers, to be sure, but their domestic presence seems to transcend the labor they perform. The Egyptians mummified them; we opt for multiplication, a rather more prosaic method of memorialization. We first own one cat, then another or perhaps two this time, and, before you know it, they have begun to multiply at a pace that soon transforms the most unlikely cat lovers among us into stereotypical crazy cat ladies. Today millions upon millions of cats live in households all over the world, claiming our attention while displaying a spirit of independence whose silky aloofness must be the envy of adolescents everywhere. But there is yet another reason for why cats must be the bane of adolescent angst in every darkened bedroom bathed in the pixilated glow of electronic screens: cats are the coolest cats in cyberspace. Cat videos and so-called lolcats (funny cat memes) make visible, nay virtual, the phenomenon of accumulation that characterizes our relationship to cats, cat lovers finding safety in the extraordinary numbers cat sites routinely register on unsuspecting hit counters. Yet lolcats fill cyberspace in a way that real cats do not fill our world, not even the streets of Rome, the city of cats. Unlike lolcats, which make some of us ooh and ah and laugh all at once, real cats make us terribly uneasy, which may be the real reason for the popularity of cats in cyberspace. Indeed, to say that cybercats are uncanny is inaccurate; they are our crude attempt to cope with the uncanniness of real cats.

"When I play with my cat," Michel de Montaigne once memorably wrote, "who knows if I am not a pastime to her more than she is to me?" (1965, 331). Cats have always had a special fascination for humans: they are enigmatic creatures that seem to question the right of humans to think, as though their mere presence inspired philosophers to explore the nature of reality or to ponder the very existence of a soul. Our curiosity about them may well be our only way to match their own curiosity about us since cats are curious in ways that would seem to go beyond the attention a predator must pay its prey. Philosophers, in any case, have always had much to say about cats, sometimes using them to illustrate philosophical conceits and sometimes using them as tropes for concepts that seem to lie beyond our grasp.

No statement has been as influential in the history of twentieth-century analytical philosophy than "the cat is on the mat," which appears under different guises in the work of philosophers such as G. E. Moore, Bertrand Russell, Ludwig Wittgenstein, and J. L. Austin, to name only the most salient. The cat in the utterance seems to be merely incidental to the philosophical problems being discussed and could presumably be replaced with any other noun. Yet, the insistence with which it is used suggests that there is something about the cat's presence on the mat that already makes it somewhat elusive, for to assert that the cat is on the mat, as opposed to, say, the book is on the mat, is already to propose that it may not be so at all, that it could be there one minute and not the next, like the Cheshire cat's smile.

But the philosophical use of cats is not restricted to problem-solving in analytic philosophy. Continental philosophers also employ cats to stage philosophical problems that are not premised on usage. Jacques Derrida, for instance, uses the uncanny experience of seeing his cat seeing him when he comes out of the shower (a real cat on the real bath mat) to launch his meditation on animals in *The Animal that Therefore I Am...* (2008) [*L'Animal que donc je suis...* (2006)]. The book's title in French plays on the double meaning of "je suis," which is the first-person conjugation of both the verb "to be" (*être*) and the verb "to follow" (*suivre*). The title both addresses the cat and refers to it indirectly, the "donc" suggesting a conclusion from observation, as though having his cat see him being seen were, much like in Montaigne, an occasion to wonder about who is (following) whom. To remark that both continental and analytical philosophers use cats to philosophize may not amount to a formula for the consilience of two philosophical traditions that have evolved along separate conceptual paths—speciating from a common felid origin?—but it is nevertheless worth noting that cats are the privileged philosophical animals in both traditions. Cats are cool in English and in French!

Schrödinger's cat, another elusive conceptual cat, is famous for precisely being elusive. Its name comes from Erwin Schrödinger, who, aside from coming up with the paradox involving a cat to which he gave his name in 1935, must have been a cool cat himself given that he was into taming waves and even won a Noble Prize for his efforts. The paradox that bears his name has to do with the idea that a quantum system (say, an atom) can exist as a combination of different possible states at the same time, what physicists call quantum superpositions, until it is observed. In order to show how absurd this idea seemed to him, Schrödinger came up with a thought experiment in which a cat could be considered to be simultaneously dead and alive under certain conditions. Imagine a cat sealed in a steel chamber containing small amounts of radioactive material that, if triggered by the cat, could kill it. If we were to follow the logic of quantum superpositions, the cat in this scenario would be simultaneously dead and alive until the moment the chamber was opened and the results observed. The precise outcome may be unknown, but, as Schrödinger's thought experiment suggests, there are only two possibilities regardless of whether we observe the cat or not: the cat is either dead or alive. Quantum physicists still debate the merits of Schrödinger's cat, and, given its cultural staying power, we can only conclude that it is the cat, rather than the physics, that has kept the paradox alive.

Yet cats are not only philosophical in their curious detachment. Cats are also playful and affectionate, often prized for their companionship, and, especially, for their soft fur. There is something arresting about their cold beauty but more so when it is accompanied by soft purring and whiny meows. Their generally likeable disposition often makes them good though hardly unobtrusive companions, their likability often enhanced by a hint of naughtiness that some humans find just delightful. As Dr. Seuss's "Cat in the Hat" memorably puts it: "I know it is wet/ And the sun is not sunny./ But we can have / Lots of good fun that is funny!" To be sure, cats are contradictory creatures: housebroken but not exactly eager to learn stupid pet tricks; warm and fuzzy, yet seemingly indifferent to our sentimental attachment to them; clean and self-grooming, yet also hairy and prone to drag half-eaten mice into the den. They have keen eyesight and enviable hearing, yet we are never sure if they recognize us for ourselves or if we are to them interchangeable beings, tolerable to the precise extent that we provide nourishment and shelter. It is a wonder that we think we have invented them at all. Night prowling seems always to trump selective breeding when it comes to cats. Perhaps in this sense they are the democratic answer to the purebred horses and Kennel Club tagged dogs of the more privileged domesticated classes. Cats, in any case, are a living reminder of the strangeness inherent in our domestication of a species that, at times, seems to have domesticated us.

Not all cats are domestic, of course; felids come in many different sizes and shapes, with spots or without them, and they sometimes bear stripes of different colors. Lions, tigers, leopards, cheetahs, jaguars, bobcats, pumas, lynxes, and many other wild felids have troubled the imagination of humans, at times through the justified fear they inspire, at times by dint of their majestic beauty. Big cats are the principal attraction in zoos, circuses, and royal trophy rooms alike, as though taming, training, caging, or embalming them made us all feel as big and strong and beautiful as they are. For this reason, they are often used in political discourse as symbols of power. This does not make them any less enigmatic, of course, as the mythological figure of the Sphinx makes clear. In its different iterations, the Sphinx is as fierce as a lion, but also just as troubling as a house cat (or a cat-in-the-hat) with its puzzling riddles and in its uncanny roles as oracle and gatekeeper. One of the very first pictures painted by humans is the multifaceted panel of lions found in the caves at Chauvet in southern France, which dates back to 30,000 BCE. In this Paleolithic image, lions are depicted giving chase to bison and, since the archeological record suggests that early humans did not in fact hunt lions, the image can be read as a sort of tribute or paean to their hunting prowess. Awe, fear, and veneration represent our own contradictory feelings toward wild felids. Too fierce to domesticate, yet so fundamentally similar to our domesticated cats that we think we ought to be able to pet them, as many a zoo tragedy has recently, and disastrously, made visible.

Cats of all types have fueled the human imagination from the beginning, appearing in myths, stories, and fables as figures for a form of animality that remains fundamentally enigmatic. Dogs, horses, rabbits, turtles, and even elephants are no less different from us than are felids but they are certainly a lot less mysterious. Accordingly, philosophers, poets, and witches have had much to say about them, creating a formidable corpus of felid tales that, like the felids of which they speak, come in many forms, genres, and tropes. It is as though the number of tales we tell ourselves about cats were in inverse proportion to the quantity of knowledge we gather in writing about them. Indeed, to take comprehensive stock of felid tales would be a task akin to herding cats. In what follows, I therefore examine a small sample of cats (a destruction, we might say) with little hope of solving the mysterious nature of felids. I aim instead to describe some of the tropes by or through which we take account of our relation to cats so as to suggest a few reasons for why cats trouble our imagination and sometimes make us approach our own condition with a sense of ennui, dread, and self-loathing.

## Kool katz

Italo Calvino's "The Garden of Stubborn Cats" forms part of *Marcovaldo*, a collection of stories first published in Italian in 1963. The stories follow Marcovaldo, an unskilled laborer living in an industrial city in northern Italy in the years following World War II, as he tries to make his way in an inhospitable urban world from which nature seems to have disappeared. In "The Garden of Stubborn Cats," Marcovaldo realizes that there are in fact two cities coexisting side by side: a vertical city for humans, and a "counter-city" or "negative city" inhabited by cats that exists in the former's interstices. Cats have been forced into the spaces that separate buildings, moving as through an invisible "network of dry canals" that subtend the human city. Marcovaldo first discovers the city of cats when he follows a tabby he has befriended during his lunch break. One day, the tabby takes him to a fancy restaurant where, through transoms that surround a domed skylight, Marcovaldo and the cat are able to look into the dining room and spy the waiters as they carry trays full of delicious food. The tabby is keen on raiding the restaurant's kitchen, but Marcovaldo is particularly taken by the sight of a fish-tank filled with live trout. He fetches his fishing tackle and, by carefully dropping a line from the transom to the dining room, he manages to catch a fat trout, which he then pulls out of the restaurant, creating in the process the impression that the trout is flying through the air. The tabby seizes the fish before Marcovaldo can unhook it, however, and runs away with his prize.

Following the fishing line through the city in search of the now twice stolen fish, Marcovaldo happens upon the garden of a crumbling villa, the only green area left in the city's center.

> And in this garden, perched on the capitals and balustrades, lying on the dry leaves of the flower-beds, climbing on the trunks of the trees or the drainpipes, motionless on their four paws, their tails making a question-mark, seated to wash their faces, there were tiger cats, black cats, white cats, calico cats, tabbies, angoras, Persians, house cats and stray cats, perfumed cats and mangy cats. Marcovaldo realized he had finally reached the heart of the cats' realm, their secret island.
>
> (Calvino 1983, 106)

This "secret island" is a Utopian space in the middle of the city that gathers within its confines a community of cats; a space that, unlike the vertical human community that surrounds it, finds in nature, however "dry," a leveling force that brings together all manner of cats. The cats, for all that, remain cats, furiously fighting each other for the spoils of the tabby's catch as well as for the "strange rain" of fish-bones, -heads, and -tails that cat-loving "little old women" throw over the wall to feed their protégés.

But they are not the only humans who are connected with the garden. When Marcovaldo tugs at the fishing-line in an effort to recover his trout, a window suddenly opens out into the garden and a pair of skinny hands, holding a pair of scissors and a frying pan, manage to steal the fish once again before Marcovaldo can recover it. The now thrice stolen fish, the old cat ladies tell him, will be used to feed a mysterious Marchesa who owns the villa and to whom no one has spoken in a very long time. Passersby have different and sometimes conflicting things to say about the villa's owner: some maintain that she has resisted the advances of developers in order to save the cats; others that she would sell if she had the chance since she could not care less about the cats. Marcovaldo decides to settle the question of whether or not the Marchesa is a lady by tapping on the window from which the pan shot out to catch the stolen fish. The Marchesa reluctantly tells him that she hates the cats and that she has repeatedly tried to leave the villa but the cats always prevent her from leaving. "They keep me a prisoner, they do, those cats!" she tells Marcovaldo. She also tells him that a developer once came to her with a generous contract in hand in order to persuade her to sell the house. She was eager to sign, but the cats stopped the man before she could sign the papers.

The suggestive similarity between the two names notwithstanding, Marcovaldo and the Marchesa move in different directions in the narrative. Some time after the episode of the trout, Marcovaldo hears that the Marchesa has died and, by the following spring, a new building is beginning to be erected on the property. But the cats are still there, upsetting the work of the builders and fighting for their right to their garden. The cats' act of resistance, the ending implies, will be successful and their "secret island" will prevail in the face of urban encroachment just as it did when the Marchesa was still alive. Though we are not privy to Marcovaldo's reaction to the cats' actions, we are free to surmise in the context of the story collection as a whole that, at least for him, who has never really taken to city life, the utopia of cats represents the triumph of imagination over reality, and of the victory of individual agency over the logic of corporate mobility. The "stubborn" cats of the story's title are stubbornly feline and this is what allows them to combat, however modestly, humans' appropriation of nature.

It is the enigmatic nature of the cats in this tale that is arguably responsible for their survival. The surprising and incongruous presence of a cat in the city initially compels Marcovaldo to follow the tabby. Similarly, the humans who feed the cats over the garden wall as though they were offering them a tribute presumably do so because their presence is to some degree mystifying. But the story also implies that in arousing humans' curiosity about their place in the city, the cats are also responsible for our own survival since their resistance makes visible our role in destroying nature. The figure of the enigmatic cat seems to embody the structural principle whereby rhetorical tropes tell us things we would not otherwise notice about the world as we go about our daily lives. Cats, in this sense, can be said to exist as living tropes, compelling us to associate otherwise disparate elements together in new surprising configurations. To the extent that Calvino's story is about resistance, the trope of the enigmatic cat (the trope of a trope) reveals the power of rhetorical figures in staging political acts of the sort the cats perform in preventing humans from destroying nature.

Cats create a similar distancing effect in Japanese writer Haruki Murakami's novels, many of which feature cats that are either lost, or that, in getting lost, lead humans to surprising discoveries. In a chapter titled "Time For the Cats to Come" in Murakami's novel *1Q84* (2009–2010), Tengo, one of the novel's two protagonists, finds himself with time on his hands and decides to take a train from Tokyo to Chikura, the town where his father lives in a sanatorium.[1] Tengo's father, a retired fee collector for NHK (Japan's national broadcasting company), is suffering from dementia and may not be able to recognize his son, who, in any case, is none too eager to see him in part because they have never been close. On board the train, Tengo reads a story titled "Town of Cats." The story, which has been translated into Japanese from the German in the novel, is about a young man who spends his holidays traveling by train without a fixed destination, stopping at stations that seem interesting to him, staying for a few days, and then boarding the train again. In the story, he gets off at a station that he finds appealing and soon realizes that the town is completely deserted. Deserted, that is, except for the cats that run it. "When the sun starts to go down, many cats cross the bridge into town – cats of all different kinds and colors. They are much larger than ordinary cats, but they are still cats" (Murakami 2009–2010, 502). In shock, the young man climbs the bell tower in the center of town and begins to observe the cats as they go about their daily business, some sitting at their desks in the town hall, others tending shop or stopping to have a drink with a friend. At dawn, the cats cross the bridge once more and go home to sleep. The young man spends the day in the deserted town and, at night, returns to the bell tower to observe the cats' activities. The train stops at the station twice every day, but the young man decides to stay put, curious about how the town is organized and ready for adventure.

On the third day, the cats smell his presence. They follow the scent directly to the bell tower where the young man is hiding, but, when they get there, they don't see him. He is as puzzled as the cats are since he is not invisible. The next day, he decides to leave the town but the train no longer stops at the station. He realizes that he will never be able to leave the town, that this is "the place where he is meant to be lost" (504). Tengo reads the story again and is struck by this phrase, which "attracts" him in the same way the town of cats "attracts" the story's protagonist before he alights on it. Tengo looks out of the window of his own train and realizes that the industrial landscape that speeds by outside is no less fantastic than the town depicted in the story. When he arrives at the sanatorium where his father lives, he finds it difficult at first to recognize him since in old age he has begun to resemble a cat with "extremely long and thick eyebrows," "large, pointed ears," and a "reddish black tinge" on the round nose (507). His father does not seem to recognize Tengo yet pointedly tells him that he is "nothing," which makes Tengo want to leave, but, like the young man in the cat story, he is curious to know more and decides to stay. The question of Tengo's paternity is one of the novel's narrative engines so his curiosity is understandable and might explain why it is peaked when his father seems to be making a point of not acknowledging him. Later, when his father asks him to read a story, Tengo reads him the cat story he has read on the train. Tengo's father, who turns out to be an attentive listener despite his senility, asks him a number of questions about the story—do the cats have television? Did the cats build the town or did they occupy a town built by humans?—that, in turn, lead to more questions and enigmatic pronouncements by both father and son until both seem to become "lost" in each other's discourse. In the end, the cat story seems to operate as something of an allegory or parable in the context of the novel as a whole, offering a way to understand the condition of being "lost," a state of being shared by several of the novel's characters.

The rhetorical status of cats in Murakami is itself enigmatic since they seem to invite a series of comparisons—human town vs. cat town; human vs. cat; fiction vs. reality; father vs. son; and so on—that, rather than establishing fixed semantic associations as in, say, metaphor, expand the semantic field in a potentially endless proliferation of comparisons. The proliferation of comparisons has a deflationary effect, which, far from inspiring political resistance as we saw in Calvino, tends to suspend action altogether. At the end, we seem to be as puzzled about the meaning of the story as is Tengo's father, prompting us to ask ever more questions that create ever more comparisons. To be sure, the rhetorical ambiguity of the cats in Murakami is in keeping with the distancing effect that pervades the novel as a whole, a narrative keen on exploring the very limits of fictional invention, including the fictional invention of reality, as the Q in the title *1Q84* suggests. The cats in Murakami's novel cannot be said to embody the idea of the trope like they do in Calvino's story, but, in their sheer elusiveness (captured in the theme of loss and disorientation), they offer an important insight into the work of tropes: when it comes semantic clarity, we are like cats on a hot tin roof.

Situated somewhere between eventful reality and mundane fantasy, Calvino's and Murakami's felid tales use similar fictional registers to tell stories that represent cats as fully embodied characters that personify our view of them as enigmas. By granting them a degree of agency and subjectivity, the stories seem to both confirm and challenge our sense of what it might mean to be a cat. Calvino's cats defy the logic of urban planning and economic development by asserting their right to occupy, if not quite Wall Street, certainly a piece of land once spared by the frenzied construction of vertical structures. In Murakami's story, the cats occupy a city that has been abandoned by humans and which they now run at night. That the city now runs more efficiently than it once did can be inferred from the fact that the cats have the capacity to detect intruders—they have detected the presence of the young man even if they cannot actually see him—while the humans who once lived there must have failed to see in the presence of cats anything other than harmless companionship, much to their own detriment. In their surprising narrative turns, these stories suggest that felids might yet surprise us all.

## And Tigger too

William Blake's poem "The Tyger" is perhaps the most famous poem in the English language. It forms part of *Songs of Experience*, Blake's 1794 collection of illustrated poems, and is often read as the counterpart or obverse of the earlier poem "The Lamb," which appeared in the 1789 collection *Songs of Innocence*. The tiger and the lamb may be said to embody experience and innocence, respectively, or, more precisely, our perception of how experience and innocence ought to be symbolized. Each of the poems addresses the animal as a created being and, by extension, as the object of poetic creation. "The Tyger" opens with a question:

> Tyger Tyger, burning bright,
> In the forests of the night;
> What immortal hand or eye,
> Could frame thy fearful symmetry?

The question is addressed to the tiger as though it possessed the key to a riddle. That the poet does not receive an answer from the tiger does not discourage him from asking more questions; indeed, the poem as a whole is structured as a series of questions, none of which receive a formal answer. This could mean that we are meant to read them as rhetorical questions, for which the answers would then be too obvious to be uttered. Yet the terms of inquiry seem to suggest that the answer is not so obvious after all, since there is some hesitation as to whether the figure of the "immortal" frames the tiger's "fearful symmetry" with eye or with hand. Since the poem also frames the tiger, the hand or eye could refer to Blake himself, especially since he illustrated his own poem. The questions seem to be posed in earnest, but why pose them at all if they are so obvious? The answer is less obvious than it might appear, in part because the tiger is "fearful" and thus raises the more troubling question about why any being would create such an animal. Questions generate even more questions in a potentially endless interrogative series whose answer is perpetually postponed since none of the questions, taken at face value, can be satisfactorily answered by reference to the poem alone.

The questions become more urgent as the poem progresses, querying the tiger about its eyes (where did they burn? what hand would dare touch them?); its heart ("what shoulder and what art/ Could twist the sinews of thy heart?" lines 9–10); and its brain (in what furnace was it wrought?). Taken literally, these questions suggest that it is hard to imagine any being capable of creating such a formidable and terrifying animal. In Blake's original cosmogony, Los is often portrayed as a smith, but Los also applies to Blake himself. The poem's imagery, rather than offering answers to the questions posed, seems to give shape to the tiger's "fearful symmetry," a phrase which might also refer to the poem's own symmetry, since it begins an ends with the same stanza, except for the substitution of "Dare" for "Could" in the last verse. The repetition of "Tyger" in the first verse of each of the two stanzas, furthermore, both reaffirms and repeats the poem's percussive meter, as though it had been wrought at a forge. The hammer and anvil of the fourth stanza remind us of the poem's rhyming scheme, which is measured and constant, like the blows of a smith:

> What the hammer? what the chain,
> In what furnace was thy brain?
> 15   What the anvil? what dread grasp,
> Dare its deadly terrors clasp!

The "spears" and the "tears" that appear in the fifth stanza, moreover, resemble the tiger's stripes—"When the stars threw down their spears/ And water'd heaven with their tears" (lines 17–18)—and set up the last question of the series (it is the last one because the last stanza repeats the first stanza): "Did he who made the Lamb make thee?" (line 20).

Consonant with Blake's logic of opposites, the question the poet poses to the tiger in the last verse is the obverse of the one he asks the lamb in "The Lamb" in the poem's refrain: "Little Lamb who made thee/ Dost thou know who made thee" (lines 1–2, 9–10). The question is not marked with a question mark, as it is in "The Tyger," which suggests that the question is either rhetorical, which would need no answer, as in the first part of the poem, or merely mechanical, as in the catechism, which requires a fixed response. That the poet himself provides the answer—"Little Lamb I'll tell thee,/ Little Lamb I'll tell thee!" (lines 11–12)—suggests that the question of how to understand the question is part of the answer, as though the "little" lamb had yet to learn how to read its own symbolism. Since the answer the poet provides refers to god-as-lamb—"He is called by thy name,/ For he calls himself a Lamb" (lines 13–14)—means that the address is itself equivocal since maker and creature share the same name, as though each made the other. In this poem, the poet never takes credit for the lamb's creation as, at least implicitly, he takes credit for the tiger's creation in the "The Tyger"; the lamb already exists categorically before the poet apostrophizes it. This brief reading of "The Lamb," even in its brevity, makes evident that the stakes of reading are quite different in "The Tyger." The questions posed by the poet to the tiger are neither literal nor rhetorical but both at once, as if the poem were about the poetic invention of a trope. This is an audacious invention, as the last line of the poem suggests ("Dare frame thy fearful symmetry?" line 24), not least because it implies an antithetical relation to the creator, one that, given the poem's imagery, tends toward the Satanic. But the fact that the poem ends in a question should also give us pause since it leaves the trope (of the tiger) suspended between the image of the tiger invented in the poem and its impossible referent.

In his poem "El otro tigre" ["The Other Tiger"], Jorge Luis Borges addresses this very problem, which could be phrased as follows: if I conjure the image of a real tiger, how can I know that I will not end up with a paper tiger instead? Borges's poem brooks no questions, rhetorical or otherwise. The poem is divided into three parts of unequal length, each of which represents a different tiger, or, perhaps, a different representation of the same tiger. The first part begins with a statement: "Pienso en un tigre" ("I think of a tiger") (line 1). The setting is a library and the statement is followed by an image of the library receding into the distance at twilight to open into a scene staged at the banks of a river in India. The change of scenery is accompanied, or perhaps instantiated, by a temporal shift: the present tense in which the library is rendered gives way in line 5 to the grammatical future:

5    Él irá por su selva y su mañana
     Y marcará su rastro en la limosa
     Margen de un río cuyo nombre ignora.

     [It will move through his jungle and his morning
     And will mark his trail on the limy
     Banks of a river whose name he ignores.]

But the future tense is here ambiguous: it could mean that the tiger "will" in fact cross the jungle and approach a river, or, more likely, that he "might" do this since the future tense in Spanish can also be used to express uncertainty rather than probability of outcome. The scene of the tiger then becomes the object of speculation itself when the poet tries to interpret the image of the tiger that has materialized in the library as if conjured:

     Entre las rayas del bambú descifro
15   Sus rayas y presiento la osatura
     Bajo la piel espléndida que vibra.

     [From among the lines of the bamboo I decipher
     his stripes and I feel the skeleton
     under its splendid pulsating skin.]

The exercise is akin to a reading practice since the tiger is in its world while the poet remains at home, "en un remoto puerto/ De América del Sur" ("in a remote South American port") (lines 19–20). The first part of the poem ends with an apostrophe: "te sigo y sueño,

Oh tigre de las márgenes del Ganges" ("I follow you and dream of you, Oh tiger on the banks of the Ganges" (lines 20–21). The apostrophe eliminates the distance that separates the poet from the tiger, but also reestablishes it by invoking the banks of the river, as if to suggest that the tiger he is imagining is the real thing.

The oscillating movement between proximity and distance that characterizes the first part of the poem becomes, in the second part, an explicit, and explicitly literary, occasion for a self-reflexive meditation on poetic invention. The scenes between which this movement takes place in the second part are no longer Buenos Aires and the Ganges; the library is now "mi alma" ("my soul") and the tiger's world becomes indefinite: the encyclopedia, Sumatra, Bengal. The tiger is no longer, and perhaps never was, the tiger that roams the banks of a river; it is now "el tigre vocativo de mi verso" ("the vocative tiger of my poetry") (line 23) and "un tigre de símbolos y sombras" ("a tiger of symbols and shadows") (line 24). The literary construction of the tiger moves from the concrete to the abstract, from the definite article "el" to the indefinite "un." The poet, in the first person, owns up to the fact that he has juxtaposed the tiger of symbols to the real one ("el verdadero"), but since he is still composing poetry to describe "el de la sangre caliente" ("the warm-blooded tiger") (line 32) it is not clear if he will ever gain access to the extra-poetic tiger or if there is indeed such a thing (lines 36–39):

> ...pero ya el hecho de nombrarlo
> Y de conjeturar su circumstancia
> Lo hace ficción del arte y no criatura
> Viviente de las que andan por la tierra.

> [ ...but the fact of naming him
> And of speculating about its state of being
> Makes a fiction of art and not a living
> Creature of the sort that roam the earth.]

In the third and last part, the poet switches from the first person singular to the first person plural to describe the substance of his poetic quest, which has becomes ours as well: to look for a third tiger. The poet knows full well that this third tiger, like the others, will be a "sistema de palabras humanas" ("a system of human words") (line 42) rather than the "tigre vertebrado" (the "vertebrate tiger") (line 43) that exists "más allá" ("out there") (line 45). Yet, the poet, compelled by "algo" ("something"), will nevertheless embark on the "aventura indefinida" ("indefinite adventure") (line 46) of finding the tiger that exists without poetry. The poem thus becomes the trace of a seemingly impossible task since there is no outside to the text. We can shift the context of the utterance and imagine new ways of imagining a tiger, but the tiger, as soon as we capture it in language, will once again become a paper tiger. The point is not that there are no tigers "out there"; we know there are many that look and behave very much like the tiger Borges describes in the poem. It is rather that our ability to understand or to simply praise and admire, or perhaps even fear and hate, is already mediated by the means, the only means, at our disposal to do so – language. Far from being a problem (of reference, of realism), it is a condition of possibility, perhaps the only condition of possibility, for establishing something like a relation to a tiger. We could of course simply kill it or capture it or embalm it or perhaps even dissect it, but this would not change the fact that, mostly out of ignorance, we will always need to use figures of speech to approach the fearsome felid.

The rhetorical sophistication and aesthetic artistry of Blake's and Borges's tiger poems lend insight into the challenges posed by animals that, though familiar to us, do not seem to exist on a human scale. Tigers are fascinating in part because they dwarf us. Unable to befriend them, we are left with the weaker conceit of having to invent them in poetry if we are to relate to them at all in a non-coercive manner. Literature helps us find the sense of disproportion that often separates us from animals and, though hardly a reliable mechanism of coevolution that would eventually balance the scales, it lets us imagine a world that might yet learn to live in the discomfort born of "conjeturar" (speculating). To the extent that Borges's poem can be said to be a reading of Blake's poem, or the fact, at any rate, that the former cannot be thought apart from the latter, these poems invite speculation about poetic invention, as such, but also, literally, as a way of inventing the "other" (tiger).

## Copychats

Charles Baudelaire included three cat poems in both the 1857 and the 1861 editions of *Les Fleurs du mal* (*The Flowers of Evil*), the collection of poems that revolutionized French poetry in the nineteenth century with its combination of decadent themes and symbolist poetics. The three cat poems, XXXIV "Le Chat" ("The Cat"), LI "Le Chat" (The Cat), and LXIV "Les Chats" (The Cats), appear in the first of the six sections into which Baudelaire divides his book. Under the rubric "Spleen et Idéal," the poems in this section trace the movement of an urban poet as he is transported from anguish ("spleen") to ecstasy ("idéal") in a variety of urban contexts and settings. The cat poems do not form a coherent group within this section and are unusual, though not in this respect unique, in that they all bear the same title (with the slight variation of the plural noun in the last of the three titles). There are two poems entitled "Femme Damnées," the second of which was banned by the censors and excluded from the 1857 edition. The four "Spleen" poems, LXXV, LXXVI, LXXVII, and LXXVIII, are grouped together near the end of the section and, given the title they share, can be said to summarize the thematic thrust and symbolic texture of the book as a whole. The point of drawing attention to the curious status of the cat poems in *Les Fleurs du mal* is not to enter the critical fray concerning the so-called architecture of Baudelaire's work. Rather, it is to make the less controversial claim that the cat poems, like the cats they depict, seem to come in multiples. The poetic sequence almost offers an algebraic equation of felid presence: "Le Chat" + "Le Chat" = "Les Chats."

The first cat poem, number XXXIV, is a sonnet with a rhyming scheme that alternates between masculine and feminine rhymes and is composed of two quatrains followed by a divided sestet. The poem begins with a series of imperatives:

> Viens, mon beau chat, sur mon coeur amoureux;
> Retiens les griffes de ta patte,
> Et laisse-moi plonger dans tes beaux yeux,
> Mêlés de métal et d'agate.

> [Come, my beautiful cat, sit on my loving heart;
> Hold back your paw's claws,
> And allow me to plunge into your beautiful eyes,
> Mixed with metal and agate.]

The repetition of "mon" in the first line might suggest that the poet's cat is equivalent to his heart, or at least equally "mine," but, given the imperative that reigns over the comparison, it might make more sense to say that cat and heart come together under the aegis of love since the direction of affect in "amoureux" is ambiguous enough to allow for reciprocity. The heart loves the cat just as the cat loves the heart. The next two imperatives suggest the give-and-take of requited love with the "retiens" of the second line giving way to the "laisse-moi" of the third. The sense of mutual sincerity and restraint that characterizes the image of a cat stepping on the poet's heart with retracted claws is repeated in the next image, in which the poet asks the cat to let him plunge into its eyes. The next quatrain shifts from a visual to a tactile register, with the poet now caressing the cat with his fingers and receiving pleasure in return, as if the poet's "ma main" (my hand) were acting in response to the cat's "ta patte" (your paw) in a game of amorous exchange, as the use of the verb "palper" (grope or feel) (line 8) makes clear. This eroticized description of the poet's relation to his cat is sublimated in the sonnet's sestet with the assertive *volta* of "Je vois ma femme en esprit" ("I see my woman in spirit") (line 9). The comparison between heart and cat is replaced, or at least complicated, by the introduction of the "femme" as the principal referent of the poem's last sentence. It is the woman's gaze that is now likened to the cat's, both of which are deep and cold, yet, this time, it is the gaze (the woman's, the cat's), rather than the gazer (the poet in the first quatrain), that has become piercing "comme un dard" ("like a dart") (line 11). The comparison is further complicated by the image of the woman's body exuding a "dangereux parfum" ("dangerous perfume") (line 13) as though it were a cat, the woman's scented body ("son corps brun" or "her brown body") (line 14) now replacing the cat's electric body ("ton corps électrique" or "your electric body") (line 8). In the end, it remains unclear if the poem is about the poet's cat, which reminds him of his lover, or about his lover, whose affections the poet might wish were more like his cat's. The cat's affections, though they may be cold, nevertheless admit of reciprocity, especially when encouraged by subtle imperatives such as "viens," "retiens," and "laisse-moi."

The second poem titled "Le Chat," numbered LI, is the longest of the three cat poems in *Les Fleurs du mal*. It is divided into two unequal parts. The first part, which is composed of six quatrains, portrays the cat as a figure for poetic imagination; the second, which is made up of four quatrains, depicts the cat as a flesh-and-blood cat. The first part begins with an arresting image: a cat prowling in the poet's brain:

> Dans ma cervelle se promène,
> Ainsi qu'en son appartement,
> Un beau chat, fort, doux et charmant.
> Quand il miaule, on l'entend à peine,
>
> 5   Tant son timbre est tendre et discret;
> Mais que sa voix s'apaise ou gronde,
> Elle est toujours riche et profonde.
> C'est là son charme et son secret.
>
> [Through my brain there prowls,
> As though it were at home,

A beautiful cat, strong, soft, and charming.
When it meows, one can scarcely hear what it says

So tender and discreet is the timbre of its voice;
However angry and complaining,
Its voice is always rich and deep.
That is its charm and its secret.]

The opening image owes much of its poignancy to the fact that it is premised on two different conceits at once. On the one hand, the figure suggests that the imagination is like a cat that strolls leisurely at home emitting enigmatic sounds the poet must then interpret. On the other, it suggests that the cat forms part of the imagination, the poet having already created an image that corresponds to the way he imagines the cat, prowling and growling in his brain. The difference between the two conceits, however, collapses under the pressure of the figure of voice, which becomes the explicit subject of the first part of the poem, first appearing as "sa voix" ("its voice") and then, at the beginning of the third quatrain, having been appropriated as "Cette voix" ("This voice") (line 9). As the first part of the poem progresses, however, it becomes less clear if the voice belongs to the cat, to the poet, or to both simultaneously. The ambiguity of verses such as "Me remplit comme un vers nombreux/ Et me réjouit comme un philter" ("It satiates me like an harmonious verse/ And delights me like a philter") (lines 11–12) suggests that the cat's voice serves as both tenor and vehicle of the initial figure (a cat speaks in my brain). The slippage between figure and referent is intensified when the cat's voice is compared to the bow ("d'archet") of a violin that plays ("qui morde" or "that gnaws at") the poet's heart. It is tempting to read the reference to the violin, which is here used as a metaphor for the poet's heart, a "perfect instrument," in the context of the admittedly murky history of the use of catgut in bowstrings. It would make the cat's figurative voice coincide with something like a cat's material voice since the image would then suggest that a real (part of a) cat is being used to emit a sort of heart-music (another term for poetry). But this reading would only add to what is already there since a voice that "gnaws at the heart" unequivocally equates the material with the figurative cat.

That the second part of the poem does not mention voice is significant but not surprising, since the cat of the imagination is already a real cat at the end of part one. The cat no longer roams in the poet's brain; it now reigns over an empire ("son empire") that is as much sensual as it is spiritual ("C'est l'esprit familier du lieu" or "It is the familiar spirit of the place") (line 29). The self-reflexive movement of the second part of the poem is articulated through visual rather than aural imagery. In a manner that is perhaps more acute for the poet in the poem that it is for the philosophers who have treated the uncanny gaze of the cat (see Montaigne and Derrida, above), the poet sees the cat seeing him, or in seeing the cat sees himself, by virtue of entering the cat rather than by merely trading places with it:

> Quand mes yeux, vers ce chat que j'aime
> Tirés comme par un aimant,
> 35  Se retournent docilement
> Et que je regarde en moi-même,
>
> Je vois avec étonnement
> Le feu de ses prunelles pâles,
> Clairs fanaux, vivantes opales
> 40  Qui me contemplent fixement.
>
> [When my eyes, towards the cat I love
> Are drawn as though by a magnet,
> Come back to me submissively
> And I look inside myself,
>
> I see with amazement
> The fire of its pale pupils
> Clear beacons, living opals
> That look at me fixedly.]

The poet's eyes, drawn towards (Baudelaire cleverly uses "vers" for "towards" here, which echoes the "vers" of the first part of the poem, where it means "verse") the cat, his eyes, which are now also the cat's eyes, are directed back at him, as though he too were a cat, or the cat the poet. What we see, therefore, is an externalized version of the cat we encountered in the first part, which walked in the poet's brain. The cat comes to signify in its inscrutability the poet's puzzled regard of his own enigmatic imagination.

The third cat poem in Baudelaire's *Les Fleurs du mal* is also a sonnet. The poem is about the symbolism of cats. It compares cats to "ardent lovers" and "austere scholars" since, like them, cats lead sedentary lives and are sensitive to cold draughts. This comparison expands to describe in more detail why cats might be considered "amis de la science et de la volupté" ("friends of learning and sensual pleasure") (line 5).

The reason provided is that they like silence and seek the "horror of darkness," but also, indirectly, because they are proud. In the first tercet, the grounds of comparison shift to the representation of cats: when asleep, cats resemble "mighty sphinxes" that seem to "fall into a sleep of endless dreams" ("s'endormir dans un rêve sans fin") (line 11). The last tercet appears to continue the comparison between cats and sphinxes established in the first tercet when it uses the phrase "magic sparks" ("d'enticelles magiques") (line 12) to describe their "fertile loins" and the phrase "particles of gold" ("parcelles d'or") (line 13) to describe the spark in their eyes, which is itself compared to "fine grains of sand" ("sable fin") (line 13). But the comparison becomes unstable since it is not clear if the figures "sand," "gold," and "sparks" are interchangeable (that is, describe each other) or express a quality or qualities of the parts of the sphinxes, or of the cats, they modify: loins and eyes.

In a celebrated reading of this poem, Roman Jakobson and Claude Lévi-Strauss shed light on the ambiguity of reference in Baudelaire's poem. The preponderance of "synecdochic tropes" in the poem (that is, of figures that take the part for the whole), they claim, accounts for the imprecision of the images, which shift progressively from the darkened interiors of the first part to the brighter exteriors of the second half of the poem. Similarly, the "proud" passivity of the cats that dominates the first part turns in the second part into the more active assumption of a pose or stance that, though stationary, inspires "endless dreams." The difference between empirical and mythological representations of the cats is articulated by the shift from metaphorical to metonymical descriptions, from a comparison with types (scholars, lovers) to parts of bodies (loins, pupils). In their reading, these rhetorical procedures demonstrate the importance of opposites in Baudelaire's poetics (multitude vs. solitude; interior vs. exterior; dark vs. light; etc.). Jakobson and Lévi-Strauss do not mention the opposition human vs. animal in their reading, a surprising omission given that the poem is structured through the explicit comparison between cats and humans (scholars, lovers). They mention that the figure of the cat is closely linked to the figure of the woman in Baudelaire's cat poems, a critical commonplace that, however accurate, is insufficient. In order to understand the importance of the animal–human distinction in Baudelaire's poem, we must first turn to another story about cats that had a transformative effect on his own poetry.

When Baudelaire first read Edgar Allan Poe's story "The Black Cat" (1843) he had a shock of recognition. The story had appeared in translation in a French newspaper in 1847 and, upon reading it, Baudelaire thought he had found a veritable soul mate. The famous last line from "Au Lecteur," the opening poem in *Les Fleurs du mal*, – "Hypocrite lecteur, – mon semblable, – mon frère!" ("Hypocritical reader, my double, my brother!) – could well have been directed at his own self as reader of Poe. "The Black Cat" was the first Poe story Baudelaire had ever read and, as he later told his friends, it was as if he had found a version of himself in Poe's writings. Poe was not only interested in some of the same themes in which he was interested; he used words that Baudelaire himself would have used. That the story is about a black cat makes this well-known anecdote all the more interesting for being doubly uncanny. It is not clear whether Poe's story directly influenced his cat poems, but Baudelaire had already translated some of Poe's works into French when *Les Fleurs du mal* was first published. It is nevertheless suggestive to think of Poe's black cat as the first in the literary clowder that gathers in Baudelaire's pages; it suggests, among other things, that cats come in multiples.

Poe's story, naturally, features not one but several black cats. The story, which is narrated in the first person, begins with a description of the narrator's "docility" and "tenderness of heart" towards animals. His favorite among the animals his parents give him is a black cat he names Pluto. They become inseparable companions. Once married, however, the narrator's disposition undergoes an abrupt transformation under the influence of the "Fiend Intemperance." He is now irascible and cruel and takes to abusing his great friend Pluto. Returning home "highly intoxicated" on one occasion, he gouges out one of Pluto's eyeballs. Though he is aware of his malice, he continues to torment the poor cat until one day he finally hangs it from a tree. He claims that it is his "perverseness" that is to blame and, when his house catches on fire, he cannot help but consider it an act of retribution. Among the cinders of his destroyed house, he discovers a plaster wall that has survived the fire on which an image of his cat, with a rope around its neck, can be clearly discerned. He is puzzled but, somewhat reasonably, he concludes that the neighbors must have thrown the dead cat through the window to alert him about the fire and that the fire in turn must have burnt the imprint of the cat's body on the newly plastered wall with the help of the ammonia emanating from the carcass.

Haunted by Pluto's "phantasm," by which word the narrator seems to mean both the mental image of the cat as well as its ghostly presence, he decides to adopt a new cat. He finds a cat in a "den of more than infamy" whose resemblance to Pluto is uncanny. The second cat is black, and, remarkably, it is also missing an eye. The most conspicuous difference between the first black cat and the second is that the latter has a white patch on its breast whose outline gradually comes to resemble the "GALLOWS!" (Poe 1991, 188, emphasis in the original). A more subtle difference between them is that Pluto is referred to as a "he" whereas the new cat is a "she." Tormented by his own sense of perverseness yet genuinely annoyed by the new cat, he jumps at the chance of getting rid of it when one day the cat chances to accompany him to the cellar. He raises an axe and is about to brain the poor creature with it when his wife intercedes and prevents him from striking. In a mad rage, he buries the axe in his wife's brain instead. He resolves to immure the dead wife in a false chimney whose bricks can be easily moved. The plaster with which he covers the new brickwork cannot be distinguished from that which covers the adjacent walls. Even though it reminds us of the plaster imprinted with Pluto's image in the ruins of the old house, and, by extension, the new cat's white patch on which the gallows is figured, the new plaster does not in itself bear the mark of the protagonist's gruesome deeds. The telltale sign materializes itself a few days later when the police, unexpectedly summoned to the house, hear the cat's agonized howl coming from behind the wall. In the end, the narrator, who we learn has been writing this story from prison, where he awaits his own death, realizes that the cat has been playing with him all along for it is he who has been entombed while still alive: "the hideous beast whose craft seduced me into murder, and whose informing voice has consigned me to the hangman" (191).

Jakobson and Lévi-Strauss do not mention Poe in their reading of Baudelaire's "Les Chats," but to the extent that their reading is premised on the prevalence of synecdochic tropes in the poem, we might understand the dismemberment of figures as the equivalent of the cats' dismemberment in Poe's story. This would mean that Baudelaire incorporates into his poems' rhetorical disfiguration the themes Poe explores in his story. We might even go further and suggest that all of Baudelaire's cat poems are premised on the figuration of dismemberment if we consider, among others, the image of the cat prowling the brain in poem LI, the trope of the disembodied voice in poem XXXIV, or the attention to eyes, paws, and fur in both of them. In Poe's "The Black Cat," we even find an image that, albeit in a less macabre register, appears in the first of Baudelaire's cat poems: "its vast weight…incumbent eternally upon my heart" (1991, 188). However direct the links that connect Poe to Baudelaire may actually be, the important point here is that they share a view of the symbolic significance of cats in the literary treatment of the idea of self-consciousness. Indeed, the rhetorical disfiguration of the cats in Baudelaire's and Poe's texts tell us something about the strange relation, or, better, the relation of strangeness, that obtains between humans and felids. The eerie effect created by these texts no doubt depends in part on the stereotypical view of cats (especially black ones) as figures of ill omen or as witches' familiars. But this effect is also a deliberate attempt to disfigure traditional literary conventions, part of the post-Romantic project we call decadence. Cats, as I hope these readings have shown, are not incidental to this project; they offer with their uncanny presence a unique perspective on the way nature is denaturalized in decadent writing as a strategy to make visible the animality of humans. These texts, moreover, show that this strategy predates the formal assimilation of Darwin's theory of evolution in nineteenth-century political culture. In Poe and Baudelaire, the cat stands as a figure for a human predicament, which can be described as the ontological incompatibility of acute self-consciousness with animal nature. The figure of the cat offers no solutions to this predicament even as it gives us, with its enigmatic presence, consciousness of its existence.

## The cat's pajamas

Grouped under the title "The Lives of Animals," two chapters of J. M. Coetzee's 2003 novel *Elizabeth Costello* are devoted to the question of the animal: the first is titled "The Philosophers and the Animals," and the second "The Poets and the Animals." These chapters were originally conceived of as lectures, which Coetzee delivered in person at Princeton University in 1997 as part of the Tanner Lectures on Human Values. Coetzee's lectures were in fact readings of a fictional representation of a series of lectures that Elizabeth Costello, the novelist and protagonist of the novel, delivers at Appleton College, the academic institution to which she has been invited to deliver the annual Gates Lectures, and where her son John works as an assistant professor of physics and astronomy. Like Coetzee, Costello is a well-known novelist who has been invited to lecture at a university based on her literary reputation, not on her view of animals. Unlike Coetzee's, Costello's lectures are not fictional though they are engaged in fiction, or, more generally, literature. The similarities are suggestive, but we are meant to focus on the differences; in fact, it would be more accurate to say that we are meant to focus on difference itself. The literary device Coetzee uses to make us focus on difference is focalization, by which term is meant the differential attention third-person narration places on particular characters who are not themselves narrators, such that the world that comes into being in fiction is seen through the eyes of specific characters. Indeed, the argument Costello makes in the lectures she delivers at Appleton College is premised on the literary device of focalization, a term neither Costello nor Coetzee explicitly use.

The argument hinges on a distinction Costello makes between different ways of representing the world. Philosophers use reason, while poets use the imagination. She acknowledges that philosophers have been at the forefront of animal rights discourse, but Costello believes that reason is not conducive to understanding the lives of animals. In her lecture, she uses the example of Red Peter, the protagonist of Franz Kafka's short story "Report to an Academy," to show that an ape can be plausibly represented as a thinking being, even if the story he tells is the story of learning to use human reason. She also cites Thomas Nagel's essay "What Is it Like to Be a Bat?" to refute the view that we cannot know what it is like to be an animal for that particular animal by introducing the concept of the "sympathetic imagination." For Costello the novelist, the imagination knows no bounds and, in order to prove it, she tells her audience about one of her own novels, *The House on Eccles Street*, in which she imagined what it would be like to be Marion Bloom, a character James Joyce invented in his novel Ulysses. "If I can think my way into the existence of a being who has never existed," Costello argues, "then I can think my way into the existence of a bat or a chimpanzee or an oyster, any being with whom I share the substrate of life" (Coetzee 2003, 80). When we repair on the fact that Coetzee is doing exactly the same thing with Elizabeth Costello, it becomes clear that he is constructing this elaborate hall of mirrors with a lecture on lectures that talk about more lectures to make us aware of the abrupt shifts of perspective, or, to use the term I introduced above, of focalization, required when we employ the sympathetic imagination.

But it is not enough to make visible the insufficiencies of reason by laying claim to the priority of the sympathetic imagination. One must also show how it works. Costello uses Rilke's "Der Panther" ("The Panther") and two poems by Ted Hughes, "The Jaguar" and "Second Glance at the Jaguar," as examples of the sympathetic imagination in action. It is curious that Costello, and, for that matter, Coetzee, should use three feline poems to show how poets imagine animals sympathetically. They are perfectly fine poems, to be sure, but why these and not others? Is it because cats are themselves the embodiments of a kind of uncanny doubling that reminds us to shift our perspective? All three poems are staged at the zoo, which is understandable given that Rilke and Hughes would have most likely only been able to contemplate these "exotic" animals first-hand at a zoo, but perhaps this circumstance also explains why Costello would choose them: cages act as framing devices that compel us to think sympathetically, and thus with a sense of perspective, about those trapped within. Furthermore, we are only privy to a partial account of Costello's comments on these poems because the chapter in which they are discussed, like the one before it, is in fact focalized through John's perspective, and he happens to have been detained at a department meeting and has only been able to join his mother's seminar *in medias res*.

She is discussing Rilke's poem when he enters. Costello seems to be using the German poet as a negative example: just like those animal tropes that are used as stand-ins for human qualities, the panther, she claims, "is there as a stand-in for something else" (95). This "something else" is something like arrested force. This is how Rilke's poem expresses it:

5    Der weiche Gang geschmeidig starker Schritte,
     der sich im allerkleinsten Kreise dreht,
     ist wie ein Tanz von Kraft um eine Mitte,
     in der betäubt ein großer Wille steht.

[The soft pace of the smooth strong stride,
as it turns itself into the smallest circles,
is like a dance of strength around a center,
in which a mighty will stands paralyzed.]

Costello is of course right in reading the panther as a "stand-in" for "something else"; that is, as a metaphor. But the poem is not unsympathetic to the panther; it suggests if nothing else that its powerful body is trapped in a cage that does not let it be itself. The image of the panther circling itself further suggests that this entrapment has become part of its very shape; it seems to circle into itself in order to contain or trap its own strength. It is true that the poem does not give us a satisfactory answer to the question Costello is implicitly posing in her reading of it—whether this way of representing an animal is sympathetic—but for Rilke to even begin to know what it is like to be a panther he needs to use the poetic resources available to him in his language. It may well be a cliché to say that the caged panther is on the verge of exploding with energy, but the image of encirclement Rilke deploys to express it also begins to trap the cliché as well, as the last "paralyzed" suggests.

Costello's readings of the two Hughes poems are more sympathetic. She suggests that Hughes is writing against Rilke and, at least thematically, the first jaguar poem, "The Jaguar," does seem to be antithetical to Rilke's portrayal of the caged panther. The poem gives credit to the jaguar for not giving up. The other cages at the zoo may well be paintings on nursery walls, so quiet and lifeless they seem. The jaguar, in contrast, is "hurrying enraged" in his prison. For Hughes, to imagine what it would be like to be a jaguar is to endow the animal with imagination:

> He spins from the bars, but there's no cage to him
>
> More than to the visionary his cell:
> His stride is wildernesses of freedom:
> The world rolls under the long thrust of his heel.
> 20    Over the cage floor the horizons come.

For Costello, Hughes is attempting to imagine a different kind of "being-in-the-world," an existence that is kinetic and not abstract (95). To be sure, the scene Hughes imagines for the jaguar is more appealing than is the one Rilke imagines for the panther, but this may be so only on account of the fact that the jaguar is both "enraged" at being in a cage and engaged in dreaming, like a "visionary," of being elsewhere. But is this image not just as clichéd as Rilke's? And if it is not, it is at least a more comforting portrayal of the fate of caged animals, a portrayal that imagines the jaguar acting as we would act in the same situation, provided we were all visionaries.

Costello argues that Hughes's jaguar poems are a record of an engagement with the animal as an embodied being rather than as an abstract idea. Yet, the second of Hughes's jaguar poems, which Costello mentions but scarcely reads, engages precisely in the kind of abstract idea she claims he resists. To the extent that the second poem represents a "second glance" at the jaguar, it is natural that it cover some of the same ground as the first, describing in more detail this time its movements inside the cage. The status of its "visions," however, is more ambiguous in this poem since Hughes describes its bodily movements using metaphors that seem to originate in the poet who contemplates the jaguar rather than in the jaguar itself. Consider the images Hughes employs to describe the jaguar's stride:

> A terrible, stump-legged waddle,
> Like a thick Aztec disemboweller
> Club-swinging, trying to grind some square
> Socket between his hind legs round,
> 10    Carrying his head like a brazier of spilling embers,
> And the black bit of his teeth, he has to wear his skin out,
> He swipes a lap at the water trough as he turns,
> Swivelling the ball of his heel on the polished spot,

Showing his belly like a butterfly,
15    At every stride he has to turn a corner
In himself and correct it.

The comparison between jaguar and Aztec priest is gratuitous since it is not the jaguar itself that seems to conjure such an image but the abstract idea of the jaguar used as a totemic animal. The Aztecs, as Hughes must have known, wore jaguar skins on their bodies in ritualistic practices. To describe the jaguar as an Aztec disemboweller, therefore, is to describe the caged jaguar as though it were wearing its own skin in some sacrificial pageant. The image is arresting, but it hardly corresponds to the "jaguarness" of the jaguar that Costello finds in the poem. The initial comparison between the jaguar and the wearer of a jaguar skin is rendered more complex by the use of different images to describe different elements of the jaguar's stride. The last line of this sentence seems to echo Rilke's poem but, in echoing it, it does not go much beyond it.

The point of reading the feline poems alongside Elizabeth Costello is not to show that her readings are false or inadequate. It is to suggest that the poetic engagement with animals is inevitably mediated through tropes, some of which may well bring us closer to the body of the animal than others but none of which will entirely disappear. In this sense, Costello's readings of these different feline poems remain underdeveloped in that the problem with using tropes to describe animals does not hinge on the difference between abstract and concrete representation; the problem lies in the ability of figures to instantiate a change of perspective, or, put in the terms I used above, to motivate a shift of focalization. From this perspective, Coetzee's use of felid poems is salutary since the cat, the cat that sees me seeing it, already troubles in its own "catness" the distinction between focalized and focalizer.

## Catcalls

Philosophers tend to name their own cats after concepts: Derrida named his cat Logos; Sartre named his cat Nothing; Foucault named his cat Insanity. Poets name their cats after their own works: Mark Twain named his cat Huckleberry; Becket named his two cats Murphy and Watt; George Bernard Shaw named his Pygmalion; Alan Ginsberg named his Howl; Don DeLillo named his Mao II; Haruki Murakami named his Kafka; Borges named his Aleph; Cortázar named his Bestiario. Something funny could probably be said about the different strategies poets and philosophers adopt in the pursuit of self-regard through their cats, but the more interesting fact about the different ways poets and philosophers have of naming their cats is that it is just not all that interesting. So much for the originality of poets and philosophers.

The question of naming cats, however, is in itself an interesting question to consider in closing since it captures our relation to cats in a pithy and perhaps figurative but in any case particularly revealing manner, since to name a cat is to domesticate it. The first thing to note is that most of the cats in the texts I have read in the present chapter are not named, Poe's Pluto standing as the one exception that proves the ruling pattern of featuring nameless cats in felid tales. Indeed, the logic of not-naming obeys the general purpose of many of the texts under discussion: namely, the appraisal of what it might be like to think, act, and feel like a cat, great and small. The act of naming, moreover, corresponds to what J. L. Austin called performative speech acts, utterances that in saying something actually do something, like naming. Among the negative examples Austin uses in formulating the conditions under which an utterance performs an act is the phrase cited at the opening of this chapter: "the cat is on the mat." (A phrase, incidentally, that we can now call a philosopheme, which is not to be confused with, but is certainly related to, a lolcat). For Austin, the "cat is on the mat" is not subject to belief conditions; under the pressure of performatives it is simply an act of insincerity to say that the cat is on the mat but I do not believe it is. Naming, then, is a performative operation in part because it is not subject to true/false criteria to determine whether someone or something or perhaps a cat is actually named. The name sticks or it does not stick, but, under ordinary circumstances, a cat's name is neither right nor wrong. Poets and philosophers notwithstanding, cat names resist connotation.

In *Old Possum's Book of Practical Cats* (1939), T.S. Eliot meditates at length on the naming of cats but maintains that cats have three kinds of names. In "The Naming of Cats," the book's opening poem, Eliot describes them in order: the first type of name includes "sensible every day names," the sorts of names you would use to refer and perhaps even to address the family cat; the second type includes "particular," "peculiar," "dignified" names that "never belong to more than one cat"; the third type, known only to cats, is an "ineffable effable/ Effanineffable/ Deep and inscrutable singular Name" (Eliot 1939 [1971], 149). Eliot's word play, sensibly pitched to his intended audience of children as nonsense, is significant in at least one respect: it makes visible the fact that naming in effect needs no words. The cat names Eliot employs in the book—a book that may be said to be about the naming of cats—make us aware that even the second type of name is nothing but action rendered conspicuous. Here's a sample: Growltiger, Rum Tug Tugger, Mungojerrie, Rumpleteazer, Old Deuteronomy, Macavity, Skimbleshanks, and Bustopher Jones. These names, like all names, only refer to an individual in the act of being used to refer to that individual, even if there are many individuals with the same name. Proper names, in this sense operate much like pronouns, except of course that they are very specific pronouns, or specific enough at least to be useful in distinguishing individuals in a specific context. There may be millions upon millions of Michaels, for all we know, but it is likely that you will only ever need to refer to one or two members of this particular set in any given situation. In the case of Eliot's cat poems, the names themselves (names of the second type, at least) are so particular as to be invented every time they are used. Indeed, the act of naming in Eliot's poems is both a poetic function and an act performed, unbeknownst to humans, by the cats themselves, if we take the third type of name to be a common act performed by pensive cats. It is probably true, as Wittgenstein famously claimed, that if a lion could talk we would not understand him. But this is the case less because we are not participants in the language games lions play amongst themselves; it is because our names and their names must necessarily act in different ways.

In the preceding readings, I have focused on some of the rhetorical and figural strategies writers have used to treat the peculiar relation that binds humans to felids. One of the most common strategies is the attempt to use rhetorical figures to try to imagine what it would be like to inhabit the life of a particular cat. The cats' enigmatic responses to this attempt often disrupt the figural relay established between human and feline to create effects of doubling and estrangement that are aptly captured in the Freudian term "the uncanny." But to the extent that this effect is inevitable—or so, at any rate, suggests the voluminous literary archive pertaining to felids—then we cannot understand the relation as exclusively mediated by rhetorical tropes; we must also consider the role of acts in the construction of something like a relation between felids and humans. Naming is one such act but there are many others, and it is in literature where, like Borges's poet, we must embark upon the "aventura indefinida" ("undefined and indefinite adventure") of catching our cat in the act. Acts and cats, if nothing else, share the same letters and, as acrostics, may as well be said to create each other in the indefinite adventure of catachresis, of which cats, as the name of the trope suggests, are the naturally inadequate embodiments.

# Note

1 This chapter was excised, reconfigured, and published separately as a story under the title "Town of Cats" in the September 5, 2011 issue of the *New Yorker.*

# Works cited

Austin, J. L. *How to Do Things With Words.* Second ed., eds. J. O. Urmson and Marina Sbisà. Cambridge: Harvard U. P., 1975.

Baudelaire, Charles. *The Complete Verse.* Ed. and trans. Francis Scarfe. London: Anvil Press, 1986.

Blake, William. *The Complete Prose and Poetry of William Blake.* Eds. David V. Erdman and Harold Bloom. New York: Anchor Book, 1988.

Borges, Jorge Luis. "El otro tigre." In *El otro, el mismo.* Buenos Aires: Emecé, 1969.

Calvino, Italo. *Marcovaldo, or The Seasons in the City,* trans. William Weaver. New York: Harcourt Brace Jovanovich, 1983.

Coetzee, J. M. *Elizabeth Costello.* London: Penguin, 2003.

Derrida, Jacques. *The Animal that Therefore I Am,* trans. David Wills. New York: Fordham University Press, 2008.

Eliot. T. S. *Old Possum's Book of Practical Cats. In The Complete Poems and Plays, 1909–1950.* New York: Harcourt Brace Jovanovich, 1971.

Hughes, Ted. *Collected Poems.* Ed. Paul Keegan. New York: Farrar, Straus and Giroux, 2003.

Jakobson, Roman and Claude Lévi-Strauss. "Baudelaire's 'Les Chats.'" In *Language in Literature.* Eds. Krystyna Pomorska and Stephen Rudy. Cambridge: Harvard University Press, 1987.

Montaigne, Michel de. *The Complete Essays of Montaigne,* trans. Donald A. Frame. Stanford: Stanford University Press, 1965.

Murakami, Haruki. *1Q84,* trans. Jay Rubin and Philip Gabriel. New York, Vintage, 2009–2010.

Poe, Edgar Allan. "The Black Cat." In *Selected Tales.* The Library of America. New York: Vintage, 1991: 182–191.

Rilke, Rainer Maria. "Der Panther"/ "The Panther." In *Prose and Poetry,* trans. J. B. Leishman. The German Library. New York: Continuum, 1991.

# 6   Animal revolutions (allegory and politics)

In his essay "The Politics of Literature," Jacques Rancière defines politics as an activity whose aim is to reconfigure the distribution of the perceptible. Political activity entails introducing new objects and new subjects onto a common stage, thereby making visible what was invisible and making "audible as speaking beings those who were previously only heard as noisy animals" (2011, 4). In Rancière's formulation, a "politics of literature" implies that literature intervenes *as* literature in the political process, helping to determine what is visible and what is audible. But what if the "noisy animals" Rancière invokes in his formulation were themselves to enter the political stage under a new dispensation in which a newly reconfigured distribution of the perceptible made them "audible as speaking beings"? And what role would literature play in this political process? In this politics-to-come, animals would be visible and audible and would thus have to be counted in the political process. We would even have to be open to the possibility that the newly perceptible language of animals would have been at least in part made so by something like animal literature. To engage with this possibility implies reconfiguring our perception of animals as well as our understanding of what literature is and of what it does.

But animals of course are already audible *in* literature, if we would only care to listen. The copious catalogue of howls, barks, meows, growls, purrs, chirps, warbles, tweets, and the many other audible voices of the "noisy animals" that inhabit the texts I have analyzed in these pages would suggest that in order to make animals count politically, we must first reconfigure the distribution of the perceptible *within* literature. This reconfiguration implies a politics of literature that is in turn based on a politics of reading since animals have been speaking in literature from its inception, even if they have not always been audible. Indeed, the categorical distinction Rancière makes between "speaking beings" and "noisy animals" is merely a symptom of the generalized repression of animals in literature as well as in its criticism. Perhaps it was not always so, but animals can hardly be said to count in literature as we perceive it. We can all surely name one or two literary animals, and, if pressed, perhaps even a handful, but we are also just as likely to dismiss them as little more than idealized children in animal dress and confine them to the realm of, well, children's literature, which is precisely what we tend to do. But to the extent that literature can be construed as that discourse which makes animals speak—the speaking animal is literature's founding invention, something like a "literareme" or basic unit of the literary—this dismissal suggests that animal speech is also a "mute language," to use the term Rancière coins to designate the silent discourse with which modern literature gives voice to otherwise inaudible objects of representation. He does not mention speaking animals, but if the speaking animal is that which makes literature literary, then perhaps in order to make animals count we must perceive literature anew, learning to listen to the mute speech of literary animals.

The texts I will read in what follows have all to do with counting; with how we account for animals, how we count them, and how we imagine animals might count themselves. I will focus on two types of texts: texts that treat undesirable animals—animals, that is, that do not normally count—and texts that treat heterogeneous groupings of animals—animals, that is, that demand to be counted. The emblematic figure for the first type is the "vermin" or *Ungeziefer*, the term Franz Kafka uses to describe Gregor Samsa in *Die Verwandlung* [*The Metamorphosis*] (1915). The second type is the animal collective, multispecies animal sets that can be found on a farm, in the jungle, at the zoo, or in the laboratory. Both tropes, the vermin and the animal collective, offer possibilities for counting politically, but each approaches counting from a different perspective: vermin tend to be individualized as figures of abjection excluded from political calculation, while animal collectives usually bear the figurative burden of social movements. As this description already suggests, both types of representation lend themselves to allegorical readings. Allegory still tends to be understood as a didactic rhetorical structure by means of which we give shape to otherwise ambiguous qualities and situations through personification: love, justice, courage, etc. From this perspective, the two types of animal texts I have isolated can be interpreted as existential parables (through this allegoreme: "the dehumanization of the modern subject") or political fables (through this allegoreme: "sovereignty as animal power"). The point is not to resist these readings which at times can hardly be avoided, as in Orwell's *Animal Farm*, which hungrily invites an allegorical reading of authoritarianism. The challenge is to read these allegories closely, literally, and skeptically so as to complicate or disrupt the referential inferences we tend to draw when we consider animal imagery as simply imagery, as though animals could only count symbolically. Many of the texts I will be reading in this chapter already go some way in deconstructing allegory, of course, fast though their critics might still cling to the lifelines thrown by symbolism. It is almost impossible to hear what animals are saying above the din that fills criticism with platitudes rather than platypuses, hearsay rather than heifers and Jerseys, pieties rather than pythons, clichés rather than critters, values rather than voles. It is nevertheless important to keep in mind that counting animals is a human prerogative and that the texts under discussion are literary texts that always imagine animal agency in excess of its animality.

## La cucaracha, la cucaracha…

In a recent survey of American attitudes toward wild and domestic animals, the cockroach was found to be the least popular among the usual vermin suspects, including the rat, the rattlesnake, the wasp, the bat, and the mosquito (Kellert 1988). The unpopularity of the cockroach is surprising only in the context of its longevity, since it has been around for far longer than humans and will in all likelihood outlive us. This is one of the premises of the Pixar film *Wall-E* (2008) which features a cockroach as the last surviving living being on an ecologically devastated earth until Wall-E, the film's robotic garbage compactor, finds a plant.[1] Cockroaches are indestructible, both on earth and in the cultural imaginary of its human inhabitants. Yet, despite their staying power, cockroaches are almost invisible and, with one notable exception, virtually inaudible in literature. Indeed, cockroaches may well be considered the lumpenproletariat of the zoomorphic text, counting for nothing in their abject condition as the unwelcome companions of human misery and decay, for when they do appear in literature they tend to be there to produce recoil rather than sympathy. Here is the paradox of the cockroach: it literalizes a condition of alterity that can only be brought to cultural attention by virtue of being literary.

That animals should be made to carry the figurative burden of human otherness in literature is of course not surprising, given that the human–animal divide is produced as an effect of what philosopher Giorgio Agamben has called the anthropological machine (see Chapter 1). The anthropological machine creates, on the basis of false or empty comparisons, hybrid figures whose function is not the blurring of categorical difference but its reaffirmation. Animalized humans (slaves, barbarians, foreigners) are excluded on the basis of their otherness, and anthropomorphic animals come to stand in for the radical alterity of the human-as-animal, the conceptual underpinning in the development and implementation of biopolitics. The concept of animality, as Keith Thomas has helpfully noted, emerged in the context of exclusionary practices among humans in the seventeenth and eighteenth centuries in England:

> Men attributed to animals the natural impulses they most feared in themselves – ferocity, gluttony, sexuality – even though it was men, not beasts, who made war on their species, ate more than was good for them, and were sexually active all year round. It was as a comment on *human* nature that the concept of "animality" was devised.
>
> (1996, 40–41, emphasis in original)

Yet the "otherness" of the animal is not often encoded as otherness: dogs, cats, horses, and songbirds tend to be portrayed in literature as familiar beings whose strangeness (the fact that they are animals) only compels us to examine our own ideological investments, psychic cathexes, and physical predicaments in an oblique and thereby simplified manner. If the assimilation of animal otherness into familiar patterns of moral and political instruction, a process Derrida has called "affabulation," manages to abstract animals out of their animality, what then of the other of the animal? Are there animals that are more radically other than the blanket otherness that the term "animal" (or "animot") would seem to imply? Harriet Ritvo has argued that "anthropocentric binaries" used to classify animals (edible vs. inedible, useful vs. useless, ugly vs. beautiful, wild vs. domestic) were instrumental in maintaining a strict division between human and non-human animals (1987). The historical apportioning of animals into degrees of otherness would therefore suggest that counting animals is a political project that extends into the distribution of the perceptible within the animal world itself; and the others of the animal world are, well, vermin.

Kafka's *Die Verwandlung* [*The Metamorphosis*] (1915), the famous story of a transformation, itself marks a transformation in the representation of animals in literature. Before Kafka, animals had never been literalized as animal figures. This is of course not say that animals had never before been used to represent human attributes, attitudes, and abstractions, nor that animals had never before been represented for their own sake. In Kafka, however, we have a rare figurative feat in which animals are represented literally as animals that acquire human form in order to express their animality. Prominent figures from Kafka's texts such as the ape Red Peter, Josephine the mouse, the animal in the burrow, the dog and its investigations, are all captured struggling with their identities as animals in a way that may resemble and resonate with humans but which never comes to replace their sense of themselves as other.[2] In Gregor Samsa, the protagonist of *The Metamorphosis*, Kafka achieves a delicate balance between representing animals as animals, and humans as the animals we always already were.

The transformation from human to animal Gregor Samsa undergoes is far less radical than the term "metamorphosis" suggests. Indeed, *Die Verwandlung*, the German title of Kafka's tale, can be read as an ironic rendering of its plausible alternative, *Die Metamorphose*, which would have echoed the more mythically laden title of Ovid's tales, traditionally translated into German as *Metamorphosen* rather than, say, *Verwandlungen*. Gregor Samsa is already an animal when the story begins, and thus the transformation to which the title refers could therefore be construed as entailing the long-drawn process of assimilating the fact that he is now the insect his family, his employers, and the world already know he is. The "becoming-vermin" of the vermin, to use the awkward but suggestive nomenclature formulated by Gilles Deleuze and Félix Guattari (1987), is a process of literalization, a figurative transformation in which a substitution (a person is called an animal) becomes naturalized (the person is the animal) and cultural categories are taken for natural ones.

The first thing to note about the monstrous vermin (*"ungeheures Ungeziefer"*) into which Gregor Samsa finds himself transformed as he wakes up from unsettling dreams (*"unruhigen Träumen"*) at the beginning of Kafka's text is that it is difficult to classify. The text may be said to be an attempt to count, or account for, the vermin, as if the absurdity of the transformation were not only that Gregor is now an animal, but also that he has turned into an animal that cannot be precisely classified, even if we accept the commonly held view that he has indeed become a cockroach. Gregor attempts to describe himself—that is, to give an account of himself as an animal—from the moment he awakes from his dreams to the very end of his troubled life, but is unable to name the vermin into which he has been transformed. He now has a "vaulted brown belly, sectioned by arch-shaped ribs," "many" "squirming" "little" legs, an "elastic" back, "very strong" jaws, antennae, "bulging" eyes, and when upright reaches up to a doorknob in height (Kafka 1915 [1996], 3, 6, 8, 11, 16, 18). The cleaning woman who finally disposes of him at the end of the story is the only one to try to give it a name, to identify the animal as a recognizable species: "Come over here for a minute, you old dung beetle!" and "Look at that old dung beetle!" (33). Although the reference (*Mistkäfer* in German) is admittedly ambiguous since this is the friendly banter of an unfazed servant rather than the descriptive language of a naturalist, the cleaning woman's address at least acknowledges his existence, whatever the classification he may merit. That Gregor counts for the cleaning woman but ceases to count for others suggests that they now occupy similar social positions, which means that neither of them really counts; they are the vermin proletarians of their respective social systems.

Gregor Samsa's transformation is one of de-socialization. When he awakes transformed into an insect, he is still preoccupied by the exigencies of his human life: the train he has missed, the responsibility he has taken upon himself as his family's principal income earner, his ambiguous status at the firm for which he works as a traveling salesman, his sister's musical promise, and so on. But gradually he begins to lose interest in the family's doings and begins to devote most of his energies to satisfying his simple insect needs. This process of de-socialization, however, cannot be described as a retreat from life itself. His sense perception is no less sharp, and perhaps even more vital, than it was when he was a human, even if it is radically altered. After he is wounded when he drags his wide body through the narrow doorway to his room, he realizes that he now heals very rapidly (18). He also realizes that he can now devour food he had initially found repulsive when his sister first served it to him "with eyes streaming with tears of contentment" (18). He begins to see "things even a short distance away less and less distinctly" (21), and even takes to crawling "crisscross" along the walls and the ceiling:

> He especially liked hanging from the ceiling; it was completely different from lying on the floor; one could breathe more freely; a faint swinging sensation went through the body; and in the almost happy absent-mindedness with which Gregor felt up there, it could happen to his own surprise that he let go and plopped onto the floor.
>
> (23)

The paratactic quality of the first four clauses in the period, each rhythmically following the next, gives us the impression that Gregor is indeed swinging from the ceiling, while the last and longest clause traces the trajectory of his fall. Indeed, Gregor has become the living answer to a question he may only have asked rhetorically: what is it like to be a vermin?

There is perhaps no better way to answer this implied question than in the language of the being Gregor is now fated to embody, a language we can now refer to as a vermin vernacular. He realizes soon after his transformation that, even though he can still understand human speech, humans can no longer understand him: "[T]hey no longer understood his words, though they had seemed clear enough to him, clearer than before, probably because he had grown accustomed to them" (11). His manager, who has come to see why Gregor, always so punctual, has failed to show up at the office, is the first to realize that he is different: "'That was the voice of an animal,' said the manager..." (10). And though Gregor understands human speech, he also realizes that he now understands it differently. The first word he hears from humans is not even a word; it is the "Oh!" his manager utters, which to Gregor "sounded like a rush of wind" (12). He recites a long speech in response to the manager's speechless utterance and then realizes that it "had possibly – indeed, probably – not been understood again" (14). He attempts to speak to his mother—"Mother, Mother," said Gregor softly and looked up at her (14)—but cannot wait for her to answer as he begins to snap uncontrollably at the coffee dripping from the table, at which action she screams as if on cue. His father emits an "intolerable hissing sound" (14) as he tries to corral Gregor back into his room with his cane, perhaps in an attempt to communicate with his son in the manner of a tourist who tries to make himself understood by raising the volume of his voice. The father's voice, which "did not sound like that of only a single father," still manages to drive Gregor back into his room. The slapstick quality of Kafka's elaborate mise-en-scène is qualified by the pathos that accompanies Gregor's attempts to connect using speech with the human world to which he knows he will never again belong. As Gregor ceases to speak he instead begins to write on the walls: "[H]e left behind traces of his sticky substance wherever he crawled" (23).

Gregor eventually ceases to count for his family, which seems to be thriving in his absence, and becomes ever less audible and visible. At one point his father pelts Gregor with apples, one of which becomes permanently lodged in his exoskeleton and renders him suddenly sluggish. Lodgers are brought into the household and their wolf-like furriness (all three have long beards and chew their food noisily) provides a categorical contrast to Gregor's insectile inertness. When the lodgers ask Gregor's sister to play the violin, Gregor is unexplainably drawn to the family room: "Was he an animal, that music could move him so?" (36). The lodgers threaten to move out when they see him, and even his sister, who has up to this point been his staunchest champion, finally realizes that he has to go. But Gregor has already become an absence, as Kafka's increasingly distant use of free indirect discourse in the above quotation makes clear in squirming detail. Not even music can save him from the dust heap of his own human history.

We can think of this process as a form of "deterritorialization," the term Gilles Deleuze and Félix Guattari (1986) employ to describe the manner in which texts, or concepts, retreat from the dominant narrative. Kafka's work, in their reading, represents a "minor" literature because it is written in the dominant language from a minority perspective. *The Metamorphosis* can be usefully classified under the category "minor literature" because its politics consist in bringing an individualized subject position to bear on the ideological construction of minority status. At the same time, it plays a collective role to the extent that it speaks for the minority position that the subject happens to occupy. This could apply to both Kafka, who wrote in German though he lived in Prague and spoke Yiddish at home, and to Gregor since he uses a vermin vernacular whose plaintive tones, if not the "words" themselves, he has learned to use at his family home.

The category of "minor literature" also applies to the work of Clarice Lispector, who wrote in the Portuguese used in her adopted country Brazil, though she was an Ukrainian Jew by birth. Moreover, her most famous novel, *A paixão segundo G.H.* [*The Passion According to G.H.*] (1964), uses a vermin vernacular insofar as it too features a cockroach trapped in a room. In Lispector's novel, narrative attention is trained almost entirely on a cockroach, or more precisely, the narrative's attention is devoted to the attention the protagonist trains on the severed body of a cockroach. The disjunction between the narrative's attention and the protagonist's creates a space of representation that may be called mystical (this is one possible reading of the novel's title), or perhaps existential in a non-technical sense, but which in any case details the process whereby the protagonist becomes disfigured. This process of disfiguration unfolds through a form of self-reflection, but it is a form of self-reflection that is displaced, first by the mode of self-regard—the protagonist begins to see herself as others see her— and then by the referent she employs to externalize the insights she gains about herself in this way. It is in this latter form of displacement that the cockroach becomes significant, but not because a relation of equivalence is established between the insect and the human; rather, the peculiar form of embodiment that the segmented cockroach represents becomes important for G. H., as though the two parts of the dying cockroach each corresponded to the two initials by which she identifies herself. Before suggesting how this indirect form of identification tells us something important about the vermin vernacular, it is important to analyze the first form of displacement since it represents the narrative's *fabula* (or story) rather than its *syuzhet* (or plot), two aspects of the narrative structure that constitute the formal correlatives of the two parts of the cockroach that stand in for the protagonist's two initials.

The story is told retrospectively one day after the events being narrated have taken place. The narrator explicitly tells us that the story is about loss: "I become scared when I realize that over a period of hours I lost my human constitution" (Lispector 1988, 6). This loss is of a nature such that the narrator doesn't know what "form to give to what happened to me" (6), as though the story (*fabula*) could have no plot (*syuzhet*). In reflecting upon the function of form, she considers whether her present form, which she experiences as "perdition and madness," will ever be "humanized life again" (6). But perhaps her humanized life was all too human: "Humanized life. I had humanized life too much" (6). But it soon becomes clear that to this sense of loss one must add other losses since the action occurs almost entirely in the empty maid's room of an elegant penthouse apartment in Rio de Janeiro where everything, including the narrator, exists "in quotation marks" (23). The protagonist, whom we know only by the initials embossed on her luggage, has fired her maid the previous day and has now come to clean what she expectantly thinks will be a messy room. Instead, she finds an impeccably clean room, a room that looks as if it were located in an "insane asylum from which all dangerous objects have been removed" (30), though she also refers to it as a "minaret" (32), an "empty stomach" (34), a "cubicle" whose "innards had dried and shriveled up" (35). She opens the door of the wardrobe, sticks her head in, and sees a cockroach slowly moving towards the light: "By its enormity and slowness, it must have been a very old cockroach" (39).

G.H., as it turns out, has a "primeval horror" of cockroaches that has motivated her to learn a lot about them, but which has also prevented her from ever having to "come face to face" with one (39). For G.H., cockroaches are both obsolete and still living, prehistoric beings that have survived unchanged for millions of years. They are hateful, in part, because they are "miniature versions of a huge animal" (41). Apprehensive about the insect's movements inside the wardrobe, G.H. asks: "what is the only sense a cockroach has? attentiveness to living, inseparable from its body" (43). Only armed with this rather Heideggerian view of animal existence, G.H. is ill equipped to deal with the fact that the cockroach is beginning to come out of the wardrobe:

Antes o tremor anunciante das antenas.
Depois, atrás dos fios secos, o corpo relutante foi aparecendo.
Até chegar quase toda á tona da abertura do armário.
Era parda, era hesitante como se se fosse enorme de peso. Estava agora quase toda visível.

(Lispector 1964, 35)

[First the annunciatory flutter of the antennae.
Then, behind those dry threads, the reluctant body started to appear. Until almost the whole thing was right at the opening of the wardrobe door.
It was grayish, it was hesitant, as though it carried enormous weight. It was now almost completely visible.]

(Lispector 1988, 44)

The paratactic quality of the passage corresponds, or at any rate makes patent, the segmentation of the cockroach's body, which, like the fragmentary structure of the text as a whole, serves to illustrate the protagonist's disfiguration. She slams the door on the cockroach and, feeling that she has done something to herself, observes that the insect's front half is sticking out of the door and that it is still alive. Thinking that the cockroach is only stuck in the door, she decides to apply more pressure on the wardrobe's door so as to crush it but suddenly realizes that the cockroach is staring at her with its "shapeless face" (47). Even though she has never been "face-to-face" with a cockroach before, she has an inkling of its symbolism, or at least of its literary lineage: "It was a cockroach as old as a salamanders, and chimeras, and griffins, and leviathans. It was as ancient as a legend" (47). The face suggests to her the face of a "dying mulatto woman" (48). Its eyes in fact look like cockroaches: "Two cockroaches mounted on the cockroach, and each eye reproduced the entire animal" (48). The *doublement* or doubling up of this meta-cockroach is of course reproduced in the text, both in the story's spatial distribution, through the carceral spaces of the closet within the maid's room within the apartment and all within quotation marks, as well as in its temporal structure since the "ancient" legend of the cockroach is both yesterday's story and today's plot.

Yet, this form of figural displacement does yet correspond to a transformation of humanized life. The process begins when the cockroach itself begins to change: the "pulp started slowly to come out of the cockroach I had smashed, like out of a tube" (54). It is the disfiguration of the cockroach itself—the fact that it is literally losing its shape—that prompts the protagonist's reflection about her own identity, neatly captured in the image of a tube being squeezed. The image is repeated, as though the pulp still oozed: "The cockroach's pulp, which was its insides, raw matter that was whitish and thick and slow, was piling up on it as though it were toothpaste coming out of the tube" (54). The protagonist undergoes a transformation that she likens to having her life squeezed out of her as though she, like the cockroach, were a tube of toothpaste. But her identification with the cockroach exceeds the one-to-one correspondence we might expect in an allegory. This excess of signification is expressed not solely as a confusion of reference and referent; it is also brought about by the introduction of extra-allegorical elements whose relation to either the cockroach or the protagonist is hardly straightforward. Consider this passage:

> Eu corpo neutro de barata, eu com uma vida que finalmente não me escapa pois enfim a vejo fora de mim – eu sou a barata, sou minha perna, sou meus cabelos, sou o trecho de luz mais branca no rebôco de parede – sou cada pedaço infernal de mim – a vida em mim é tão insistente que se me partirem, como a uma lagartixa, os pedaços continuarão estremecendo e se mexendo.
>
> (Lispector 1964, 65)

> [I, neutral cockroach body, I with a life that at last is not eluding me because I finally see it outside myself – I am the cockroach, I am my leg, I am my hair, I am the section of brightest light on the wall plaster – I am every Hellish piece of myself – life is so pervasive in me that if they divide me in pieces like a lizard, the pieces will keep on shaking and writhing.]
>
> (Lispector 1988, 57)

In this passage, the protagonist explicitly embodies the cockroach. But this form of personification is unstable, and she soon personifies different entities in a proliferating series of identifications that is never anchored in a given term, as would be the case in anthropomorphism, in which the human is always a given. The "I" is coupled to multiple predicates—"my leg," "my hair," "the section of brightest light on the wall plaster," etc.—but none of these amounts to a new identity. It is only in the form of metaphor (she is like a lizard) that she can express her own disfiguration as a form of dismemberment.

In the end, this figural play proves to be inadequate, and the protagonist realizes that in order to know what it is like to be a cockroach, she has to ingest it:

I knew that I would really have to eat the cockroach mass, and all of me eat it, even my very fear eat it. Only then would I have what suddenly seemed to me to be the anti-sin: to eat the cockroach mass is the anti-sin, sin that would kill myself.

(157)

It is tempting to read this passage as a religious allegory in which the ingestion of the body of the cockroach constitutes a profession of faith: the implied transubstantiation transports the protagonist to a form of "passion" that is both passive and impersonal. The text's religious imagery seems to justify such a reading, but the allegorical relays that would make this reading plausible reach a limit in the materiality of the act of eating a dead or dying cockroach. The text does not actually describe the act of eating, nor, for that matter, does the protagonist herself. It is an act that has transpired but about which nothing can be reported. It is an empty space that cannot be filled, not even by the retrospective narrative. We can understand this moment as a "secret" if we understand the secret as that unfathomable otherness that cannot be accessed, not even by language.

Fôra mais uma vertigem, pois que eu continuava de pé, apoiando a mão no guarda-roupa. Uma vertigem que me fizera perder conta dos momentos e do tempo. Mas eu sabia, antes mesmo de pensar, que, enquanto me ausentara na vertigem, "alguma coisa se tinha feito."

(Lispector 1964, 167)

[It had been more like a dizzy spell, for I was still on my feet, my hand propped against the wardrobe. A dizzy spell that had made me lose track of the moments, of time. But I knew, even before thinking, that, while I had been gone in the dizzy spell, "something had happened."]

(Lispector 1988, 159)

The enigmatic "something had happened" is as close as G.H. can come to articulating her passion, the quotation marks that surround the phrase signaling—if not quite encasing, like the cockroach's exoskeleton, its "pulp"—a secret that brings about her transformation. That this transformation is material, rather than spiritual, as the language she uses to come to terms with it would suggest, becomes clear when the act of eating a cockroach is disengaged from its figural trappings, and the allegory ceases to coincide with its referential structures, evacuating in the process any religious determinations that would reinscribe it as a passion. The materiality of the "pulp" constitutes a linguistic event whereby the initials "G" and "H" are transformed into marks that identify the protagonist as a living being. Put differently, this means that the sort of transformation we have come to expect in human–animal metamorphoses, from Ovid to Kafka, is here itself transformed into a linguistic act, making visible the rhetorical alchemy that allows us to imagine what it would be like to be an animal. When the animal whose life we aim to imagine is a vermin instead of, say, a jackal, the anthropomorphism against whose pressure we push in an effort to "embody" the animal in its own terms reasserts itself as a rhetorical operation that is categorically linguistic. Sometimes, the vermin text is literally a vermin text.

## The rat pack

Rats have a bad rap: this is both justifiable (they are the principal carriers of diseases that have literally plagued humanity for centuries) and ironic (they have evolved among humans and thrived on our garbage, and can thus be said to reflect the condition of human communities). Fear and loathing thus characterize our relation to rats in equal measure. It is therefore not surprising that literature avoids them like, well, the plague. In Albert Camus's 1947 novel, *La Peste* [*The Plague*], rats are portrayed as both the carriers of disease (the population of the Algerian city of Oran is decimated by an outbreak of the bubonic plague), and, in the text's allegorical circuits, as the figurative vehicles for exposing the social contagion of fascism. The rats in Camus's novel, however, do not for all that bear any of the formal marks we tend to associate with literary characters; they are neither audible nor visible, other than as corpses. They are hidden in the text, perhaps like the narrator, Dr. Rieux, who makes himself known as the narrator of this "chronicle" only at the end of the novel. To the extent that the rats that begin to appear in Oran, first in small numbers and then in veritably epidemic proportions, are dead or dying, it is death that makes visible what was once hidden. Yet, after they are collected and burned—thereby spreading the disease to humans—the rats cease to have any role in the text, which directs its attention to a group of humans who may or may not act "like" rats, but who nevertheless contribute to eradicating the disease transmitted by the rats. The rats infect the text, but like the disease they transmit, they only count once they are eliminated.

Very few texts have granted rats anything resembling subjectivity. Robert Browning's poem "The Pied Piper of Hamelin" aptly captures the abject character of our representations of rats:

10   Rats!
     They fought the dogs, and killed the cats,
     And bit the babies in the cradles,
     And ate the cheeses out of the vats,
     And licked the soup from the cook's own ladles,
15   Split open the kegs of salted sprats,
     Made nests inside men's Sunday hats,
     And even spoiled the women's chats,
     By drowning their speaking
     With shrieking and squeaking
20   In fifty different sharps and flats.

This is the second of the poem's fifteen parts and the only one to describe them directly, if by "directly" is understood a mode of description that in recounting the acts they perform (biting, eating, licking, spoiling, drowning, shrieking, etc.) in fact avoids noting their size, their shape, their appearance; that is, it avoids representing them as rats. The fact that all the rats' actions are enumerated in the past tense, moreover, suggests that the rats are themselves elusive, or at least no longer present. The representational avoidance in the poem is further expressed in the way the stanza's first line, "Rats!," seems to get lost in the semantic alternatives that appear in the repetitive, and well nigh elementary, rhyming scheme: cats, vats, hats, chats, flats, as if the representation of rats could only be stomached by means of euphemism. The absence of rats in Browning's poem is of course consonant with the poem's narrative, which tells the story, familiar to every schoolchild, of a musical rat exterminator who rids the town of Hamelin of its rats, and, at least momentarily, of its children as well, since their abduction becomes the only means at the piper's disposal for obtaining compensation for services rendered. But the absence of rats in Browning's poem, like the town council's reluctance to pay the pied piper, is also in keeping with culture's aversion to rats. Even acknowledging their presence constitutes an affront to human sensibilities.

Sociobiologists will sensibly argue that our disgust for rats, and hence our reluctance to grant them representational space, is justified on evolutionary grounds. We have the Black Plague to remind us that our own survival depends on avoiding rats, even if medical science, such as it was in fourteenth-century Europe, could not account for the fact that the zoonotic pathogen responsible for the plague is carried by fleas that are in turn borne by rats. Whatever medical reasons exist for avoiding rats, there are certainly plenty of other reasons for trying to steer clear of them, not the least of which is that they tend to live among that which we have already tried to avoid, namely our garbage. As Mary Douglas has shown in *Purity and Danger*, many of our taboos follow a differential logic whereby "ideas about separating, purifying, demarcating, and punishing transgressions have as their main function to impose system on an inherently untidy experience" (2002, 4). In order to establish a semblance of order, differences need to be exaggerated and hierarchies created so as to maintain them. From this perspective, the human avoidance of rats responds not only to putative evolutionary pressures, but also to political exigencies whose logic cannot be reduced to the propagation of genetic advantages. I hope it is not controversial to note in this context that our political activity often works against our own best interests, ideologies of selfishness notwithstanding.

Rats, in this reading, are thoroughly socialized rodents, not only in the sense that they live in highly organized colonies, but also in that these colonies are directly implicated in human communities on which they depend. It is perhaps only in Disney, with the emblematic rodent Mickey Mouse as its big cheese, that a rat can become fully integrated into the human community. The story of Remy, the cooking rat in *Ratatouille* (2007), is a story of assimilation in which our abhorrence of rats is portrayed as social prejudice. Remy's supremely sensitive sense of smell separates him from his siblings, who seek satisfaction in scraps rather than seasoning. Remy defies all odds by becoming a great chef, and, in the process, integrating his extended family into human society. Human society, in turn, must overcome its own prejudices (hyperbolically though neatly captured in the name of the food critic, Anton Ego), and come to accept that rats can not only handle food but also manipulate it (rats' paws are oddly human-like) into delicious dishes. Remy is a foodie not only because he is French (despite his irrepressibly American hipster accent), but also because his taste in food is a supplement to his ratness.

Rats' hunger is manifested in a very different register in David Mann's film *Willard* (1972), which is perhaps more famous for having been described by Gilles Deleuze and Félix Guattari in their essay "Becoming-Intense, Becoming-Animal, Becoming-Imperceptible…" than for its rather limited commercial and critical success. The story, as recounted by Deleuze and Guattari, centers on the relation between Willard, an office worker who lives with his mother, and Ben, a rat he has saved from his mother's destructive impulses. Willard's mother dies, and he is left alone with Ben and his growing rat pack. He is in danger of losing his house so he takes Ben and the rat pack to the home of the greedy businessman who covets it. The rats kill him. One day, Willard inadvisably takes Ben and Ben's companion to his office, where he is forced by his coworkers to kill his companion. Naturally, Ben is not happy. Willard then enters into a romantic relationship with a coworker, who happens to look like a rat. When Willard decides to take her home, Ben sees an opportunity for revenge, but instead of attacking Willard's companion to even the score, Ben lures Willard into the basement, where he is summarily killed by the rat pack.

Deleuze and Guattari gloss this film as an illustration of the "becoming-rat" of Willard, who, hard as he has tried to remain attached to human community, must be absorbed willy-nilly into the pack (1987, 233). The rat pack undermines the values of family, conjugal love, and career by constituting an assemblage that "deterritorializes" Willard from the signifying projects that would otherwise condemn him to relive in the context of the office romance the unresolvable Oedipal drama of his childhood. In this scenario, the rat pack is a political force because it disrupts the logic of resemblance by virtue of which capitalist society protects and preserves its relations of production. Rats are apt conceptual vehicles for the purpose of dismantling the existing order, not least because they have been categorically excluded from human signifying systems; they are always already deterritorialized, to put it in somewhat clumsy but accurate terms.

As these examples illustrate, rats are paradoxical creatures: at once excluded from human forms of representation (that is, inaudible within the distribution of the perceptible, to use Rancière's formulation), and yet persistently invoked as figures of marginalization. Although rats are just as socialized as dogs and cats—they live within human communities rather than in the wild—rats, unlike dogs and cats, do not count for humans, except as reminders of what it is like to *not* count. In this sense, rats can be said to occupy the very border that separates the perceptible from the imperceptible, which is the same as saying that they are thoroughly political creatures. This paradox provides the backdrop for Günter Grass's postmodern novel *Die Rättin* [*The Rat*] (1987).

In Grass's novel, rats have taken over a post-apocalyptic, post-human world. The She-rat of the title is first introduced in the form of a Christmas gift, the somewhat eccentric wish of the novel's protagonist, a writer, much like Grass himself, who wants a rat as the inspiration for a poem he is writing on the "education of the human race" (Grass 1987, 1). The rat soon begins to haunt the narrator in his dreams and fantasies and, indeed, to take over the narration. Her stories—"No end to what the She-rat knows!" (4)—provide a natural as well as a literary history of rats on earth, but they are also meant to account for their future survival. Ever since they were rejected by Noah when he was loading the Ark, rats have been unfairly marginalized: "Already the prejudice had taken root. Hatred from the start, and the urge to eradicate what gives people that retching sensation" (4). Having survived the Flood by building tunnels whose openings were plugged with decomposing animals, the rats became humankind's indestructible companions, living off the garbage humans have always produced. Unlike the rats in George Orwell's *1984*, which produce abject terror in Winston, the rats in Grass's novel, whose action symbolically takes place in 1984, are sympathetically if unsentimentally portrayed.

In the novel, the tenacity of rats is expressed in the manner in which the She-rat seems to burrow under the novel's many narrative strands, competing with the poet protagonist for narrative authority, and impinging on the human voices that bear witness to the dehumanization of the world. One of the literary devices Grass employs to create a sense of disorientation is irony, here understood as a disruptive force that interrupts the illusion of narrative continuity and aesthetic totality that gives shape to our view of life as an organic whole. The figure of the She-rat—"Rättin" is a neologism in German—neatly captures the text's ironic stance in the awkwardness of its referent. Grass himself is not immune to the She-rat's ironic interventions, of course, and, Oskar Matzerath, the perpetually young drummer in Grass's 1959 novel *The Tin Drum*, enters the novel as a 60-year-old film producer with prostate problems who is traveling to Poland to celebrate his grandmother Koljaiczek's 107th birthday. The brothers Grimm, now state functionaries in charge of preventing deforestation, mingle with the characters with whom they peopled their fairy tale forests to make a film about the destruction of the environment, creating in the process a surreal proliferation of referential relays that renders the distinction between fact and fiction virtually inoperable. "'All power to the fairy tales,'" the text declares, the double quotation marks suggesting the potentially abyssal fate of all figurative constructs, as though each meaning had a mirror image that was in turn reflected in another mirror (255). Another tale, this time the story of the pied piper of Hamelin, appears as part of the forged frescoes painted by Lothar Malskat, a character whose real-life referent deliberately added anachronisms to a series of frescoes in Lübeck Cathedral which he was ostensibly restoring. But perhaps the story most effectively skewered by the persistent burrowing of Grass's ironic She-rat is the story of the Apocalypse itself, which in this disorienting text can no longer simply be dismissed as a fiction.

The deliberate confusion the text creates between fact and fiction, fairy tale and reality, representation and simulacrum becomes one of the narrative's explicit thematic pursuits since the narrator and the

She-rat are figured as truth-tellers who are not shy about telling lies if this will serve to expose other lies. This form of negative knowledge, perhaps best understood in a Nietzschean "extra moral sense" (though now surely also understood in the more problematic context of the author's own surprising revelations concerning the fact that he joined the Waffen-SS during World War II), informs the narrative's accusatory tone and fuels its incendiary indictments. "Again the She-rat laughed in her own way... but then stored-up bitterness restored her gravity. The rats and the Jews, the Jews and the rats are to blame" (99). The She-rat's abrupt shift from laughter to gravity captures the novel's impatience with deep-seated prejudices and complacent political attitudes. The chiasmic relation between rats and Jews in this quotation is significant in this regard since it does not describe a relation of identity, as in anti-Semitic discourse, but one of interchangeable association. The rhetorical coupling of Jews and rats is monstrously offensive when it follows the logic of substitution, as in metaphor or epithet; the chiasmus, in contrast, proposes something closer to empathy in that it places each of its terms in the other term's position. But this empathic association, of course, only makes sense provided we look favorably upon rats, which, as the novel amply suggests, is hardly a given. We might begin to do so, however, if we regard rats as the animals they are and not as the symbols they have become. Tropes expose other tropes just like lies expose other lies. Indeed, Grass's entire oeuvre might be understood as just such an attempt because many of his books, such as *The Flounder* (1977), *Dog Years* (1963), *Cat and Mouse* (1961), and *From the Diary of a Snail* (1972), feature animals whose voices he seeks to make audible. In an interview in the *Paris Review*, Grass was asked if there was a special reason for focusing on animals. Grass replied: "This world is crowded with humans, but also with animals, birds, fish, and insects. They were here before we were and they will be here should the day come when there are no more human beings."[3]

The rats try to warn humans of their impending doom by staging a protest but, like the rats of Hamelin, the humans in the novel seem to be heading towards their inexorable doom as though following in bewildered awe the command of a higher power. The rats survive the nuclear holocaust by digging themselves into the earth. Digging is the evolutionary advantage that has allowed them to survive not only the Flood, but also the mass extinction of the dinosaurs, which they weathered by digging themselves into their eggs. Rats come to miss humans after humans have managed to annihilate themselves, an event the novel refers to as "The Big Bang." They miss human garbage, to be sure, but they also miss humans' ideas.

When the earth has once again begun to thrive now that humans can no longer pollute it, the rats begin to develop suspiciously human-like notions such as religion, yet, "doomed to walk in the footsteps of man" (Grass 1987, 329), they begin to act on these notions. Hominoid rat hybrids called "Watsoncricks" (after James Watson and Francis Crick, the scientists who uncovered the molecular structure of DNA) begin to appear and the rats, in order to preserve intact the image of humans that they still harbor, must destroy them. "By saying yes to the rat component in us, we are becoming truly human. And because we are aware of our human component, the rat component has become essential to us" (329). In the end, the rats' survival suggests that the strange chiasmic inversions of rat and human that occur in the post-Apocalyptic world—a rhetorical strategy similar to the one that associates Jews and rats in the quotation above—offers hope for our present survival as animals among other animals. Rat politics in Grass's work is a politics of attrition that makes visible humans' suicidal attitude toward the natural world.

Grass offers a sobering lesson in animal sympathy but does not for all that solve the paradoxical political status of rats, since in making an argument about their surprising resilience he is also suggesting that this is precisely surprising to the extent that they do not really count for us. But the paradoxical status of rats can never be satisfactorily solved since their presence is also discursive, performing a defining structural role that characterizes modern politics. Michel Foucault argues that the new model of political organization based on discipline that came into being at the end of the eighteenth century was founded on a medical principle. Whereas townships had been able to control diseases such as leprosy by means of exclusion, the plague required an entirely different political dispensation. The plague, as Foucault describes it, "gave rise to disciplinary diagrams" that called for the strict spatial partitioning, careful surveillance, and detailed inspection that came to characterize "disciplined society" (1975, 231). To say that rats are behind the development of Panopticism, Foucault's term for the institutionalized process of subjectivation under surveillance, is of course excessive. But, like all conspiracy theories, it reveals in its attempt to place blame on a single agent or agency the sort of paranoia that would in fact require surveillance. For rats make evident one of the aspects of discipline that remain unaccounted for in Foucault's formulation: that it makes a strict division between humans and animals. Animals, it follows, must occupy the place of lepers in this historical scheme, which explains why rats must be categorically excluded from surveillance if the mechanisms that have been put in place to eliminate them are to bear fruit within the human community. Extermination, like the figure of the Pied Piper reminds us, is the only option available to the logic of discipline. The persistence of rats in human communities, however, suggests that they might play a different political function. It is to another Foucauldian political model, the model of biopolitics, that we must now turn to better understand the role of animals in the political world of humans.

## Jungle fever

H. G. Wells's *The Island of Doctor Moreau* (1896) has often been read in the context of the anti-vivisectionist movement, one of the most important animal rights campaigns in nineteenth-century Britain. The movement's most eloquent champion, Frances Power Cobbe, founded the Victoria Street Society in 1875, an organization that is still in operation today under the rather more descriptive name of NAVS, the National Anti-Vivisectionist Society, on the principle that animal vivisection had to be abolished. Through the publication of pamphlets that vividly exposed the pain and suffering to which animals were subjected during surgical procedures that required them to remain conscious, the anti-vivisectionist movement was largely responsible for the successful passage of the 1876 Cruelty to Animals Act. The act restricted, but did not ban, the use of animals in scientific experiments. According to the Act—which interestingly only covers "living vertebrate animals"—the physical suffering endured by the animal should be minimal and is justified only if it serves a purpose in the pursuit of "physiological knowledge" or the "alleviation of suffering" (39 and 40 Vict., Public Acts, c. 77).

To read Wells's novel in the context of the history of the anti-vivisectionist movement is both justified and understandable since it offers a chilling portrait of a vivisectionist. But Wells's portrayal of Dr. Moreau is more complicated, not least because Wells himself was a cautious supporter of animal experimentation throughout his life. Having been trained by T. H. Huxley, Wells remained committed to the narrative of scientific progress biologists advanced as they promoted Darwin's theory of evolution. Indeed, in a 1927 article, Wells criticized the anti-vivisectionist movement, which he stereotypically though not inaccurately characterized as a movement composed of women pet-lovers, by arguing that the pets of "careless women" are themselves "products of a ruthlessly dysgenic breeding industry which sacrifices vigour and vitality to minuteness, quaintness, and delicious ugliness" (Wells 1896 [2009], 245). In addition, Well's novel is arguably about the limits of scientific experimentation and the unsavory extremes to which practices such as vivisection can be carried out by unscrupulous and crazed megalomaniacs, rather than about the more narrowly construed question of the morality of vivisection. Wells's Dr. Moreau belongs to that small cadre of "mad scientists" who operate at the margins of the modern literary canon and include such minatory figures as Mary Shelley's Frankenstein, Hawthorne's Rapaccini, Stevenson's Dr. Jekyll, Fritz Lang's Rotwang, and Kubrick's Dr. Strangelove. Furthermore, to the extent that Dr. Moreau, unlike all these other mad scientists, experiments with animals suggests that the anti-vivisection movement serves more as the occasion for the narrative that unfolds on a remote island than as the focus of the text's advocacy or political commitments.

Wells's novel, I would like to suggest, can be more profitably read as a biopolitical tale in which the border separating human from animal is blurred and then retraced, as though by means of a humanizing form of surgery, on the body politic. Animal experimentation is of great interest in the context of biopolitics because it forms part of a wholesale effort to medicalize life and thereby regulate it on the order of species living and at the scale of population. The figure of the mad scientist becomes important in this context since the aberration of the mad scientist's practice highlights nothing so much as normative medical categories by virtue of violating them. Vivisection is premised on the idea that human physiology can indeed be studied by proxy using live animals, as though at the level of physiology the distinction between human and non-human animals were, at least momentarily, or theoretically, suspended. Vivisection, in other words, represents a state of exception in which "bare life," to use Giorgio Agamben's term, is killed only the better to regulate it outside the anatomical theater.

Wells's novel is a political fantasy that takes place on an unnamed island in the Pacific where Dr. Moreau, a once famed London physiologist whose career was wrecked by a pamphlet that made public his vivisectionist practices, conducts surgical experiments on animals with the aim of shaping them into humans. The novel formalizes the re-inscription of the human/animal divide as a moving border existing within the human. Insofar as Moreau's experiments are premised on what he calls the "plasticity of living forms," the novel subscribes to the notion that species life is itself fluid, and individual species mere formalizations of a "bare life" that can be rendered bare by what Moreau calls the "bath of burning pain." The power wielded by Moreau on his island, moreover, is quite literally a form of biopower since it operates in excess of any sovereign right he might have arrogated to himself, and takes life as both its object and as its objective. Pain is both the means by which Moreau produces new life forms and the instrument of sovereign power on his island.

The narrator, Prendick, who has arrived on the island after being shipwrecked, assumes upon meeting the Beast People that they are the abominable result of experiments conducted on humans. Since the Beast People can speak English but are not fully aware of their status, Moreau feels compelled to use Latin to set Pendrick straight: "He coughed, thought, then shouted: 'Latin, Prendick! Bad Latin! Schoolboy Latin! But try to understand, *Hi non sunt homines, sunt animalia qui nos habemus* ... vivisected. A humanizing process. I will explain. Come ashore" (Moreau 1896 [2005], 67). Moreau has learned to shape individuals belonging to a wide range of species into humans by surgical procedure, but the process he has been trying to perfect on the island can in theory be used to shape any living form whatsoever, including monstrous beings and entirely new hybrid species:

> I might just as well have worked to form sheep into llamas, and llamas into sheep. I suppose there is something in the human form that appeals to the artistic turn of mind more powerfully than any animal shape can. But I've not confined myself to man-making. Once or twice...
>
> (73)

Despite the success he has achieved in "man-making," however, Moreau's experiments seem to have reached a limit beyond which he cannot proceed. This limit is a zone of indistinction in which the various attributes that have traditionally been used to mark the human/animal divide (hands, rationality, emotions) prove to be the stubborn reminders of species-specific differences that cannot be homogenized through surgery.

> The human shape I can get now almost with ease, so that it is lithe and graceful, or thick and strong, but often there is trouble with the hands and claws – painful things that I dare not shape too freely. But it is in the subtle grafting and reshaping that one must needs do to the brain that my trouble lies. The intelligence is often oddly low, with unaccountable blank ends, unexpected gaps. And least satisfactory of all is something that I cannot touch, somewhere – I cannot determine where – in the seat of the emotions. Cravings, instincts, desires that harm humanity, a strange hidden reservoir to burst suddenly and inundate the whole being of the creature with anger, hate, or fear.
>
> (78)

The Beast People tend to revert back to their animal origins as though the "inside animal" within the animal remained beyond the reach of Moreau's scalpel. Moreau poses the problem of reversion as a scientific problem, but the implications are thoroughly political since it is the population of Beast People on the island (numbering in the hundreds now) that has to be controlled. The mechanisms of political control Moreau has put into place through the ritualized iteration of a series of laws and prohibitions ("Not to go on all-Fours," "Not to eat Flesh or Fish," "Not to Claw bark of trees," etc.) are disciplinary in nature, designed to train the Beast People into adopting a self-regulative regime that could in theory lead to subjectivation, and in which the possibility of punishment is always present.

Moreau is killed in the end by one of his own creations in a violent reaffirmation of wild animality. The biological seems to trump the social; the biopolitical the disciplinary; the population the individual. Moreau's experiments make visible that life is everywhere subject to a degree of manipulation in part due to its biological "plasticity," much in the way in which the body in a state of exception can be made to bear the traces of its political exclusions. In the event of death, in the non-sacrificial putting-to-death of the outcast, of the figure Agamben calls the *homo sacer*, we reach the threshold of the body's death but, in being final and unpredictable, death also becomes the grounds for a form of political rationalization that counts on life. The political dimension of Moreau's experiments become clear when Prendick returns to civilization and notices that everyone forms part of a sort of Beast People:

> My trouble took the strangest form. I could not persuade myself that the men and women I met were not also another, still passably human, Beast People, animals half-wrought into the outward image of human souls; and that they would presently begin to revert, to show first this bestial mark and then that.

(116)

But what Prendick describes is a much more troubling specter that the novel does its best to suppress, and that is racism. Foucault asks: "How can the power of death, the function of death, be exercised in a political system centered on biopower?" For Foucault, the answer is racism: biopower inscribes racism as the basic mechanism of power. Racism is a means of introducing a break into the domain of life that is under power's control: the break between what must live and what must die. Within the biological continuum appears the human race of races, the distinction among races, the hierarchy of races: it all fragments the field of the biological. It creates a biological-type caesura within a population, which henceforth appears to be a biological domain. This allows power to treat a population as a mixture of races, or, more precisely, to treat the species, to subdivide the species it controls, into the subspecies known, inaccurately, as races. Under biopower, racism is the precondition for exercising the right to kill.

Wells's novel fits into a pattern of social evolutionism that, at the end of the nineteenth century, became a set of notions (hierarchy, struggle, selection) that allowed, more that an allegoreme, a "real way of thinking" about the relations between colonization, the necessity for wars, criminality, the phenomenon of madness, mental illness, the history of society's classes, and so on. Racism, in this context, becomes the mechanism whereby biopower is set to work on the population, not (or not only) as a top-down governmental policy, but rather as a discourse that justifies all sorts of national projects since it first develops with colonialism (with colonizing genocide) and continues in the conduct of war. Racism, according to Foucault:

> justifies the death-function in the economy of biopower by appealing to the principle that the death of others makes one biologically stronger insofar as one is a member of a race or a population, insofar as one is an element in a unitary living plurality.
> (1975, 258)

Rudyard Kipling's *Jungle Books* can be situated within the biopolitical framework of colonialism. As is well known, Kipling's Mowgli stories present a natural or naturalized environment in which animals appear as though they were acting as animals for a human audience of one. Like menageries and the circus, Kipling's naturalized representation of a "wild" social community blurs the human–animal distinction by creating social relations among different species within an anthropocentric worldview. To be sure, as a wild child, Mowgli belongs to a longstanding tradition that extends from classical antiquity to Rousseau, but he is also presented as a hybrid species, a man-cub raised by wolves and trained in animal behavior by a bear, a panther, and a snake.

Mowgli's hybridity can be usefully contextualized within the history of zoological classification, which, as Harriet Ritvo notes, marks the distance separating different human groups. In nineteenth-century iconography, for instance, the Irish were routinely made to bear an unflattering resemblance to the great apes, an all too common representational strategy of racist ideology. More generally, however, the fascination with hybrids and cross-breeding among the Victorians, even though often proven to be hoaxes, unsettled the ostensible species barrier that separated humans and animals. In the Victorian imaginary, the connection between humans and our non-human "cousins" (Ritvo's term) could occasion a wide variety of hybrids, many of which were the product of suggestion, representation, or resemblance. For Ritvo, these connections show that "similarity remains as firmly embedded in contemporary culture as does the scientific and theological assertion of difference" (2004, 66).

The process of instruction whereby Mowgli learns to act like an animal is not only what may be thought of as instinctual – though here the distinction becomes harder to make. In addition to having to learn to satisfy basic biological needs, he also needs to be socialized into what the stories call "The Law of the Jungle." This law constitutes a code, part moral, part political, that is used to guarantee the survival and peaceful coexistence of different privileged species in a circumscribed territory simply referred to as "the jungle" that has remained for the most part untouched by humans, as though its borders coincided with the human/animal divide itself. Mowgli, of course, has crossed the border, but so has Bagheera, the black panther, who was born in human captivity and therefore knows the ways of men. Mowgli is an adept pupil—language is, of course, never a problem—but Baloo, the bear who teaches the Law of the Jungle to the wolf pack as a whole, realizes that Mowgli, as a man-cub, must learn a great deal more than the other cubs.

> The boy could climb almost as well as he could swim, and swim almost as well as he could run; so Baloo, the Teacher of the Law, taught him the Wood and Water Laws: how to tell a rotten branch from a sound one; how to speak politely to the wild bees when he came upon a hive of them fifty feet above ground; what to say to Mang the Bat when he disturbed him in the branches at mid-day; and how to warn the water-snakes in the pools before he splashed down among them.
>
> (Kipling 1998, 23)

Baloo is not shy about using corporal punishment to get his pupil to learn what he calls the "Master Words of the Jungle." His face, Bagheera notices one day, is bruised: "Better he should be bruised," replies Baloo, "from head to foot by me who loves him than that he should come to harm through ignorance" (25).

Mowgli's training involves making the body repeat, in the mechanical fashion of industrial time, a repertoire of actions premised on their reproducibility. Despite his docility, however, there is an unsocializable remainder, a human quality that escapes the Law of the Jungle and which leads to a series of misrecognitions that both blurs and, in blurring, reasserts an essential difference separating human from non-human. (Despite his great affection for Mowgli, for instance, Bagheera knows that he is incapable of looking him in the eye.) But the scene of misrecognition that makes most dramatically visible that zone of indistinction between humans and non-humans is the episode in which the Monkey People, the Bandar-log, abduct Mowgli and carry him through the tree tops to an abandoned human city that lies beyond the jungle's limits. The grey apes occupy a space that exists categorically outside the Law of the Jungle. The Monkey People, as Baloo puts it to Mowgli, who has been keen to play with them, are outcasts.

> They have no speech of their own, but use stolen words which they overhear when they listen, and peep, and wait up above in the branches. Their way is not our way. They are without leaders. They have no remembrance. They boast and chatter and pretend that they are a great people about to do great affairs in the jungle, but the falling of a nut turns their minds to laughter and all is forgotten.
>
> (26)

Monkeys are neither part of the jungle nor part of the human world; they occupy a border zone of indefinite animality that separates them from all other species, including humans since they may well be recognizable as human "cousins," to use Ritvo's term, but they are also categorically non-human. Indeed, the monkeys perform a kind of humanity to which they cannot in the end aspire, since they lack their own language, have no history, and are always seeking the attention of the other animal species. They are, in other words, imperfect humans whose sub-humanity makes them not only undesirable, but also dangerous because they follow no law and exist in great numbers.

To read the representation of multi-species animal collectives in Wells's and Kipling's novels as biopolitical allegories premised on the use of racist categories is to question the cultural logic whereby interspecies relations come to stand in for social relations among humans. Consider the DreamWorks Animation film *Madagascar* (2005). In the film, a sort of zoological road movie, four performing animals—a giraffe, a zebra, a lion, and a hippopotamus from New York's Central Park Zoo—reluctantly find themselves on a ship bound for Africa. A team of penguins from the same zoo highjack the ship in the middle of the ocean with the intent of steering it toward Antarctica, dropping overboard in the process the crates in which the four friends have been stowed. The crates wash ashore in Madagascar, where the four friends encounter a community of lemurs that live under the constant threat of the fossa that live on the other side of the island. The story is structured through a series of encounters between different sets of animals: the multispecies zoo set, the penguin set, the lemur set, the fossa set, and, somewhat on the margins, the human set. Its structure could be visualized as a Venn diagram in which the action takes place at the intersection of the different sets. The narrative problem is whether the heterogeneous zoo set can meaningfully intersect with the homogeneous sets. To the extent that the zoo set stands in for contemporary New York—the characterization of the four friends is premised on these facile stereotypes: the neurotic Jewish giraffe; the funny black zebra; the lion-as-king-of-Broadway; the motherly black hippo—the ability of its elements to interact with those of all the other sets rests on the idea of multiculturalism. Predictably, the narrative problem is never solved, or rather is solved in advance, since it soon becomes clear that the four friends, though in different degrees attracted to life in the wilderness, are not "wild" animals at all and must find a way to get back to civilization, under whose aegis the integrity of the sets will presumably be preserved. This is a discouraging resolution in that, if we read it allegorically, we end up with a parable of American exceptionalism through multicultural inclusiveness in a world of exclusionary sameness. But this resolution can only be understood in these terms if we take into account the rather obvious fact that animals are being used to stage this story since it is the very notion of difference, or of the difference of difference, that the film is structuring as biological fact. The zoo set is meant to represent all other sets, but only as long as it does not intersect with any other set.

But it is in the film's sequel where the biologization of political categories by means of animal representation becomes most evident. *Madagascar: Escape 2 Africa* (2008) continues the adventures of the four friends, this time as they "escape" from Madagascar "2" Africa on a plane piloted by the penguin team. In this sequel, the elements of the zoo set encounter other sets of which they could be elements, which is to say that the lion encounters a pride of lions, the zebra a crossing of zebras, the hippo a bloat of hippos, and the giraffe a tower of giraffes. This new situation alters the terms of comparison among the original sets and creates a new narrative problem: how is the heterogeneous zoo set to remain a set under the pressure exerted by the homogeneous sets to which each element belongs? Phrased in the film's own terms: is the bond that binds the four friends stronger than their nature as animals? One possible outcome is the dissolution of the heterogeneous zoo set: the very idea of the "zoo" no longer obtains since the four friends' return to their origins in Edenic Africa implies the end of the zoo's representational *raison d'être*. Conceptually, the zoo, like Noah's Ark, ought to include representative elements of all possible animal sets in order to become a unique set that is also the intersection of all sets. Another possible outcome is the expansion of the zoo set to include the totality of the multiplicities obtaining in each of the homogeneous sets, becoming in effect a union of animals (the "Animal Kingdom") as the individual elements return to their "wild" sets, but since the different animal species in the film actually live in a "natural preserve," the expansive narrative solution simply expands the zoo set. The failure of this solution becomes evident in a scene that might have once been described as an equine, but also Gidean, *mise-en-abyme* in which the zebra, having initially joined his crossing joyfully, finds that he has lost his sense of individuality in the pack, a situation which the other zebras in the set take literally by miming him so that even his friend the lion is now utterly unable to tell him apart from the other zebras. But the expansive solution fails for another reason: the union of all sets, now known as "Africa," is threatened from without by human poachers, and from within by human tourists such that the human–animal distinction is reinstalled in the union of all sets through narrative conflict.

The makers of the film find a narrative solution to the problem of preserving the integrity of the zoo set under the added pressure of the human set by making it a homogenous set. We already had an inkling of this predictable though for all that no less troubling outcome in the representation of the human set: the human set is conceptually a heterogeneous set since it consists of a multicultural touring group, but, to the extent that they enter into conflict with the "Africa" set, they function as a separate, and thus homogenous, set. Since both the zoo set and the human tourist set are both from New York, this process of homogenization can be understood culturally under the rubric of the "melting pot," even as the difference between animal characters and human characters remains representationally strict. But the filmmakers use another narrative vehicle to achieve the homogenization of the zoo set: the marriage plot. The giraffe and the hippo, as it turns out, have always loved each other and must now, naturally, get married.

At first blush, the marriage plot seems to offer an adequate narrative solution: there is something salutary about abstracting human social and racial differences so as to overcome prejudice and consolidate democracy, which, to the degree that it is based on equality, understands itself as a homogeneous social set. But, to the extent that the animal characters in the film are racially and ethnically marked—the hippo is anthropomorphically coded as a black woman; the giraffe as a Jewish man—the social differences that interracial marriage is meant to overcome are in fact re-encoded as biological sets whose elements can never intersect. Put differently: to represent racial identity in terms of species difference is to confuse cultural with biological categories. This category mistake, as these animal texts make evident, forms the very grounds upon which racial thought is constructed under biopower, which must now be understood to depend in its implementation on the use of animal figures, or, better, on the figure of the animal: the idea of race is only intelligible as a correlate of the animal–human divide.

## Some animals are more equal than others

No modern text combines more effectively the seductive logic of allegory with a political understanding of its ideological effects than George Orwell's *Animal Farm* (1945). The text has long been read as a thinly veiled allegory of the Stalinist purges and a trenchant satire of totalitarianism. It follows, in this regard, a long tradition of satirical writing in which animals are used to illustrate human folly. Book IV of Jonathan Swift's *Gulliver's Travels* (1726) immediately comes to mind when we think of this tradition, but it is Thomas Taylor's satirical, and indeed Swiftian, pamphlet *A Vindication of the Rights of Brutes* (1792) that is the closer predecessor to Orwell's text. Taylor makes an argument *ad absurdum* against Mary Wollstonecraft's *A Vindication of the Rights of Women* (1792) that if women have rights, then animals ought to have rights as well, from which we ought to infer that, since it is absurd for animals to have rights, then it is equally absurd to suggest that women could ever claim to have rights. The violent and eager sexism of this text does not prevent Peter Singer from citing it in his groundbreaking book *Animal Liberation* (1975) as an example of an argument whose own absurdity had become only too obvious in the context of the women's liberation movements of the 1960s and 1970s. For Singer, it is not a matter of asserting, against Taylor, that animals ought in fact to have the same rights as women, but rather of using it to show that the sexism that had once made plausible the sort of argument Taylor made is of a piece with the discriminatory attitudes toward animals that inform what he calls "speciesism."

Under the rubric of the first chapter's title, "All Animals are Equal," Singer makes an argument for extending the basic principle of equality to animals by taking the premises of Taylor's argument literally. If all men and women have equal rights, then animals ought to have them as well; indeed, all animals are equal. Singer's formula, as we shall see in more detail below, repeats the last of the Seven Commandments the animals living on Orwell's Animal Farm (previously known as Manor Farm) originally formulate as the principles of what they call Animalism, the revolutionary ideology that has driven them to topple the humans who exploit them. That the animal's seventh commandment, famously corrupted into the rather more Orwellian "All Animals are Equal but Some Are More Equal than Others" at book's end, became, through Singer's use of it, something like the rallying cry of the modern animal rights movement is in keeping with Singer's efforts to literalize our relation to animals, to make them more real. To be sure, this is a salutary development in the history of human–animal relations because we are always at risk of reifying our relation to animals by treating them literarily—that is, imaginatively as tropes—and thereby distancing ourselves from the plight of "real animals" (the other great rallying cry of the animal rights movement). But this is a risk we must take if we are to advance animal politics, understood in the context of the present argument as the counting of animals in a newly reconfigured distribution of the perceptible. Orwell helps us in this regard because, if nothing else, *Animal Farm* is a study in the allegorical imbrications of political discourse.

Orwell's novel stages the animal rebellion on a modest scale; that is, on an English farm. The animals correctly assert that the work they perform only benefits humans:

> Man is the only creature that consumes without producing. He does not give milk, he does not lay eggs, he is too weak to pull the plough, he cannot run fast enough to catch rabbits. Yet he is lord of all the animals.
>
> (Orwell 1945 [1996], 6)

Addressing them as "comrades," Old Major, the oldest pig in the farm, urges the farm's animals to rebel against the "tyranny of human beings" (7). The farmer who owns Manor Farm gives them an opportunity to do just that when, returning one day to the farm after a particularly lengthy drinking spree in town, he finds that his animals are up in arms about the fact that he has neglected to feed them. The animals attack him and run him off the farm, after which they solemnize the occasion by writing with almost perfect orthography the seven commandments of Animalism that will guide their conduct in the newfound community, which will henceforth be known as Animal Farm. It is perhaps superfluous to mention under this head that Orwell's seven commandments resemble the various laws that codify behavior among the Beast People in Wells's novel, and rule the conduct of animals in Kipling's jungle stories, but it is nonetheless worth remarking that this resemblance is itself indicative of the political character of the trope of the animal collective. Each according to its abilities, the animals organize themselves into committees (an Egg Production Committee is instituted for hens, for instance, and a Whiter Wool Movement for sheep) such that the division of labor often coincides with the natural relations of production that already operate on the farm.

The pigs, "generally recognized as being the cleverest of the animals" (14), do not perform physical labor, but, since they have taught themselves to read and write, become instead the self-proclaimed leaders of the farm. Led by three charismatic pigs named Napoleon, Snowball, and Squealer, the animals are initially very productive, with the work on the farm proceeding "like clockwork." Some of the animals begin to notice that the pigs get more than their fair share of the products of their collective labor, but it is the tensions that grow between Napoleon and Snowball, rather than the injustice of the unequal distribution of goods, that sows trouble on Animal Farm. Snowball is the more articulate of the two pigs but Napoleon the more ruthless and, after a series of open conflicts concerning the construction of a wind mill, Snowball is chased off the farm by the fierce dogs Napoleon has been secretly training as a means of asserting his power. Though now exiled, Snowball is still remembered as a hero of the Battle of the Cowshed, the confrontation that delivered the animals from human tyranny.

One need not try to match the three pigs with Stalin, Trotsky, and Lenin to understand that, once Napoleon is in total control of the farm, the commandments will undergo subtle qualification—"No animal shall sleep in a bed *with sheets*" (48); "No animal shall drink alcohol *to excess*" (75); etc.—nor to realize that the rules of conduct the pigs had originally devised in their idealist phase soon become meaningless. Employing appalling political tactics to appease his allies and intimidate his rivals, Napoleon prevails over all the other animals, his schemes progressing virtually unhindered until the political order he has established comes to resemble the old human order the animals had fought to overturn. At the end, Napoleon and the other pigs are indistinguishable from the humans against whom they once rebelled, taking it upon themselves to walk on two legs while trying to squeeze ever more profit from the farm. The new dispensation is neatly captured in the slogan that appears on the tarred wall on which the original seven commandments had once been painted: "all animals are equal, but some animals are more equal than others."

Told in this manner, the story of *Animal Farm* unsurprisingly reads like an allegory of totalitarianism, which it certainly is. It could be reduced to this: Stalinism installs a brutal political order in the name of equality, based on the confusion of social for natural categories.

Orwell's use of animal figures to illustrate Stalin's ruthless treatment of enemies, real and perceived, equates political violence with a certain form of animality. This Hobbesian equation is of course not new, but his use of the animal collective as a trope for society does introduce a set of variables to the equation that have wide-ranging implications for animal politics, which henceforth ought not be thought apart from politics as such. Consider the two versions of the Orwellian formula: the first version, "all animals are equal," is incontrovertible if we read it allegorically as a founding principle of animal rights. If we read it literally, as Singer does, there may be some disagreements as to how we ought to treat animals, but it speaks, in the spirit if not to the letter, of a broad consensus that animals ought to be treated humanely.

But if we read Orwell's first formula literally from the point of view of animals, the meaning is quite different since it is patently false that animals are equal, or indeed that they ought to be considered equal. In all fairness, Singer and other animal rights philosophers such as Tom Regan and Mary Midgley make distinctions about sentient and non-sentient animals, proximate and distant animals, distinctions that would suggest that not even they take the formula literally. To take it literally is to subscribe to the notion that there is no difference among animals, that the word "animal," as Jacques Derrida's strange term "animot" neatly captures, is a word that reduces difference to sameness. It is of course true that animal rights philosophers who advocate for animal equality refer to equality as a political principle rather than as a biological concept, but it is equally true, though in more urgent need to be asserted, that these two categories are not easy to disentangle, especially in the context of biopolitics.

No one would want to endorse Orwell's second formula, of course, but read literally, as in taking "some animals are more equal than others" to mean that there are in fact differences within the multiplicity of the living that is encompassed by the term "animals," the formula prompts us to reflect upon the fact of difference as a guiding principle in our relations to animals. Surely, cockroaches are as different from rats as humans are from frogs; it is just that we tend to group differences together when we invoke "equality" as a principle to guide our relation to animals. Should difference become our guiding principle in our relation to animals then Orwell's second slogan, "some animals are more equal than others," could be understood as a rallying cry for counting animals. The question of what the phrase "more equal" might mean when it is invoked would then be settled on the grounds of equal access to difference rather than on the exclusionary practices such invocations usually imply. If Orwell's tale can be construed as satirizing a certain reconfiguration of the perceptible in which pigs count more than other animals, it is also the case that it literalizes the fact of difference. Animal revolution may well be a utopian construct—and Orwell is, if nothing else, a formidable critic of utopian thinking—but it is not for all that an absurd notion when we reflect on the fate of animals in factory farms. I am invoking "real" animals here not to disqualify allegorical representations *tout court*, including Utopia; rather, I am drawing attention to the fact that even factory farms operate on the basis of a narrative structure that relies on the figurative representation of animals. When Noelle Vialles describes the way we refer to the killing, flaying, and butchering of animals in abattoirs as complex rhetorical operations involving the use of litotes, euphemism, and metaphor—she calls flaying a "patient metamorphosis"—she is drawing attention to the fact that allegorical practice subsumes the most fraught of our relations to animals. Orwell's use of animals to satirize political constructs, like Thomas Taylor's before him, has lost its polemical power not because he was wrong to condemn Stalinism but because he used animals to do so.

The two types of tropes I have examined in this chapter, the vermin and the animal collective, propose different ways of counting politically. Vermin are categorically excluded from society and thus come to justify discipline as a means of subjectification that would invent humans as the non-vermin. Animal collectives operate on biopolitical principles of division that entail using biological categories for political purposes. In both cases, the distinction between human and animal is preserved: in the first case it is strictly maintained as an inside/outside binary, while in the second it is incorporated as an internal feature of human biology. The literary texts I have read lend themselves to allegorical readings not only because animals can be used to illustrate political arrangements; they are allegorical because animals form the very foundations upon which politics is built. Politics is that form of organization whose purpose is to distinguish us from animals. We might yet learn to read allegory as a fundamentally political rhetorical figure through which our relation to animals is continually negotiated. We need literature to learn this impossible lesson.

## Notes

1 Two cockroach films worth mentioning in this context are *Joe's Apartment* (1996, dir. John Payson) and *Twilight of the Cockroaches* (1987, dir. Hiroaki Yoshida). Narrated from the perspective of the cockroaches, both films are premised on the idea that cockroaches are not given enough credit; that is, that they have no voice to make themselves count.
2 The stories I am referring to are: "A Report to an Academy" ["Ein Bericht für eine Akademie"] (1917), "Josephine the Singer, or the Mouse Folk" ["Josefine, die Sängerin oder Das Volk der Mäuse"] (1924), "The Burrow" ["Der Bau"] (1931), and "Investigations of a Dog" ["Forschungen eines Hundes"] (1922).

3 *Art of Fiction* No. 124. *The Paris Review*. Available at: www.theparisreview. org/interviews/2191/the-art-of-fiction-no-124-gunter-grass.

## Works cited

Agamben, Giorgio. *The Open: Man and Animal*, trans. Kevin Attell. Stanford: Stanford University Press, 2004.

Browning, Robert. *Robert Browning's Poetry*. New York: W. W. Norton, 2007.

Camus, Albert. *The Plague*, trans. Stuart Gilbert. New York: Vintage, 1991.

Deleuze, Gilles and Félix Guattari. *Kafka: Toward a Minor Literature*, trans. Dana Polan. Minneapolis: University of Minnesota Press, 1986.

Deleuze, Gilles and Félix Guattari. *A Thousand Plateaus*, trans. Brian Massumi. Minneapolis: University of Minnesota Press, 1987.

Douglas, Mary. *Purity and Danger*. London: Routledge, 2002.

Foucault, Michel. *Discipline and Punish*. New York: Vintage, 1975.

Grass, Günter. *The Rat*, trans. Ralph Manheim. New York: Harcourt, 1987.

Grass, Günter. *The Tin Drum*, trans. Ralph Manheim. New York: Vintage, 2005

Kafka, Franz. *The Metamorphosis*, trans. and ed. Stanley Corngold. New York: W. W. Norton, 1966.

Kellert, Stephen R. "Human–Animal Interactions: A Review of American Attitudes to Wild and Domestic Animals in the Twentieth Century." In *Animals and People Sharing the World*. Ed. Andrew N. Rowan. Hanover: UP of New England, 1988.

Kipling, Rudyard. *The Jungle Books*. Ed. W. W. Robson. Oxford World Classics. Oxford: Oxford University Press, 1998.

Lispector, Clarice. *A Paixão Segundo G. H.* Rio de Janeiro: Editôra do Autor, 1964.

Lispector, Clarice. *The Passion According to G.H,* trans. Ronald W. Sousa. Minneapolis: University of Minnesota Press, 1988.

Orwell, George. *Animal Farm*. New York: Harcourt Brace, 1996.

Orwell, George. *1984*. Modern Classics. London: Penguin, 2004.

Rancière, Jacques. "The Politics of Literature." In *The Politics of Literature*, trans. Julie Rose. Cambridge: Polity Press, 2011.

Ritvo, Harriet. *The Animal Estate: The English and Other Creatures in the Victorian Age*. Cambridge: Harvard University Press, 1987

Ritvo, Harriet. "Our Animal Cousins." *Differences: A Journal of Feminist Cultural Studies*, (15).1 (2004): 48–68.

Singer, Peter. *Animal Liberation*. New York: Ecco, 2001.

Stanton, Andrew. *Wall-E*. Disney, 2008.

Swift, Jonathan. *Gulliver's Travels*. Penguin Classics. London: Penguin, 2001.

Thomas, Keith. *Man and the Natural World*. Oxford: Oxford University Press, 1996.

Taylor, Thomas. *A Vindication of the Rights of Brutes*. London: Edward Jeffery, 1792.

Vialles, Noelle. *Animal to Edible*, trans. J. A. Underwood. Cambridge: Cambridge University Press, 1994.

Wells, H. G. *The Island of Dr. Moreau*. London: Penguin Classics, 2005.

Wells, H. G. *The Island of Dr. Moreau*. Toronto: Broadview Press, 2009.

Wollstonecraft, Mary. *A Vindication of the Rights of Women*. World's Classics. Oxford: Oxford University Press, 2009.

# Glossary

**"affabulation"**   Jacques Derrida's term for describing the fabulous or fictional quality of many of the narratives inscribed within political discourse to naturalize otherwise artificial and/or historical realities based on moral fables, most often those involving animals.

**allegory**   a narrative figurative construction often used for didactic purposes, whereby a story or character is made to represent an alternative story or character. Historically associated with the personification of abstract qualities (love, charity, pity, purity), though more recently thought to be the rhetorical matrix which sustains the theory of tropes.

**"animot"**   term coined by Jacques Derrida to draw attention to the fact that humans use a single word ("mot" in French) to describe animals ("animaux") as though the vast multiplicity of the living could be encompassed by a single word. [See Derrida, *The Animal that Therefore I Am*]

**Anthropocene**   term coined by atmospheric chemist Paul Crutzen to denote the current geological epoch in which humans have left an indelible environmental trace upon the planet.

**anthropocentrism**   the idea whereby humans (*anthropos*) see themselves as the center of explanation with regards to nature and the cosmos.

**anthropodenial**   according to primate ethologist Frans de Waal, the reluctance among scientists to learn about animals through anthropomorphism.

**anthropological machine**   term used by Giorgio Agamben to describe the discursive apparatus created by Western culture to create a categorical distinction between humans and animals. [See Agamben, *The Open*]

**anthropomorphism**   from *anthropos* (man) and *morphe* (form). Historically, a heresy whereby God was represented in human form.

For Mary Midgley, it is one of the roots of our attitude of sovereignty toward nature. It is nevertheless inevitable, as some scientists have asserted, since to represent non-humans (artistically, scientifically, politically, ethically) is to use human means to do so.

**antonomasia** a rhetorical operation whereby a generic or definitional term is used instead of a proper name—the Bard for Shakespeare– or a proper name is used to express a general idea—a Scrooge for a miser.

**bare life** a term Giorgio Agaben develops to describe a form of existence stripped of political determinations that exists in a zone of indistinction and continuous transition between humans and animals.

**Bildungsroman** (from the German: novel of formation or education). The most important novelistic genre of the nineteenth century centered on a young protagonist as he or she tries to make his or her way in the world. A coming-of-age novel.

**biopolitics/biopower** Michel Foucault's term for the political logic that focuses on the biological conditions of the population and rationalizes government action on the basis of the statistical capture of life's functions (birth rates, health risks, mortality, fertility, etc.).

**catachresis** a trope without an adequate referent in reality; an aberrant trope. Examples include: the "leg" of a table; the "face" of a mountain; the "dressing" on a salad. It is not the case that these figures are "wrong"; in fact, we use them all the time. It is the case, however, that when we do use them we are in fact using figures to refer to things or situations that don't themselves have their "own" words to refer to them.

**chronotope** term coined by Mikhail Bakhtin to describe the narrative nexus of a novel in which time and space (chrono-tope) coordinates determine the shape and direction of the story. Some examples include: the road, the ship, the castle, the ballroom, the spa.

**enstrangement** Viktor Shklovsky's term for the literary effect whereby a given referent seems "strange" or "removed." From the Russian "ostranenie," which is a neologism Shklyovsky coined to describe the "strangeness," or better, the "making-strange" of certain literary situations, characters, or events. We owe the translation of "ostranenie" as "enstrangement" to Benjamin Sher.

**eugenics** program of selective breeding and sterilization among humans designed to favor certain traits over others. Francis Galton, Darwin's cousin, was the first to seek its implementation.

*fabula* **(story) and** *syuzhet* **(plot)** terms used by Russian Formalists Viktor Shklovsky and Vladimir Propp to distinguish between the raw materials of a story (*fabula*) and their narrative organization (*syuzhet*).

**FIDO** (free indirect discourse *obligé*)  term used in this book to describe cross-species, third-person narration in which the opinions, feelings, and thoughts of an animal are perforce expressed by humans as though they were being articulated by said animal.

**focalization**  a narratological term originally coined by Gerard Genette that is used to describe the manner or perspective from which a narrative is presented.

**governmentality**  Michel Foucault's term for the institutionalized political logic, often but not exclusively premised on biological categories, that gives rise to modern regimes of power.

**irony**  drawing on the writings of the Jena Romantics, Paul de Man defines irony as a "permanent parabasis"; that is, as a perpetual interruption. Irony interrupts the illusion of narrative continuity or realistic illusion by introducing a different discourse or frame structure.

**JAX® mouse**  an animal model developed by C. C. Little at the Jackson Laboratory in Maine for use in cancer and genetic research.

**literareme**  a neologism, analogous to "idologeme" or "allegoreme," intended to describe the talking animal as a basic unit of literary discourse. There are of course many other literaremes – indirect speech, characterization, meter, etc. – but none among them is more visibly literary, nor more visibly discredited, than the giving of voice to animals.

**minor literature**  the term Gilles Deleuze and Félix Guatarri use to describe literature written in an dominant language from the perspective of its minority use.

**narratable**  a term coined by D. A. Miller to designate the structural principle of closure in narrative, whereby certain stories are retrospectively deemed worthy of being told and while others languish.

**natureculture**  Donna Haraway's term for describing the intermingling and interdependence of biological entities (human and non-human) and technological apparatuses in everyday life, such that it has become increasingly difficult to isolate cultural from natural attributes.

**OncoMouse™**  A transgenic mouse model developed to conduct research on human breast cancer by Harvard University and DuPont.

**parataxis**  the staccato grammatical fragmentation of larger discursive units into smaller, simpler ones.

**picaresque**  Spanish literary genre from the sixteenth century in which a young protagonist, the "pícaro" (or rascal) that gives the genre its name, makes his way in a corrupt world by dint of cunning, trickery, and even treachery. Examples include: The anonymous *El lazarillo de Tormes* (1554); Mateo Alemán's *Guzmán de Alfarache* (1599); and Quevedo's *El buscón* (1604). [See Bildungsroman]

**speciesism**　term coined by Peter Singer to describe a form of discrimination based on species, like racism is a form of discrimination based on race and sexism one based on gender.

**structure of feeling**　phrase coined by Raymond Williams to describe the social experience of subjects living under specific historical circumstances.

**subjectivation**　Michel Foucault's term, elaborated in *Discipline and Punish* (1975), for the process whereby subjects are disciplined under a regime characterized by Panoptic surveillance. The subject, Foucault writes, becomes the "principle of his own subjectivation" (202–203) under surveillance.

**synecdoche**　a literary trope that uses a part to signify the whole.

*syuzhet* **(plot) and** *fabula* **(story)** See *fabula* **and** *syuzhet*

**territorialization/deterritorialization**　Deleuze and Guattari use these paired terms to describe the subject's assimilation into, or rejection of, the great "molar" powers of family, career, and love, all of which tend to provide structures that sustain the capitalist order.

**uncanny**　Sigmund Freud coined the term "Unheimlich" (rendered as "uncanny" in English by Alix Strachey, Freud's first translator, and subsequently adopted by other translators) to describe the eerie feeling one experiences when one sees oneself as a stranger (as in a shop window, for instance), and then generalized as a concept to include phenomena that distort one's sense of self.

*volta*　the *volta* (from the Italian "turn") most often occurs between the octet and the sestet in the Petrarchan sonnet, and between the 8th and 9th, or the 12th and 13th, lines of the Shakespearean sonnet, but it can actually occur anywhere in the sonnet. The *volta* marks a turn—thematic, grammatical, logical—in the development of the sonnet.

# Suggested reading

Acampora, Ralph. *Corporal Compassion: Animal Ethics and Philosophy of Body*. Pittsburgh: University of Pittsburgh Press, 2006.

Adams, Carol J. *The Sexual Politics of Meat: A Feminist-Vegetarian Critical Theory*. Cambridge: Polity, 1990.

Agamben, Giorgio. *The Open: Man and Animal*. Stanford: Stanford University Press, 2004.

Armstrong, Philip. *What Animals Mean in the Fiction of Modernity*. London: Routledge, 2008.

Bagemihl, Bruce. *Biological Exuberance: Animal Homosexuality and Natural Diversity*. New York: St. Martin's Press, 1999

Baker, Steve. *Picturing the Beast: Animals, Identity, and Representation*. Champaign: University of Illinois Press, 2001.

Baker, Steve. *Artist Animal*. Minneapolis: University of Minnesota Press, 2013.

Baker, Steve. *The Postmodern Animal*. London: Reaktion Books, 2000.

Bataille, Georges. "Animality." In *Theory of Religion*, trans. Robert Hurley. New York: Zone Books, 1992.

Beer, Gillian. *Darwin's Plots: Evolutionary Narrative in Darwin, George Eliot, and Nineteenth-Century Fiction*. Cambridge: Cambridge University Press, 1983.

Berger, John. "Why Look at Animals?" In *About Looking*, ed. John Berger. New York: Pantheon, 1980.

Boggs, Coleen Glenney. *Animalia Americana: Animals Representations and Biopolitical Subjectivity*. New York: Columbia University Press, 2013.

Brown, Eric C. *Insect Poetics*. Minneapolis: University of Minnesota Press, 2006.

Brown, Laura. *Homeless Dogs and Melancholy Apes*. Ithaca: Cornell University Press, 2012.

Burt, Jonathan. *Animals in Film*. London: Reaktion Books, 2002.

Calarco, Matthew and Peter Atterton, eds. *Animal Philosophy*. London: Continuum, 2004.

Calarco, Matthew. *Zoographies: The Question of the Animal from Heidegger to Derrida*. New York: Columbia University Press, 2008.

Cavell, Stanley, Cora Diamond, John McDowell, Ian Hacking, and Cary Wolfe *Philosophy and Animal Life*. New York: Columbia University Press, 2008.

Clark, Stephen R. L. *Animals and their Moral Standing*. London: Routledge, 1997.

Coetzee, J. M. *The Lives of Animals*, ed. Amy Guttman. Princeton: Princeton University Press, 1999.

DeGrazia, David. *Taking Animals Seriously: Mental Life and Moral Status*. Cambridge: Cambridge University Press, 1993.

Deleuze, Gilles and Félix Guattari. *Kafka: Toward a Minor Literature*, trans. Dana Polan. Minneapolis: University of Minnesota Press, 1986.

Deleuze, Gilles and Félix Guattari. *A Thousand Plateaus: Capitalism and Schizophrenia*, trans. Brian Massumi. Minneapolis: University of Minnesota Press, 1987.

Derrida, Jacques. "'Eating Well,' or the Calculation of the Subject." In *Who Comes After the Subject*, ed. Eduardo Cadava, Peter Connor, and Jean-Luc Nancy. New York: Routledge, 1991.

Derrida, Jacques. *The Animal That Therefore I Am*, trans. David Wills. New York: Fordham University Press, 2008.

Derrida, Jacques. *The Beast and the Sovereign, Vol. 1*, trans. Geoffrey Bennington. Chicago: University of Chicago Press, 2009.

Derrida, Jacques. *The Beast and the Sovereign, Vol. 2*, trans. Geoffrey Bennington. Chicago: University of Chicago Press, 2011.

Diamond, Cora. *The Realistic Spirit: Wittgenstein, Philosophy, and the Mind*. Cambridge: MIT University Press, 1995.

Foucault, Michel. "Man and His Doubles." In *The Order of Things: An Archeology of the Human Sciences*. New York: Vintage, 1970.

Foucault, Michel. *The History of Sexuality, Vol. 1: An Introduction*, trans. Robert Hurley. New York: Vintage, 1978.

Foucault, Michel. *Discipline and Punish: The Birth of the Prison*, trans. Alan Sheridan. New York: Vintage, 1995.

Foucault, Michel. *"Society Must Be Defended": Lecture at the Collège de France, 1975–1976*. New York: Picador, 2003.

Francione, Gary L. *Animals, Property, and the Law*. Philadelphia: Temple University Press, 1995.

Francione, Gary L. *Animals as Persons: Essays on the Abolition of Animal Exploitation*. New York: Columbia University Press, 2008.

Franklin, Sarah. *Dolly Mixtures: The Remaking of Genealogy*. Durham: Duke University Press, 2007.

Fudge, Erica. *Animal*. London: Reaktion Books, 2002.

Fudge, Erica. *Pets*. Stockbridge: Acumen, 2008.

Guerinni, Anita. *Experimenting with Humans and Animals: From Galen to Human Rights*. Baltimore: Johns Hopkins, 2003.

Ham, Jennifer and Matthew Senior, eds. *Animal Acts: Configuring the Human in Western History*. New York: Routledge, 1998.

Haraway, Donna. *Simians, Cyborgs, and Women: The Reinvention of Nature*. New York: Routledge, 1991.

Haraway, Donna. *The Companion Species Manifesto*. Chicago: Prickly Paradigm, 2003.

Haraway, Donna. *When Species Meet*. Minneapolis: University of Minnesota Press, 2008.

Hearne, Vicki. *Adam's Task: Calling Animals by Name*. New York: Harper Collins, 1991.

Heidegger, Martin. *The Fundamental Concepts of Metaphysics; World, Finitude, Solitude*, trans. William McNeill and Nicholas Walker. Bloomington: Indiana University Press, 1995.

Heise, Ursula. "The Hitchhiker's Guide to Ecocriticism," *PMLA* 121(2): 503–516, 2006.

Heise, Ursula. *Sense of Place and Sense of Planet: The Environmental Imagination of the Global*. Cambridge: Oxford, 2008.

Horkheimer, Max and Theodor W. Adorno. "Man and Animal." In *Dialectic of Enlightenment*. New York: Continuum, 1995.

Irigaray, Luce. "Animal Compassion." In *Animal Philosophy: Ethics and Identity*, eds. Peter Atterton and Matthew Calarco. London: Continuum, 2005.

Kean, Hilda. *Animal Rights: Political and Social Change in Britain since 1800*. London: Reaktion Books, 1998.

Keete, Kathleen. *The Beast in the Boudoir: Petkeeping in Nineteenth-Century Paris*. Berkeley: University of California Press, 1995.

Kuzniar, Alice. *Melancholia's Dog*. Chicago: University of Chicago Press, 2006.

Latour, Bruno. *Politics of Nature*. Cambridge: Harvard University Press, 2004.

Lemm, Vanessa. *Nietzsche's Animal Philosophy: Culture, Politics, and the Animality of the Human Being*. New York: Fordham University Press, 2009.

Levinas, Emmanuel. "The Name of a Dog, or Natural Rights." In *Difficult Freedom: Essays on Judaism*, trans. Sèan Hand. Baltimore: Johns Hopkins University Press, 1990.

Lippit, Akira. *Electric Animal: Toward a Rhetoric of Wildlife*. Minneapolis: University of Minnesota Press, 2005.

Lucht, Marc and Donna Yarri. *Kafka's Creatures: Animals, Hybrids, and Other Fantastic Beings*. Plymouth: Lexington Books, 2010.

MacIntyre, Alisdair. *Dependent Rational Animals*. Peru, IL: Open Court, 2001.

McHugh, Susan. *Animal Stories: Narrating Across Species Lines*. Minneapolis: University of Minnesota Press, 2011.

Midgely, Mary. *Beast and Man: The Roots of Human Nature*. London: Routledge Classics, 1995 (first published in 1978).

Midgely, Mary. *Animals and Why They Matter*. Athens: University of Georgia Press, 1983.

Miller, John. *Empire and the Animal Body: Violence, Identity and Ecology in Victorian Adventure Fiction*. New York: Anthem, 2012.

Norris, Margot. *Beasts of the Modern Imagination*. Baltimore: Johns Hopkins University Press, 1985.

Nussbaum, Martha. *Frontiers of Justice: Disability, Nationality, Species Membership*. Cambridge: Harvard University Press, 2007.

Palmer, Claire. *Animal Ethics in Context*. New York: Columbia University Press, 2010.

Pick, Anat. *Creaturely Poetics: Animality and Vulnerability in Literature and Film*. New York: Columbia University Press, 2011.

Rader, Karen. *Making Mice: Standardizing Animals for American Biomedical Research, 1900–1955*. Princeton: Princeton, 2004.

Regan, Tom. *The Case for Animal Rights*. Berkeley: University of California Press, 1983.

Ritvo, Harriet. *The Animal Estate: The English and Other Creatures in the Victorian Age*. Cambridge: Harvard University Press, 1987.

Rohman, Carrie. *Stalking the Subject: Modernism and the Animal*. New York: Columbia University Press, 2009.

Rose, Nikolas. *The Politics of Life Itself*. Princeton: Princeton University Press, 2007.

Rothfels, Nigel. ed. *Representing Animals*. Bloomington: Indiana University PRess, 2002.

Rothfels, Nigel. *Savages and Beasts: The Birth of the Modern Zoo*. Baltimore: Johns Hopkins University Press, 2002.

Serpell, James. *In the Company of Animals*. Oxford: Blackwell, 1986.

Shehan, James J. and Morton Sosna, eds. *The Boundaries of Humanity: Humans, Animals, Machines*. Berkeley: University of California Press, 1991.

Singer, Peter. *Animal Liberation*. New York: Harper Collins, 1975.

Soper, Kate. *What is Nature? Culture, Politics and the Non-Human*. Oxford: Oxford University Press, 1995.

Steeves, Peter H., ed. *Animal Others: On Ethics, Ontology, and Animal Life*. Albany: SUNY University Press, 1999.

Sunstein, Cass R. and Martha C. Nussbaum, eds. *Animal Rights: Current Debates and New Directions*. Oxford: Oxford University Press, 2004.

Tyler, Tom. "If Horses Had Hands…" *Society and Animals*, 11(3): 267–281, 2003.

Vint, Sheryl. *Animal Alterity: Science Fiction and the Question of the Animal*. Liverpool: Liverpool University Press, 2010.

Weil, Kari. *Thinking Animals: Why Animal Studies Now?* New York: Columbia University Press, 2012.

Wolfe, Cary. *Animal Rites: American Culture, the Discourse of Species, and Posthumanist Theory*. Chicago: Chicago University Press, 2003.

Wolfe, Cary, ed. *Zoontologies: The Question of the Animal*. Minneapolis: University of Minnesota Press, 2003.

Wolfe, Cary. *What is Posthumanism?* Minneapolis: University of Minnesota Press, 2010.

# Index

# Taylor & Francis eBooks

---

## Helping you to choose the right eBooks for your Library

Add Routledge titles to your library's digital collection today. Taylor and Francis ebooks contains over 50,000 titles in the Humanities, Social Sciences, Behavioural Sciences, Built Environment and Law.

**Choose from a range of subject packages or create your own!**

### Benefits for you

- » Free MARC records
- » COUNTER-compliant usage statistics
- » Flexible purchase and pricing options
- » All titles DRM-free.

> REQUEST YOUR **FREE** INSTITUTIONAL TRIAL TODAY
>
> **Free Trials Available**
> We offer free trials to qualifying academic, corporate and government customers.

### Benefits for your user

- » Off-site, anytime access via Athens or referring URL
- » Print or copy pages or chapters
- » Full content search
- » Bookmark, highlight and annotate text
- » Access to thousands of pages of quality research at the click of a button.

## eCollections – Choose from over 30 subject eCollections, including:

| | |
|---|---|
| Archaeology | Language Learning |
| Architecture | Law |
| Asian Studies | Literature |
| Business & Management | Media & Communication |
| Classical Studies | Middle East Studies |
| Construction | Music |
| Creative & Media Arts | Philosophy |
| Criminology & Criminal Justice | Planning |
| Economics | Politics |
| Education | Psychology & Mental Health |
| Energy | Religion |
| Engineering | Security |
| English Language & Linguistics | Social Work |
| Environment & Sustainability | Sociology |
| Geography | Sport |
| Health Studies | Theatre & Performance |
| History | Tourism, Hospitality & Events |

For more information, pricing enquiries or to order a free trial, please contact your local sales team:
**www.tandfebooks.com/page/sales**

**Routledge**
Taylor & Francis Group

The home of
Routledge books

**www.tandfebooks.com**